MW01165505

THE STRUGGLE OF JEWISH YOUTH FOR PRODUCTIVIZATION:

THE ZIONIST YOUTH MOVEMENT IN POLAND

ISRAEL OPPENHEIM

EAST EUROPEAN MONOGRAPHS, BOULDER
DISTRIBUTED BY COLUMBIA UNIVERSITY PRESS, NEW YORK

1989

EAST EUROPEAN MONOGRAPHS, NO. CCLXXIII

TABLE OF CONTENTS

PREFACE

The pioneering Zionist youth movements, and especially that of Poland, played a central role in fulfilling the aims of the Jewish national movement. Though it has not yet been investigated in depth, there is no doubt that their contribution to the formation of the life-styles of a number of sectors of the national life during the British Mandate in the Land of Israel was significant and even central. This was especially so in the realm of settlement, which in no small measure determined the boundaries and shape of the State of Israel during the first decades of its existence. The uniqueness of the youth movements did not express itself in new ideological abstractions but in the realization of the national and social aims as formulated by the Zionist and Socialist Zionist ideologies.

One of these central goals was the productivization of the Jewish people in order to create an agricultural and working class in the Land of Israel. To achieve this, it was necessary to change the Jewish society's attitude toward manual labor. Indeed, educating to physical labor as a social and spiritual national value and as an impetus to the rebirth of the Jewish people in the Land of Israel, was at the core of the educational doctrine of these youth movements. And the major vehicle for this was the hakhshara kibbutz which, in the thirties, spread to most of the places of Jewish settlement in Poland. The aspiration to productivization drew its nurture from varied ideological sources and in most of the youth groups was combined with an eclectic, Socialist, collectivist outlook. The aim of this education for productivization was two-fold: it was to serve as a vehicle for moving the masses of Jewish impoverished, petit-bourgeois

Jewish youth who could find no place in the Polish economy which was especially hard-hit by the world-wide economic crisis because of its backwardness, and as a result of the increasing policy of discrimination by the country's regimes.

For this youth to identify with these goals, Jewish society's traditional hierarchy of values which the youth shared, i.e., of looking down upon the laborer and the agricultural worker, had to be changed. The main educational efforts of the youth movements were invested to this end. The aspiration was to equip the trainees to fulfill the Zionist Socialist national and social goals in the Land of Israel. From this point of view, the education toward productive labor was a vehicle only. There was, however, an additional aspect: the collectivist training was also seen as an end in itself, as an example of the future egalitarian society.

The very fact that the hakhshara kibbutzim took root throughout Poland when the Jewish situation in general and that of Jewish youth in particular was worsening significantly, resulted in the hakhshara's fulfilling a function beyond that of its original goals. It was seen by various circles of the Jewish community in Poland as a conscious, organized expression of the processes of productivization in Jewish society that had begun in the second half of the 19th century after the crisis which had effected Eastern European Jewry as the East European countries made the transition from a semi-feudal to a capitalistic economy. The kibbutz member's relative success in penetrating the labor market previously closed to the Jewish worker was proof in certain circles that even in times of severe crisis it is possible to break through the limited framework of the traditional Jewish occupations. Therefore, various ideas were raised for the productivization of the masses of Jewish youth in the collective hakhshara kibbutzim without relation to the Zionist goals in the Land of Israel; rather, that it prepare them for absorption into the existing economy beyond the earlier restrictive limits. The attitude of the pioneer Zionist youth movements to these suggestions was ambivalent. On the one hand, they took pride in having proven that a social change could be wrought within the Jewish youth even in most trying times, and that they could succeed with the small expenditures of the hakhshara kibbutzim while the veteran Jewish organizations such as ORT and others who managed to serve only limited groups of Jews were expending huge sums. On the other hand, they were convinced that the chances for the successful productivization of the Jewish youth without any relationship to the broad national and social goals, were slim.[1]

It is our pleasant task to thank the Yivo Institute for Jewish Research which graciously permitted us to include herein the main points of the material published in our article in the book on the Jews of Poland.[2] We also wish to thank Nathan H. Reisner for the translation from the Yiddish.

INTRODUCTION

The Halutz (pioneering) movement, in all its manifestations, has from its inception been the radical wing of the Jewish national movement. Attempts at avant-garde self-realization accompany Zionism from its very outset.

Genetically and historically, Zionism is a part of the general modern national liberation process of the oppressed peoples of Europe. In the case of the Jews, it is expressed in the aspirations of certain segments of the population, especially among the youth, to exchange the old traditionalist expectations of waiting for the Messiah for that of voluntarist activism, with the goal of altering the fate of the Jewish people both individually and collectively. This new approach meant replacing the Messianic traditionalist and religious principle with a secular one which also contains pseudo-Messianic elements as part of a national ideality of the Nation as a collective redeemer.

Being part of the general, more encompassing national awakening, Zionism also bears a specific immanent character, as the reaction of a minority group against alien oppression and hatred. At the same time, it is characterized by a fear of utter decline, disintegration and assimilation as a result of the dispersion of the Jewish people throughout the world.

* * * * *

From the beginning, the Zionist movement was organically linked with aliyah (immigration) to the Land of Israel and with attempts to establish

1

a Jewish agricultural economy on individual bases at the time of the First Aliyah.[1] The first collective economy was established during the period of the Second Aliyah.[2]

The He-Halutz movement adopted the ideological foundations of Zionism in general, and later, those of Labor Zionism in particular. It identified fully with the Zionist analysis of Diaspora reality and with Zionist social and political goals as a solution to the Jewish problem. Thus the pioneer movement did not find it necessary to create its own theoretical, ideological principles outside of the Zionist and Zionist-Socialist movement.

Nonetheless, the pioneer movement is a unique phenomenon within Zionism. Its distinction lies in its concept of "hagshama"—practical realization of its national goals and ideals.

To a great extent, the pioneer movement in all its ramifications was an expression of protest against the hollow slogans of Zionist parties and organizations, which preached the importance of aliyah and land-settlement, but did almost nothing to attain that noble goal.[3]

By emphasizing activism as a revolutionary force that changes human society, the pioneer movement in Russia and subsequently in Poland as well, exhibited tendencies to disparage those theoretical and ideological constructions that were isolated from concrete life-situations and did not require implementation. The position of the pioneer movement toward theoretical considerations may therefore be characterized as follows: in the main, it recognized the importance of theory as a tool of the trade, i.e., not as an abstract essence, but rather as an expression of the spirit of the times as understood by the leftist Hegelians, namely, as a means of acknowledging reality in order to change it.

In addition, the conditions of its work and efforts did not enable the pioneer movement to develop a distinct Zionist or Zionist-Socialist worldview, since all its energy was concentrated on the practical work of establishing the hakhshara—the vocational and ideological preparation—of Zionist pioneers, building and strengthening the ideological foundations within an organizational framework, educating the youth toward self-realization, as well as on the struggle to create a place for itself within the Zionist movement.

Ideological divisions within the ranks of the He-Halutz movement itself first appeared in the later stages of its development. In the general He-Halutz movement, for example, there were differences between the majority faction which was allied with the Kibbutz Ha-Meuhad on the one side, and with the Ha-Shomer Ha-Tza'ir and Gordoniah on the other side, as well as between He-Halutz Ha-Klali and the pioneer organizations outside its ranks, which were created by different parties and which competed with the general He-Halutz: for example, the General Zionist He-Halutz Ha-Klal Tzioni, He-Halutz Ha-Mizrahi, the Revisionist Hakhshara, etc. These contending forces were, however, a consequence of the variety of Zionist currents and did not derive from He-Halutz ranks per se, whose intellectual roots lay in Zionist and Zionist-Socialist ideology.

* * * * *

"Throughout history revolutions have devoured people . . . . Our movement is based on the individual, on imbuing each person with a sense of responsibility, a sense of duty, and a sense of rights."[4] With these words a He-Halutz leader described the He-Halutz movement, emphasizing its democratic, egalitarian principles. He stressed the fact that since it is a revolutionary movement in its definition of goals and tasks, the He-Halutz movement considers its individual members as being no less important than its leaders.

This approach links the He-Halutz movement to the youth movement, i.e., although it does not accept the ideology of the youth movement,[5] halutziut (pioneering), nevertheless, also places the individual at the very center of its activity, as an active part of the collective. At the same time, He-Halutz attempts to unite the masses within its ranks, thereby synthesizing the needs of the individual with its national and social goals.

Typologically, the hakhshara may be defined as an "in-group," i.e., hakhshara centers developed based upon the following principles:

1) direct, informal relationships among its individual members, motivated not only by ideological goals but indeed, primarily, by emotional ties;

2) intensive identification of particular ideals with those which are general in scope;

3) ongoing communication among group members;

4) capacity for joint participation in communal work resulting from an inner drive;

5) intense feelings of solidarity within the group, united against external pressures;

6) absence of bureaucratic control of its members;

7) a degree of conformity of its members to group norms.

The hakhshara groups, though small and intimate during the initial years of the movement, followed a polycentric model. Instead of the authority being vested in one leader, it was distributed informally among group and individual members. The strength of the hakhshara lay in the personalities of individuals—in their behavior and in their mode of life, serving as an example to the other members of the group.

As the movement grew and embraced the masses, its internal structure changed to a certain extent. Relationships between the members and the leadership became more formalized. This created an apparatus which, at times, lost direct contact with its individual membership. On the other hand, there was a constant member turn-over, as old members with long service to the movement immigrated to the Land of Israel, and as new members replaced them in the group. The resulting provisional nature of the hakhshara structure prevented the He-Halutz movement from becoming an extreme, formalized bureaucracy. Moreover, its democratic egalitarian, and avant-garde elements acted as a counter-balance to the above-mentioned negative tendencies and manifestations.

* * * * *

The development of the He-Halutz movement in Poland between the World Wars is now a closed chapter in Jewish history, having met its tragic demise together with all of Polish Jewry. In its last phase, during World War II, the He-Halutz movement wrote the most heroic and tragic chapter in its history, as one of the major forces in the Jewish resistance movement, in the ghettos, concentration camps, and forests of Poland.

In reconstructing the history of the He-Halutz movement, the question arises as to the precise and unique nature of this movement. It was a product of its particular time, of the social, political and cultural circumstances which gave birth to it. However, it also possessed its own intrinsic values which gave it its unique complexion and which distinguished it from other social forces of its time.

The hakshsara did not arise ex nihilo. Its precursors were the pioneering groups that existed during the period of the Second Aliyah, prior to World War I. This was especially true of the Russian He-Halutz which, to some extent, had nurtured the international He-Halutz movement in general and the Polish movement in particular.[6]

After the Bolsheviks came into power in Russia, hegemony over the pioneer movement shifted from Russia to Poland. At that time, Poland had the largest and most densely populated Jewish community in the world. It then became the center of the movement and from there various initiatives emerged which spread pioneering all over the world. In addition, Poland had the largest number of pioneers and hakhshara centers.

Hakhshara groups arose spontaneously. The first we hear of them is in an article in the Yiddish press which appeared toward the end of 1916, but these were merely sporadic attempts. The first phase of actual He-Halutz history began when a provisional central committee laid the foundation for the movement and coordinated its work which lasted until 1923. During that time, the movement had an amorphous character both ideologically and organizationally.[7]

The second phase began in 1924 and lasted through the crisis of the Fourth Aliyah, which took place during 1926-1928. Certain conceptions of the kibbutz-hakhshara idea were crystallized during that period. The youth movement of He-Halutz, called He-Halutz Ha-Tza'ir (the Young Pioneer), then came into existence. This was followed by other pioneering groups: He-Halutz Ha-Mizrahi (the Religious Pioneer), He-Halutz Ha-Merkazi (the Central Pioneer, later called He-Halutz Ha-Klal-Tzioni). The Ha-Shomer Ha-Tza'ir (the Young Scouts) joined the He-Halutz on the principle of internal autonomy. The general He-Halutz movement identified itself both organizationally and ideologically with the Histadrut and the Zionist-Socialist movement.

The third and most important stage in the history of He-Halutz and the hakhshara in Poland began in 1929 and lasted almost until the outbreak of World War II. It was only at this stage that it became a mass movement with a membership of tens of thousands of young people.

Until the 1930s the pioneer movement can be viewed as an important component of Zionism, although it played a secondary role in the mainstream of Jewish life in Poland. It was only after hakhshara penetrated into hundreds of cities and towns throughout the country that it began to play an important role in the life of Polish Jewry.

All three major phases in the history of the Polish hakhshara movement
paralleled in their main features the waves of Jewish immigration to the
Land of Israel from the Third to the Fifth Aliyah. For example, the fact
that the growth of He-Halutz depended upon the Aliyot is expressed in
the following statistics: In 1919 He-Halutz had 4,000 members; after the
1923 crisis in the Land of Israel, its membership dropped to 2,000; as the
Fourth Aliyah began in 1924, the membership rose again to 12,000 members; but during the 1927-1928 crisis in the Land of Israel, membership
dropped again to about 3,000. Growth was again renewed in 1929 with
the beginning of the Fifth Aliyah; by 1935 the membership had risen to
60,000 in Poland and Galicia. During the Abyssinian War and disturbances
in the Land of Israel, the membership waned once more.[8]

The organic link between the growth of the He-Halutz movement and
the waves of immigration to the Land of Israel presents a dilemma for the
researcher. Should we analyze the movement exclusively from the point
of view of the Land of Israel, i.e., seeing it merely as an instrument and an
exponent of events in the Land of Israel? Or, should we, despite the great
influence of the Land of Israel on the development of He-Halutz, deal
with it as an independent phenomenon with its own dynamics that were
stronger than any external influences—even when the latter were most
intense? We believe the second approach to be the correct one. As a mass
movement, He-Halutz developed an intrinsic dynamic which followed its
own laws and was subjected to influences from various sources, both internal and external, in a dialectic relationship.

From the aforementioned statistics, we can infer another characteristic
feature of the development of the hakhshara and pioneering in Poland.
This may be characterized as a spiral, i.e., its growth did not progress in
a continual upward direction. Rather, every period of expansion and
growth was followed by a period of contraction. The downward dip, however, almost never dropped below the high point of the preceding stage.
The He-Halutz movement thus maintained its growth pattern despite the
various crises that arose.

* * * * *

At the very center of the He-Halutz movement stood He-Halutz Ha-Klali,
the general He-Halutz, primarily because it was the largest pioneer organization in terms of membership and numbers of hakhshara centers. A

separate chapter will also be devoted to othe pioneer-hakhshara movements: Mizrahi, General Zionists, Revisionists, etc.

From a geographical perspective as well, that part of Poland which was
under Russian domination prior to World War I was the center of He-
Halutz activity. This was because the vast majority of Polish Jewry lived
there, almost two-thirds as compared to one-third in Galicia and Silesia.

The situation was also reflected in the character and number of hakhshara centers. But beyond that, after Poland regained its political independence, historically-rooted tradition left its mark on the political party
constellation of Jewish society. Except for the Bund, most of the other
Jewish political parties and movements did not succeed in uniting organizationally, so that each region developed independently. Thus, for example, He-Halutz in Galicia bore an entirely different character than He-
Halutz in Congress-Poland. In fact, it was a separate, independent movement, with its own ideology and organizational characteristics and merits
special attention and investigation.

CHAPTER 1

THE BEGINNING

A. The Organizational Foundations Are Laid

The pioneer groups which had been organized in pre-war Russia and Poland and which carried the seeds of the later pioneer movements, disintegrated at the outbreak of World War I.[1] However, the foundations which had already been laid did not disappear entirely. As conditions changed and it became possible again to resume activity, the He-Halutz movement did not have to start from scratch, for it had an ideological tradition and past membership upon which to build. Many pioneers had been waiting for an appropriate opportunity to resume their activity. This became possible only after the Germans had occupied Poland.

The fundamental and spontaneous organization of groups of pioneers that sprung up in many regions, reflected the general atmosphere of national awakening of oppressed peoples, among them, the Jewish people. "In 1917-1918 the Jewish community is in a state of anticipation. . . . Everyone is awaiting important historical news. The Balfour Declaration has called forth a tremendous mass enthusiasm. The House of Israel is rejoicing. . . . People from far and near are uniting. The gates of redemption are open. . . . Meetings, conventions, demonstrations . . . uniting young and old. . . . There is an awakening of a revolutionary determination to act, to organize. He-Halutz groups are springing up of their own accord, without any directives and they are affiliating with the Warsaw Central Committee." In this manner one of the first pioneers describes the atmosphere within the Jewish Halutz centers in Poland where He-Halutz groups were being organized.[2]

The first organizational steps taken in the town of Bendin are described in the following manner: "Our pioneer group owes its origin to a group of former Shomrin (scouts). In October 1917, twelve of us laid the corner-stone for our organization and we soon got down to practical work. We divided our membership into two groups: one worked in a carpenter's shop and the other in a shoemaker's. We also offered lectures on Palestino-graphy and Jewish History."[3] In summarizing, we can say that, in its first stage, He-Halutz did not come about as a result of methodologically plan-ned groundwork among the Jewish youth. Rather, this youth joined the movement because of the revolutionary atmosphere within the confines of its Jewish environment, as well as because of new and impressive per-spectives that were unfolding for Zionism at the end of World War I.

The task of channeling this spontaneous development and of organ-izing the movement on a national scale was undertaken during September-October 1917[4] by the Warsaw He-Halutz, at which time the specific prin-ciples and goals were formulated. *Dos Yidishe Folk,* the weekly publica-tion of the Zionist Organization in Poland, printed an "Appeal to Pioneers" (issue 33, October 1917) in which the Warsaw pioneers proposed to take advantage of the 3rd National Convention of Zionist Organizations and to call together a conference of representatives of pioneer groups. The need for consolidation was presented in the following manner: "The war has severely affected the Land of Israel, but the awakened national will has been strengthened. Moreover, external circumstances have become more favorable for Zionism (a reference to the Balfour Declaration and to the hope that it offered). It is the duty of the Jewish people as a whole to work for its national and social renewal." The appeal emphasized that it was the special responsibility of Jewish youth to become the vanguard of this development. The He-Halutz movement was organized in other countries as well. Their goal was "to alter their present life-style and to return to our ancient soil." Only Poland was lagging behind. Its few groups were weak and divided. It became necessary for them to unite in order to expand and conduct their activity on a broader scale. It was there-fore proposed to call a meeting of the representatives of the pioneer groups. The Warsaw organization took the initiative in organizing this meeting[5] which took place seventeen days later, on the 28th of October. Its participants included members of the Warsaw He-Halutz Council together with delegates from other parts of the country. At the meeting, it was decided to form a He-Halutz Steering Committee as part of the Land of Israel Commission of the Central Committee of the Zionist Organization of Poland. A committee was elected to formulate a uniform status for the He-Halutz movement. Other recommendations were made, among them, to form a separate department for pioneers within the Land of Israel Commission of the Central Committee, its members to be elected by the pioneers and recognized by the Central Committee.[6]

In the first phase of its development, the Polish He-Halutz considered itself to be an integral part of the General Zionist Organization. Although it had a certain degree of autonomy, it did not maintain itself as an independent movement. Nor was it part of the Labor Zionist movement as was He-Halutz in Russia.[7]

SECTION 4, PARAGRAPH I of the CONSTITUTION states:

> 1. The He-Halutz is affiliated with the Zionist Organization of Poland, is administered by its own Central Committee, consisting of nine members elected at the annual Pioneer Conference, and by an additional three members that are appointed by the Zionist Central Committee of Poland.
> 2. The Central Committee is closely connected to the Land of Israel Commission of the Central Committee and engages in joint undertakings with it.[8]

The Constitution treats other organizational matters, such as setting up local branches, defining their powers, rules of procedure for changing by-laws, elections, etc. It also emphasizes that both males and females from the age of eighteen, may join the local branches of the movement.[9]

Other voices, opposed to this integrative-Zionist organizational and ideological orientation were heard at the 1st Tze'irei Tzion Party Conference which was held on the 23rd of September, 1918. One of the participants emphasized that almost all of the pioneers were members or supporters of the Tze'irei-Tzion and that if He-Halutz were to take positions counter to the spirit of the Tze'irei Tzion, the party should not permit its members to belong to it. The majority, however, rejected this proposal.[10]

Immediately after the war ended, local He-Halutz branches began to proliferate and to organize themselves along regional lines. The first regional conference took place in Bendin on the 12th of December 1918, with the participation of delegates from He-Halutz and the Tze'irei Tzion. At the conference, which lasted for two days with delegates participating from twelve local branches from Zaglembiye and the surrounding area, a committee was elected "of five representatives, that has fulfilled its responsibilities to the highest standard of performance."[11]

At the plenary sessions of the provisional Central Committee of He-Halutz, with the participation of regional delegates from Warsaw, Lodz, Sosnovitz, Shedletz, Kutno, Rodom, and Bialystok, various resolutions were passed; one of them, "to convene a national conference of He-Halutz to be held from the 12th-16th of May."[12]

This national conference opened May 14, 1919 with 32 delegates from 20 localities, representing approximately 1,100 members. Since many delegates were not able to attend, it was decided after discussion "that this gathering shall be constituted as a preliminary conference, having the power to make decisions on major issues of principle."[13] In fact, however, the conference is documented in the history of the Polish He-Halutz as being the 1st He-Halutz Conference of Poland.

The organizational report of the Central Committee makes mention of an earlier preliminary conference of He-Halutz which took place Tabernacles 1918, when the Tze'irei Tzion conference was also held. At that time a central committee was elected but the members of the provinces did not participate in the activities. Therefore, only the Warsaw members of the Central Committee actually met and they were not able to deal with the expansion of the movement. This was particularly evident after November 1918, when the pogroms, on the one hand, and the peace negotiations on the other, attracted thousands of new members in many areas to He-Halutz. Within four months, the movement grew from thirty to fifty local branches, with a membership of 4,000. It therefore became necessary to expand the Central Committee co-opting additional members. The reorganized Central Committee maintained contact with all 150 branches.[14]

The differences of opinion within the Central Committee itself and also within some of the branches led to a rift. Members who opposed an autonomous national He-Halutz organization left the movement. The question of organizational autonomy was but the first step toward complete independence from the Zionist Organization and from other Zionist and Zionist-Socialist parties. In his paper, "The Program of He-Halutz," Joseph Heftman stressed this trend toward independence. "Only with respect to the Land of Israel does He-Halutz have a point of agreement with the Zionist Organization."[16] This is to say that on all other issues it took an independent position. There were, however, opposing views that advocated continuing organizational unity between He-Halutz and the Zionist Organization.[17] Still others, in turn, opposed the "union with the Zionist Organization while favoring subordination to the World Zionist Congress."[18]

The difference of opinion on organizational structure was reflected in the resolutions. A decision was reached that He-Halutz of Poland and Lithuania be part of the World He-Halutz Alliance, which "defers to the Zionist Congress."[19] Two points of view developed regarding relations to the Zionist Organization of Poland: one favored uniting with the Palestine office of the Zionist Organization, and formulated its position in the following manner: "Agreeing in principle to uniting with the Land of Israel Office of the Zionist-Organization, the Preliminary Conference authorizes the Central Committee of He-Halutz to conduct negotiations with the Zionist Organization regarding this matter."[20]

The second point of view held that He-Halutz be a free and independent organization.[21] Inasmuch as no agreement was reached, the first resolution was passed, on condition that the issue be debated in the local chapters, while for the time being, the members of He-Halutz would negotiate with the Zionist Central Committee. The final decision was to be reached at a plenary session of the He-Halutz Central Committee together with representatives from the local branches. This session was to be held during the nationwide all-Zionist Conference.[22]

Additional organizational resolutions were adopted at the He-Halutz conference dealing with the problems of local branches, regional conferences, the powers of the Central Committee, etc.[23]

At the 4th Nationwide Zionist Conference, held in late August 1919, twenty-one He-Halutz delegates, out of a total of 282, were present. The proposal of the He-Halutz delegates that the Palestine Office be elected by the Conference, rather than by the Central Committee, was not even put to a vote. Rather, the speaker, discussing the Land of Israel problems, strongly attacked the "dilettantism of He-Halutz and demanded of the leaders of He-Halutz. . . more moderation and a greater sense of responsibility for their words and deeds."[24] Obviously, the attitude of the Zionist leaders toward He-Halutz intensified the tendency toward independence within the movement. At the 2nd He-Halutz Conference in 1921, it was therefore decided that "He-Halutz be organized as an independent inter-party organization uniting all workers. . . who are preparing for aliyah to the Land of Israel in the near future.[25]

At its 4th Conference in 1925, He-Halutz went even further in confirming its independent existence, despite attempts by the 14th Zionist Congress to split the United He-Halutz by recognizing other pioneer organizations that had been founded by various parties.[26] "The 4th He-Halutz Conference again proclaims that it is an unaffiliated organization, uniting within its ranks everyone, regardless of political point of view. He-Halutz calls upon all pioneer movements, both within and without its ranks, to unite in the He-Halutz endeavor, through the unaffiliated efforts of He-Halutz."[27] While He-Halutz is organizationally independent of any party in the Diaspora, it establishes a close relationship with the Histadrut (the Labor Movement) in the Land of Israel.

* * * * *

By the time of the 1st He-Halutz Conference in May, 1919, membership in the organization had reached almost 4,000. But toward the end of that year, the work of He-Halutz was partially curtailed "for objective reasons and also due to feelings of despair when the gates of the Land of Israel were closed to the pioneers who had already been trained to go on aliyah."[28] The reports of that summer's activities describe the disbanding of pioneer groups, in part because its members were being drafted into the army. In Bendin, for instance, only five members remained in the group. The same was true of the other areas.[29] The 1920 riots in the Land of Israel and the closing of its gates caused a weakening of the He-Halutz organizational activities. By mid-1921, however, He-Halutz had still retained 4,500 members, 1,700 of whom were working on hakhshara.[30] The Treaty of Riga, which concluded the war between Russia and Poland, opened up vast opportunities for He-Halutz in eastern-European communities, that had been incorporated into Poland.[31] In November 1922, the Vilna He-Halutz, which had up until that time functioned as an independent center in the Polish sector of Lithuania, joined the Polish He-Halutz.[32] Despite this geographic expansion, however, at its 3rd Regional Conference in June 1923, membership in the Polish He-Halutz had declined to 3,000. This number remained constant until the Fourth Aliyah, which began as soon as the Land of Israel crisis had subsided. During the subsequent five month period, membership increased to 5,000 and by the end of 1924 the Polish He-Halutz reached a total of 12,000 older members in its 425 organizational branches, and 3,500 younger members in He-Halutz Ha-Tza'ir.[33] With its organizational expansion, He-Halutz entered into a new phase.

B. Ideological Foundations

One of the most significant characteristics of the He-Halutz movement, throughout its history, was its spontaneity. The organization arose almost simultaneously in several countries, albeit under different general and specifically Jewish conditions. This led to the formulation of diverse organizational goals and points of view, particularly in the early stage of its existence.

The He-Halutz of Russia was, to a large extent, ideological and organizational heir to the pre-war pioneer groups which had been influenced by the Ze'irei Tzion movement. It had, therefore, from its very outset been nurtured by socialist roots. Its socialist character became more fully developed in the early 1920s under the leadership of Joseph Trumpeldor and his followers.[34]

The situation in Poland was, however, very different. The He-Halutz movement there was the creation of the entire Zionist movement, in all its facets and philosophical variations.[35] Its broad amorphous character was clearly expressed in the resolution adopted at its conference of May 14-16, 1919. The paragraph entitled "Supervision," states: "He-Halutz is an alliance whose goal is to realize the primary objective of Zionism: to build the Land of Israel for the Jewish people through Jewish labor," primarily work on the land.[36] Because of its general character, He-Halutz could accept as members any young people 18 years and older "who acknowledge its principles and desire to be trained in the Diaspora for future work in the Land of Israel."[37] Neither in the Diaspora, nor in the Land of Israel did this young movement identify itself with any political party of social or political goals. Regarding its position vis-a-vis other organizations, it was decided that "He-Halutz would establish contact with any organizatin that includes in its program support for the Land of Israel."[38] And, indeed, which Zionist organization did ot have as its goal "support of the Land of Israel"? In addition, He-Halutz as an organized movement did not take any official position regarding the internal political and social problems within the Jewish community of the Land of Israel itself. Nor did it take a position on interparty relations there, despite the fact that most of its members and new immigrants to the Land of Israel had come from the ranks of the Tze'irei Tzion.[39] In contrast to the Russian or Roumanian He-Halutz, avant-garde concepts were not popular within the Polish He-Halutz. In its early years, He-Halutz of Poland concerned itself only with matters of aliyah as well as with hakhshara, which trained its members for a trade. It did not educate them for living on a kibbutz, nor did it require that its membership have any specific ideological identification and affiliation.[40]

It may be said that the unique character of the He-Halutz of Poland was a result of the post-war developments of the Zionist youth in Poland. The war and the excesses that followed, shattered the very foundations of Jewish survival and shook the faith of the younger Zionist generation in the possibility of a national Jewish continuity in the Diaspora. This sector of young people was not at all as convinced of the prospects of continued Jewish national existence in the countries where they lived, as were some of the older Zionists,[41] who had devoted a grat deal of energy to "work for the here-and-now." The core of antagonism between the He-Halutz movement and the Zionist Organization with its political parties, stems from the differences that prevailed at that time and that contributed to the evolution of He-Halutz until the outbreak of the war.[42]

Characteristic for this period is the romantic call to the young people to fulfill their duty, "to change the content of their present life-style by returning to Mother Earth."[43] He-Halutz envisioned the redemption of the Jewish people through physical labor, not because there was no alternative, but because it was a positive ideal, "the ship of the future which carries us toward a concrete, peaceful, happy shore." Labor is seen not as a prosaic means of eking out a living but as an ideal for the future.[44]

The question "of labor as an all-encompassing ideal and goal," as well as its methods and organization, were at the hub of the on-going discussions by the pioneers. The discussion sessions of the Warsaw Zionist Youth Organization, Merkaz Ha-Tze'irim, which took place in September, 1917, devoted a great deal of attention to this problem. We find at the 1st Conference of the Pioneer Movement of October 26, 1917, a reflection of legionnaire influences with respect to the matter of labor organization. A proposal was made at the conference that He-Halutz become "a strongly disciplined peace-army" so that "the pioneer may be sent to the Land of Israel whenever he was needed." It was the duty of the pioneer to be ready to respond to its every call.[45] Though this proposal was rejected by a majority of delegates, it was nevertheless in itself symptomatic of the spirit of the time, for it reflected the external influences in the He-Halutz movement. There appears to be no doubt of the existence of the concept of a workers' army, in keeping with the then popular legionnaire view in Poland and elsewhere in Europe, albeit with some modifications. The He-Halutz core thinking changed from a military struggle to conquest through labor. Even more to the point: within the demands that the pioneer be duty-bound to stand in the vanguard of the movement both in the Diaspora and in the Land of Israel, lay the seeds of the avant-garde approach which characterizes the He-Halutz movement: i.e., the pioneers must be an elite group of people ready to sacrifice themselves, who march at the head of the army and lead the way. This concept, derived from the voluntaristic ideology of the Tze'irei Tzion, had at one time been prevlant in the Russian He-Halutz. However, under the leadership of Trumpeldor (who urged that He-Halutz become a mass movement) this avant-garde concept was rejected. Small wonder that the majority of the Polish He-Halutz opposed this idea from the beginning, since it was contrary to the very conceptualization of He-Halutz as a mass movement which characterized it from the outset.[46]

The discussion about the character of the movement continued. At the 1st Conference of the Tze'irei Tzion of September, 1918, Atkin presented a paper demanding the creation of avant-garde He-Halutz groups which would constitute a peace-army under military discipline.[47] The discussion continued at the 1st He-Halutz Conference of May, 1919. In his speech on the program of the He-Halutz, Joseph Heftman demanded that work be treated as a religion, as an article of faith. In order to attain the national goal of a Jewish majority in the Land of Israel, He-Halutz must be "organized as an army" in order to direct its activities for the next thirty-forty years and to fulfill its goal. And this will be possible only through disciplined Jewish labor, public works in the Land of Israel such as health-related sanitation and amelioration, etc., which would have to be put under the control of He-Halutz.[48] But this approach met with opposition.[49] There was no mention at all of the legionnaire view in the resolutions of the conference.[50] Apparently this was only a short, dramatic interlude in the history of the He-Halutz movement of Poland.[51] The ideological evolution of He-Halutz now veered in another direction toward an ever-increasing tie with the Histadrut and the Socialist-Zionist labor movements, i.e., toward a more socialist orientation. Several factors had led to this development:

a) He-Halutz had accepted radical goals from its inception. The emphasis on labor in general, and on agriculture in particular, as the most important national components, brought it into conflict with the General Zionists who were frequently satisfied with political demonstrations of a more propogandist nature without any active follow-up. The main concept held by He-Halutz, on the other hand, was "self-realization,"—a personal and national revolution of the Jewish people. This concept was the source of antagonism between those who wished to convert the national ideal into deeds, and those who used it only for propaganda, demonstrations, and "higher level politics." At first this conflict was of an organizational rather than ideological nature between the young radical wing of the Zionist Organization and its adult leadership which was more prudent and practical. After awhile, however, the internal natural development within He-Halutz, as well as external influences, transformed this difference into an ideological conflict which remained as part and parcel of the history of He-Halutz up to the outbreak of World War II.[52]

From the outset, traces of socialist leanings could be noted in He-Halutz, though they were as yet weak and nebulous. The plenary session of He-Halutz of May 24-25, 1919, in which regional representatives participated, indicated its solidarity with the ideological bases of He-Halutz which had been defined at the He-Halutz Conference held in Kharkov on January 28-29, 1918.[53] Such solidarity with the Kharkov decisions was, in our opinion, the outcome of a misunderstanding. These decisions had been the result of a compromise between the "idealistic" avant-garde conception on the one hand and "materialistic" mass aspirations on the other. Thus, for example, the essence of He-Halutz was characterized as "avant-garde by the working people who were going to settle in the Land of Israel, having as its goal the preparation of the land for the masses."[54] This decision was in sharp contrast to the mass character of He-Halutz in Poland. It was only in East Galicia that this socialistic-utopian tendency attained a more definite formulation in the resolutions adopted at the He-Halutz Conference of December 7-8, 1919. This group demanded of the Zionist Executive the "gradual nationalization of all land in the Land of Israel and all its natural resources."[55]

A step forward vis-a-vis a more realistic orientation was expressed in an article which demanded that the naive Land of Israel-romanticism be ended and replaced with a true appreciation of Land of Israel reality.[56]

A more detailed socialist orientation was urged by Israel Mereminsky in his article "Sober Idealism."[57] He insisted that instead of messianic exaltation, the end of which is disillusionment due to disappointment, the movement rely on clear and sober intelligence. After analyzing the difference between the Polish peasant and the pioneers, he stressed that the pioneers were forced into agricultural labor through necessity. "The pioneer is the victim of the difficult transition of a landless people to agricultural labor." The revolutionary task of rebuilding the Jewish reality demanded systematic preparation. Mereminsky denied the extremist view of "shelilat ha-Galut" (the negation of the Diaspora) because both the Diaspora and the Land of Israel had to be renewed. The pioneer was called upon not to be satisfied with only working the soil. He also had to take part in the struggle of rebuilding society as a whole upon new foundations. The author also denied the subjective voluntarism which was popular in some pioneering circles. He characterized this as idealization arising in a "narrow little corner" and forsaking "every societal ideal." The transition to agricultural labor, according to him, was not the result of romantic ideals, but is a compulsive societal process which has both a national and a universal aspect. "The pioneer has to struggle on two fronts: for national liberation in the Land of Israel as well as for national autonomy and social freedom in the Diaspora. Pioneers must have both national and societal goals and they must build an avant-garde in our struggle for liberty and equality . . . . We must stress not only 'the good laborer' but also 'the ideologically conscious laborer' who will not lag behind in the revolutionary struggle for the realization of our nationalism and our socialism, of our Zionist-socialist ideal."[58]

b) The evolution of the Polish He-Halutz toward a greater Labor Zionist orientation was likewise influenced by the increase in membership of the Tze'irei Tzion and Po'alei Tzion youth organizations. These two groups impelled He-Halutz toward a more radical direction and even the Po'alei Tzion groups began to express an open socialist orientation. At first this trend met with resistance on the part of those who aimed at retaining the general character of He-Halutz. The Regional He-Halutz Conference of February 28, 1921 reflected the struggle between these two trends—the overt socialist position represented by the Tze'irei Tzion and Po'alei Tzion delegates, and the so-called "social" orientation. The proposed resolution that He-Halutz prepare a labor element in order to build at socialist Land of Israel was voted down. The conference then adopted a compromise, 11 to 8, which called for a labor community in the Land of Israel. It was also decided to give He-Halutz members a socialist-Zionist education. The conference then greeted the emergence of the Histadrut and expressed its hopes for an early unification of all workers in the Land of Israel.[59] As was evident from the resolutions adopted at this conference, even the non-socialist wing of He-Halutz now come to look favorably upon the Histadrut and the labor movement.

With the exception of the Tze'irei Tzion movement, a movement with a rich pioneer tradition,[60] its influence on He-Halutz of Poland grew apace. The number of Tze'irei Tzion and Po'alei Tzion members at the conferences and congresses of He-Halutz continually grew. At the Regional Conference of the He-Halutz of Rovno on February 28, 1921, twenty-two out of thirty delegates were from the Tze'irei Tzion.[61] At the local conferences of Congress Poland, Vilna, Volhynia, and Brisk-Grodno, out of 125 delegates, forty-six represented the Tze'irei Tzion, fifteen were from the Hitashdut, twenty-one were from the Po'alei Tzion's right wing, and five were from "Dror" (the Zionist intellectual movement).[62] After the merger of the Po'alei Tzion with the Socialist-Zionist Party, and the increased contact with the labor sector in the Land of Israel, the socialist trend became dominant in He-Halutz.

c) A visibly strong influence on the ideological development of the Polish He-Halutz came from the Russian pioneers,[63] who had paused from 1919 to 1923 in various countries, including Poland,[64] enroute to the

Land of Israel and, indeed, Poland was the most important country of transit for the immigrants. Close to 1,800 Russian and Ukrainian pioneers had passed through Poland. In contrast to He-Halutz in other lands, the Polish He-Halutz was not founded by the Russian pioneers, so that from its beginning the He-Halutz of Poland had been under the influence of quite a different faction.[65] But when the Russian pioneers arrived in Poland, they brought with them the dynamics of the Russian revolutionary atmosphere, its social pathos, and its proletarian pride.

The pioneers of Russia and the Ukraine formed themselves into a separate, autonomous group, thereby increasing the organizational chaos of the Polish He-Halutz even further. Till then the country had had three separate headquarters: one in Congress Poland, one in East Poland, and one in Galicia. Now a fourth was added. This and the demand of the Russian pioneers to be sent on aliyah first, even at the expense of the Polish candidates for aliyah, led to quarrels among the various parties.

Despite these disagreements, however, the influence of the Russians on Polish pioneer-Zionist youth was quite marked. The young people saw in the Russian pioneers the embodiment of a new type of person: a revolutionary with universal ideals combined with a firmly national point of view. The Russian pioneers had brought with them some of the customs, concepts, and mannerisms of the Russian Revolution. They introduced their collective life-style into the homes of the Polish pioneers with whom they stayed. Their scorn of religion and free attitude toward sex evoked repugnance against these "tramps" among more conservative Jews, on the one hand, but on the other hand, Jewish young people viewed this new life-style as an expression of the new pioneering Land of Israel.

Within the hakhshara, this influence resulted in the stressing of difficult physical labor and proletarian pride. Whereas in Poland the emphasis had been on agricultural and craft-industrial hakhsharot, the Russian influence created in Poland a short-lived era of "hewers of wood and carriers of water."[66]

d) In his paper on *The Nature and the Principles of He-Halutz*, presented at the 2nd Regional He-Halutz Conference in July 1921, Dobkin, who was the delegate of the World Union of He-Halutz, formulated the ideological thrust of the movement: "The only way to liberate the Jewish people from national and social oppression is through Zionism, which strives to renew a free Jewish life supported by the productive foundations of labor. . . . Our Zionism stands not only for national but also for social liberation."[67] As the avant-garde of the Jewish people, He-Halutz must earnestly educate its youth to physical labor. Anyone, regardless of party affiliation, who wants to offer his life to labor may join He-Halutz. In contrast to the socialist-Zionist parties with their precisely formulated programs, He-Halutz can unite within its ranks all those who agree with its basic ideals, i.e., who believe in the imperative of changing the Jew toward identifying with hard labor and solidarity with the laboring classes in the Land of Israel." His conclusion was: "We are a labor organization and we have to strengthen labor consciousness. Each He-Halutz may take his own stand, however, in matters upon which the labor parties are not in agreement. Yet, in general, the movement must have a 'definite socialist character.'"[68]

Despite the opposition of those groups that wanted to retain the general character of He-Halutz by preventing its identification with the labor parties, the 2nd National Conference of He-Halutz, acting in the spirit of Dobkin's paper, declared that the movement is struggling together with the other Zionist-Socialist labor parties, in order to bring about the realization of the main goals of Jewish labor in the Land of Israel. It is important to stress here that the identification is an ideological rather than an organizational-political one. In this way He-Halutz remained open for membership of young people from different youth organizations and unaffiliated pioneer groups.

In summarizing the first era in the history of He-Halutz, Zalman Rvbashov stressed the following: "At its outset, He-Halutz had groped in the dark. It did not know who its friends were. Now its path is clear. The Diaspora He-Halutz is an organic part of the labor movement in the Land of Israel. Together with the labor movement, it strives to develop in the Land of Israel a society based on the foundations of justice and social equality."[70]

The ties with the Histadrut and the kibhutz movements in the Land of Israel became even stronger, until He-Halutz shed its general Zionist character and became recognized in the Diaspora as belonging to the Histadrut. In a way, this trend opposed the general emphases: i.e., of aiming to unite all the pioneers in its midst—including the religious and the General Zionist groups. These groups, therefore, soon formed their own specific pioneer organizations and established their own haksharot, separating themselves from He-Halutz.[71]

The memorandum of the World He-Halutz Congress which was sent to the 16th Zionist Congress specifically emphasized the general, unaffiliated character of He-Halutz. However, it also stressed that each of its members must recognize his close ties with the Histadrut and must participate in the campaigns of the labor Land of Israel[72] i.e, those pioneers who are not identified with labor in the Land of Israel have no place in He-Halutz despite its declared General Zionist position.

The 5th Nationwide Conference of the Polish He-Halutz of 1929 resolved that "the cultural work of He-Halutz must have as its goal the development of socialist-Zionist conviction among its members."[73]

The developmental process of He-Halutz from that of general idealism, which was amorphous, to its clear, ideological identification with socialist-Zionism, had come to a close.

CHAPTER TWO

THE STAGES OF DEVELOPMENT OF
THE HE-HALUTZ HAKHSHARA

A. A Seasonal Agricultural Hakhshara

Central to the He-Halutz idea is the concept of the dual meaning of hakhshara as a preparation for industrial, and especially, for agricultural work in the Land of Israel, as well as the means of making the Jewish economy productive in order to alter the specificially Jewish societal structure, primarily in the Land of Israel but also in the Diaspora.

The concept of making the Jewish economy productive was initiated during the period of the Haskalah (the Jewish Enlightenment). Theoretically it was claimed: the majority of Jewish people are engaged in nonproductive occupations. Their earnings have a destructive influence on the Jewish national character. These negative features, which developed due to Jewish concentration in petty commerce and middlemen fuctions, call forth hatred among the surrounding populations. This condition prevents the fulfillment of the Haskalah's goals of civil equality. Therefore, as long as Jews do not improve their condition by changing to productive work, they will not be able to enjoy equal rights.

There is no doubt that the negativistic attitude toward Jewish economic activity was engendered by various physiocratic theories which negated the

23

economic worth of trade and of the middleman, and which saw in agriculture the basic source of national wealth. The popularity of these
theories and their wide spread, stressed even further the abnormality of
the Jewish economic base. Likewise, the cult of labor on the land is tied
to the spread of the romantic attitudes of Rousseau. The organic link to
the soil was established as the chief prerequisite for the development of
spiritual, authentically national and human values. Jewish as well as non-
Jewish maskilim (enlightened ones) steadily disseminated the idea of productivization as the condition that would abolish hatred of the Jew by
the surrounding peoples and that would serve as a means of reaching full
Jewish civil and political emancipation.[1]

Zionism inherited the principle of productivization—not as a means of
emancipation in the Diaspora, but rather as the basis for the national
renaissance in the Land of Israel.

From the time of the First Aliyah and the Hovevei Zion (Lovers of
Zion) movement of the eighteen-eighties, the Jewish national movement
developed and nurtured the longing for a return to the Land and to a life
of justice and simplicity as peasants. A rich literature was created extolling
labor in general and labor on the Land in particular. This literature described in magnificent colors the joy of the agricultural worker who earns
his living from the soil and who is near to nature.

Of all the causes that brought Jewish youth to the Land of Israel during
the First and Second Aliyot, the desire to productivize and to settle the
Land was one of the most important. The transition to physical creative
work in general and to agriculture in particular was the most significant
principle in the He-Halutz movement and served as the basis of its hakhshara work.

The Zionist leaders regarded labor not only as an economic, but—much
more—as a moral imperative. The ideas of Martin Buber gave clear expression to this approach. In analyzing the concept of kibbush (conquest),
Buber concluded that neither the Turks nor the other conquerors of the
Land of Israel will reawaken the land. Neither will the power of money
accomplish this. The buyer of the object "land" becomes only the legal
owner of the land. The true conquest can be accomplished only by the
labor of the pioneers. "Labor is . . . the conquence of body and soul . . . .
It is an act of love."[2] The Jewish people would yield to temptation
just as other peoples have done if they were to conquer the Land of

Israel as "robbers or merchants. It is only the power of labor, by the power of love and longing that the Jewish people will conquer the land and redeem it."[3]

The same was expressed by David Ben Gurion, Yitzhak Ben Zvi, and Yaakov Zerubovel in organizing the He-Halutz in the United States during World War I. D. Ben Gurion emphasized: "A home is not given nor received as a gift . . . nor conquered through political documents or rights, neither is it won by money or force. A home is built and created . . . . If a people have the right to say: 'This is my home.' is is because these people have created it with their own hands . . . . The basis of a right to a land . . . lies not in the political nor in the juridical possession but only in labor. The true owners of a land are those who work it."[4]

The He-Halutz movement put the principle of physical labor and the return to labor on the soil at the core of its educational endeavors. This approach often assumed the character of a romantic myth.[5]

The hakhshara idea was based on the premise that in order for young people to realize their national and social ideals in the Land of Israel, especially that of a return to the soil, they must prepare the tools for this work while they are still in the Diaspora.

Even prior to World War I youth groups, part of the Tze'irei Tzion movement, sprang up spontaneously within Imperial Russia. They participated in the hakhsharot in order to prepare themselves to go to the Land of Israel.

At the 1906 Conference of Youth Biluim (young pioneer group in the Biluim tradition), a program was formulated which was based on the principles of the Bilu movement of the First Aliyah—principles that were similar to the later He-Halutz. Among other commitments, the young Biluim pledged themselves to learn a trade needed in the Land of Israel.[6]

The 1st Conference of Tze'irei Tzion, held in 1913 in Vienna, simultaneously with the 11th Zionist Congress, passed the following resolution: "To train potential olim (new immigrants) for the Land of Israel."[7] It also created the Palestine Bureau which was to coordinate hakhshara and aliyah activities. In the first circular of 1914, the Bureau insisted that the immigrants be organized in groups to train together for their tasks in the Land of Israel.[8] These efforts were only sporadic, being interrupted by the outbreak of World War I. After the war, the work of the hakhshara was developed on a larger scale throughout the entire Jewish world, especially in Poland, to become the most influential component of the pioneering movement in all its ramifications. Without the hakhshara, not one pioneer would have been able to go to the Land of Israel.

For some years after World War I, the He-Halutz hakhshara was synonomous with agricultural work. At the very first discussion sessions of the Warsaw Zionist Youth Organization, Merkaz Ha-tze'irim, held in September 1917, the discussants stressed the need for learning agricultural skills as the major prerequisite for going to the Land of Israel.[8] Similar demands were made by the He-Halutz Commission, elected at the Pioneers Conference of October 1917, and by the representatives of the Regional Zionist Conference, requiring that:

1. Farms be organized to train pioneers for working the soil in the Land of Israel;

2. Jewish landowners be persuaded to hire pioneers to till the soil.[9] The first overt efforts of the He-Halutz movement in Poland after World War I resulted in the creation of agricultural institutions, the first being established in February 1918 in the town of Bendin. Its founders, the young shomrin (scouts), write:[10] "in February we got a farm which had a two-acre field and two acres of gardens. The farm behind the town had a nice little one-story house. We began our work under the leadership of an experienced gardener. . . . The haverim (members) worked in two shifts of two hours each at assigned periods. . . . The work went well. The haverim found their work useful for they learned a great deal. Moreover, by working and living closely together, they developed an intimate spirit of comradery."[11] In analyzing the organizational approach of the Bendin hakhshara, we obtain a clear picutre of those aspects that were to become characteristic for other identical undertakings.[12] As a rule, these farms were but small units, no more than ten acres in size. They were of a temporary, warmly idealistic nature, lasting only a season or two, usually closing with a financial loss. The Bendin pioneers summed up their work-season, which ended December 1, 1918: "We made no profit on our farm. A great deal of damage was caused by heavy rains; in addition we were forced to hire outside workers to help us in our work."[13]

The romantically naive character of the hakhshara, which was to prepare colonizers for the Land of Israel, is apparent in the correspondence from the town of Grajevo: "On the first day, when our haverim came out with their pitchforks, they made a very good impression. The residents of the town looked with wonder at the young people of respected families cleaning and removing rubbish in the middle of the day."[14] It is hard to conceive how two or three or four hours of daily work in the fields during a period of a few short months could possibly accomplish the goal of actual preparation of workers of the soil. It may be said that the true significance of these efforts lies not so much in their occupational preparation as in their psychological and moral training—by taking these young people away from their urban milieu and transplanting them nearer to nature, as well as instilling in them a new dignity and pride in common labor—and this in a society where intellectual achievement was highly valued and physical labor was often looked down upon as an undesirable occupation.

But financial losses forced the pioneers to appeal to the Jewish public for support of their farms, so that, in its first stage the hakhshara also assumed a somewhat philanthropic character.

However, since its motives were idealistic, the movement's failures did not hinder it from further developing the concept of the hakhshara, particularly in its agricultural component.

The newspaper of the He-Halutz movement devoted a great deal of space to publicizing and justifying the need for preparing future farmers for the Land of Israel, arguing from a national and moral point of view. In one of its articles, "Our Mehtods and Goals," by CH. Z, the following is written: "The core in the life of a people, around which other layers of life are grouped, is the land."[15] "The tragedy of the Jewish people lies in the fact that the Jew has been pushed away from this core since his dispersion from the Land of Israel. The indigenous nations of the countries of the Diaspora drew their substenance from the soil, while the Jewish people were forced to create their own source of livelihood indirectly, second or third hand. It is impossible to alter the abnormal economic structure of the Jew in the Diaspora. Economic normalacy means the return to one's land, i.e., staging an economic revolution. This can be accomplished only in the Land of Israel. The preparation for this stage, through labor in general and agricultural labor in particular, can and must also be undertaken in the Diaspora."[16]

The hakhshara is identified with productivization. It widely accepted the view that the transition to labor is an historical imperative for Jewry in the post-war period, because general developments in the world indicate a tendency to push out the Jew from his already precarious economic position that had been undermined by the preceding war. The only alternative that remains is labor, but not labor accepted because of lack of choice. A spiritual and psychological revolution is a necessity, "to create a love of physical labor;"[17] i.e., to imbue labor with a mystical, semi-religious aura: "We have to stress the necessity of labor not only as a life-boat in stormy waters, but as a boat of the future which will take us toward a definite peaceful happy shore; labor, not for daily sustenance but as an ideal for the future;"[18] or: "The occupation of Jews in agricultural work is a national task. And when Jewish life will be reorganized on new national foundations, this task will receive the greatest attention."[19]

The romanticization and idealization of work on the land was tied to a particular anti-urbanization tendency expressed in an article by Tanhum Berman, "The Road to the Soil."[20] Because of the Diaspora, the Jewish people have lost a certain simplicity. The Jewish people have, indeed, developed a good sharp sense of orientation as a defense mechanism against constantly threatening dangers. Life in a ghetto atmosphere, however, has laid upon a Jew a stamp of abnormality. His economy became crippled and unnatural. The Jewish type is the antithesis of the normal human type which depends on physical labor for its livelihood and is "hard working though easy going."[21] A merchant does not sing at work while a peasant or an artisan does: "Song and labor are natural, and they come from the same source . . . and on the other hand, the nearer a person is to civilization, the further he is from nature."[22] Without doubt, an echo of attitudes is heard in the foregoing phrases which draws its sustenance from the Zionist tradition of the First and Second Aliyot, and from the ideas of the "narodnike"; perhaps even from the earlier German youth movement that saw in the city with its industrialization the cause of the alienation of people and of their estrangement from their natural source, the soil.[23]

If urbanization is a generally universal process, then the Jews occupy first place therein because they lack built-in correctives which would halt this harmful process. Total alienation and estrangement can be ended only by Zionism which calls the Jewish people back to the soil. The author stresses that labor has an impact on the emotional and physical constitution of man: "Together with other methods of sustaining life, many clearly unhealthy and unsympathetic traits of the Diaspora Jew will likewise

likewise disappear, and replacing these, the Jew will acquire, with the healthy color of his face, also the healthy outlook upon physical labor in general and of labor on the land in particular."[24]

This last sentence contains obvious apologetic features. Many anti-Jewish writings stress the harmful nature of the Jew who is supposedly by nature, "a swindler, a parasite who feeds off the labor of the surrounding peoples." The author recognizes the principal argument of the unsympathetic traits of the Diaspora Jews, but he considers them to be not the result of innate Jewish nature, rather that of the Diaspora; that is, an historic inheritance. With the success of He-Halutz and the Zionist revolution, these traits will vanish and the Jew will cease being different from other peoples: "Only by possessing a healthy agricultural class can we, in time, hope to straighten out our bent spines and crippled spirit. . . . Only the path of Jewish land and Jewish labor is the shorter and easier path to true redemption."[25]

It was this same spirit that was present at the discussions of the 1st He-Halutz Conference of May 1919. Speakers demanded that "labor become a cult." Of special importance was agriculture because "there must be a reaction against suburban life."[26] One of the resolutions of the conference, in the paragraph on the "philosophy of He-Halutz" declared:

"1. He-Halutz is an alliance that has the task of carrying out the actual program of Zionism: that of the rebuilding of the Land of Israel for the Jewish people by means of Jewish labor;

"2. He-Halutz strives to organize, disseminate, and establish the productive element for the Land of Israel. Primarily He-Halutz must form the cultured agricultural worker."[27]

In keeping with the spirit of this resolution, He-Halutz proceeded to create agricultural farms, as many as eighteen of them. But lack of funds to carry on agricultural work led to the abandonment of the farms, except for the Grochov farm established in 1919, which operated until the outbreak of World War II.[28]

The Arab attacks on the settlers of Tel Hai in the Northern Galilee on March 1, 1920, elicited a tremendous reaction among young people and hundreds of them began to join the ranks of He-Halutz. Neither the farms nor the treasury of He-Halutz could accomodate all of these new members. A new type of agricultural hakhshara, which had already existed side by side with the original He-Halutz hakhshara (although run on a more modest scale), now became the more common one. This was the seasonal hakhshara, consisting of Jewish agricultural workers on loan to Jewish farm owners. This form of hakhshara existed, with few interruptions, until the 1930's, when it was replaced by the permanent hakhshara, "hakhshara kevu'ah." Thousands of pioneers from all pioneer organizations went through this seasonal hakhshara.

Its beginnings were not auspicious. The Jewish farm owners regarded the young pioneers with suspicion and were not willing to accept them as workers, perhaps fearing that the employment growth of Jewish workers would "antagonize the Gentile workers. . . .Others, on the other hand, told us that they would hire a few pioneers on condition that they did not have to pay them wages."[29]

The same vibrations also came from Zamosc and environs which had several Jewish estates: "For two years our group of pioneers has been interceding with the Jewish farmers to hire some of us on their farms. But it was difficult because our wealthy Jewish peasants were afraid lest they be called upon to make sacrifices for the sake of the Jewish pioneer workers."[30]

After these landowners did however agree to hire pioneers as workers, they were soon convinced that, though the pioneer had no practical experience in agricultural work, yet his good will and enthusiasm were so great that, after a short but strenuous period of acclimationization, he could do the same work as the Gentile seasonal laborers. The landowners then exploited the pioneers in the worst possible way. In an article written by J. H. (Joseph Heftman—I.O.) called "Pioneers and Landowners,"[31] the author summarized the work of the pioneers on Jewish estates, a most tragic story indeed. With very few exceptions, Jewish society reacted with contempt and indifference toward Jewish labor. Many Jewish landowners shamelessly exploit the pioneers who are forced to work under the worst conditions and for the smallest wages. What is even worse, some of these providers of work are themselves Zionists. In many cases the employers do not even pay a minimum wage. At times they would withhold food even though they had agreed to provide it so that the pioneers are forced to pay for food out of their own scant funds. Their work day is from 7 A.M. to 9 P.M. The author feels such treatment is caused by the fact that the Jewish landowner looks upon the field labor of Jewish young people as an abnormal phenomenon: "Therefore they deserve to be treated with a certain contempt."[32] And this despite the fact that the accomplishments of the pioneers exceeded those of the Gentile laborers.

It might seem that such shameful treatment would call forth strikes or other forms of protest. The author, however, came to the conclusion that although these landowners behaved like animals, they gave Jewish youth the only means of training in practical agriculture. Therefore the pioneers had to remain silent and not resort to any radical counter-measures. Though this attitude was temporary and not characteristic of the pioneer movement—especially later when He-Halutz became identified with the labor movement and obligated its members to join labor unions—yet it put a weapon into the hands of He-Halutz opponents, such as the Bund and the Communists, who argued that He-Halutz was a tool in the hands of the bourgeoisie, in lowering the wages of the worker.[33]

In summary: the author of the article demanded a cahnge in this relationship: "We are not seeking privileges. On the contrary, we want the Jewish worker in the fields to receive the same treatment as the Gentile worker; we want them not to be taken for queer idealists or impractical dreamers who may be treated with contempt and underestimation."[34]

In fact, it is important to emphasize that this negativistic picture is not entirely an objective one. We found in some correspondences appearing at that time in He-Halutz publications, echoes of another positive attitude on the part of Jewish landowners toward the pioneers. For example, the pioneers of Kremenetz stressed that in their agricultural hakhshara, in a village near the city, "there were several Jewish agricultural families who treated the pioneers very kindly."[35]

Besides propagandizing for agricultural hakhshara, He-Halutz also developed a vision of a future society for those pioneers who went to settle in the Land of Israel. In agreement with the general Zionist character of the movement, He-Halutz did not educate colonists for a collective kibbutz type of life. At the time the goal of the hakhshara was to train village landowners, owners of small though modern agricultural units. It was said at the 1st he-Halutz Conference: "We must develop in the Land of Israel a class of peasant small landowners."[36]

The transition from an individual to a collective hakhshara and to exclusive kibbutz training came later. This transition came as a result of an internal development that brought He-Halutz closer to the concept of a kibbutz, and as the fruit of stronger ties with the Histadrut. It also came as a result of the influence of the Land of Israel "shelihim" (emissaries) from the kibbutz movements in Palestine: especially from Ha-Kibbutz Ha-Meuhad (the United open, non-partisan Kibbutz movement), and later from Ha-Kibbutz Ha-Artzi (the Ha-Shomer Ha-Tza'ir kibbutzim movement), and from hever Ha-Kevutzot (the Society of Small Settlements), though the first sprouts of the concept of a collective hakhshara had been evident as far back as the 1920's.[37] However, at the time, life in a collective hakhshara did not obligate a pioneer to a collective kibbutz life in the Land of Israel, as it did later, during the Fourth Aliyah, until World War II.

The period during which the agricultural hakhshara was the center of gravity of pioneer activities lasted until 1921. At that time a new chapter began in the history of He-Halutz—the new chapter of the artisan-industrial hakhshara which lasted until the beginning of 1924.

B. Training for Vocations and All Hard Physical Labor

1) "As a result of the programmatic resolution,[38] all He-Halutz members must learn one of the trades necessary for building Eretz Israel."[39]

This is the decision of the Second Nationwide Conference of He-Halutz in 1921 which opens the period of vocational training.

All the vocations needed in addition to the agricultural are listed: land and sea communication, building trades, locksmithing, carpentry, technical skills, etc. A very limited number of members are asked to learn service trades such as shoemaking, tailoring, baking etc.[40]

Members who are not working at all, it was decided, will be admitted as He-Halutz members only in exceptional cases if they can be of behavioral or organizational use to the group.[41]

It seems that under the influence of the Russian halutzim who, while in Poland, had spread the concept and ideal of physical, "dirty" work, like carrying water and hewing wood, the following resolution was also adopted: "In the hakhshara we must take pains to prepare the members *for hard physical labor* (underlined in the original, I.O.) so that when they come to the Land *they should be prepared for every work*" (underlined in the original, I.O.).[42]

The truth is that vocational training occupied a certain place in He-Halutz even when agriculture was at the center of the hakhshara work.

Already in the first regulations of He-Halutz at the beginning of January 1918, agriculture is indeed stressed as an important goal of the movement. But at the same time it is also demanded of the halutzim that they learn "various other agriculturally-related trades such as carpentry, blacksmithing, and the like," as well as skills "in every area of production," and that they also "recruit people needed for creating a new settlement— for example, for construction work, road and railroad building, stonemasonry, and the like."[43]

The correspondence from the various localities do from time to time report the creation of vocational courses, but as secondary activities and sometimes after the attempts at agricultural hakhshara failed. Such was the case in Lithuanian Brisk after the attempt to establish a farm did not succeed "and we unfortunately had to spend the entire winter sitting on our hands, though a few of us did work for owners of estates." When the winter season was over, with the help of the American Committee, they established a trade-school. The plan was to learn various trades such as being a mechanic, sewing, etc. But because of a shortage of means they had to settle for carpentry only and the consolation "that this trade is very important for the Land of Israel and does not require much time to learn."[44] There are also reports of other forms of sporadic attempts to learn trades; of some halutzim who hire themselves out as apprentices to private craftsmen.[45] The trend, however, only becomes dominant in 1921.

At the outset, the ideological basis for trade hakhshara was the need to prepare cadres for the agricultural needs of the Land of Israel which, as we have seen, was at the center of the hakhshara efforts as the basis of the national renaissance. However, there was some doubt from the start about the relevance to the Land of Israel of agricultural hakhshara in Europe because of the difference of soil and climate. At the First He-Halutz Conference, the agronomist Oppenheim responded to this positively in his report: "Organizing the Practical Work of He-Halutz."

"One often hears the question: Are the conditions of the soil the same as here? The answer to that may be: the conditions are not the same; but from that one should not conclude that one should not expand. Botany, zoology, agronomy, etc. are the same the world over, and a farmer will alwyas find a solution everywhere. What we learn here will undoubtedly be useful for us in the Land of Israel."[46]

When they came to the Land of Israel, however, the halutzim met an entirely different reality: work opportunities were not waiting for

them in the existing agriculture nor in the setting up of new rural settlements. The little work available in the old colonies was preempted by
Arabs. Furthermore, the few Jewish laborers that were there could not
support themselves because of the low pay. The few amenable collective
kevutzot, established during the Second Aliyah, could not accept the
new olim because they themselves were living on a low standard. The
country had no industry. Thus, in the early years of the Third Aliyah,
especially between 1920-1921, the largest number of olim found employment in public works, mainly in the building of roads planned and carried out by the British government.[47] The discrepancy between the
nature of the hakhshara in Poland and the sources of work in the Land
of Israel became even greater in 1922-1923, when the public government work came to an end and the employment center of gravity shifted
to construction and other trades financed and implemented by the Zionist
Organization.[48] The greatest part of the new olim was absorbed in the
city, not in the village. The workers' census of the end of 1922 shows
that only 20% had found employment in agriculture, 17% in construction,
and many more in trade and industry.[49] This reality forced He-Halutz to
create new forms of hakhshara to conform to the Land of Israel reality.

At the end of 1922, a country-wide network of hakhshara locations
was set up. The following trades were taught: carpentry, locksmithing,
construction work, etc.[50]

The trade hakhshara developed in two forms: individually, with private
artisans, and collectively, in one's own He-Halutz workshop, where social
and cultural activity was also developed. There the work was based upon
cooperative principles. Understandably, the movement leaned to the
second form because only a limited number of skills could be learned from
the private craftsmen and in most such instances there was no theoretical
education. The craftsman was in many cases not interested in teaching
the halutz journeyman the secrets of the trade. The worth of this kind of
hakhshara was therefore very limited. But the lack of its own sources of
funds to establish its own trade schools leaves He-Halutz no alternative
but to support the private trade-hakhshara.[51] Where possible, two haks-
shara options are proposed: its own trade-school and He-Halutz homes
(halutzim-houses). But, again, due to financial difficulties which do not
permit a 3-to-4-year trade hakhshara, they make do with setting up halutzim-houses with workbenches. It is stressed that the halutzim must receive

their hakshara away from their permenant residences in order to free themselves from economic dependence upon parents and the moral and societal
influences of the environment.

Since these institutions are not rentable, it is recommended, especially
during the transitional period until the members learn the trade, that the
He-Halutz Central Committee should support them until they can support
themselves.[52]

In the spirit of this recommendation, the Central Committee did establish a few central workshops where halutzim from all over Poland received
trade training. Thus it was, for example, that at the He-Halutz Central
Committee session of April 17, 1923, it was decided to create in Szyd-
lowiec (near Radom) a central locksmith shop on a cooperative basis . . .
for ten members; the working time to be twelve months; the members
to receive room and board, shoes and clothing, but they must bring their
own boots. The sums invested by the Central Committee is considered
a loan to be repaid by the ten members in equal payments here or in the
Land of Israel. Every member who will be accepted must bring with him
at least 150 kilograms of corn.[53] Members who join the locksmith shop
must be sufficiently advanced ideologically to be able to organize their
internal life and manage a pioneering venture.[54]

The third avenue for trade hakhshara was to attend the schools of
ORT, "Help through Labor," and community and other public institutions. He-Halutz has a certain reserve about this form of trade hakhshara
because, though the motive force in both ORT and He-Halutz is productivization, there does exist a principle difference between the two.
"In ORT, productivization is a means to economic independence, but for
us it is a complete *weltanschauung.*"[55]

Here, also, the paucity of funds forced He-Halutz to compromises.
Since there are not enough monies to establish their own institutions,
it is recommended that the halutzim also exploit these opportunities to
learn a trade.[56]

The resolution of the Third Nationwide Conference of the Polish He-
Halutz, in May, 1923, reflects the development of the hakhshara concept
from the Second to Third Conference. The third session decides to especially concern itself with individual hakhshara, for the trade-hakhshara
with the artisans and estate owners is the greatest percentage of the entire
hakhshara.[57] Among other things, the Conference demanded that the

Central Committee and the local Committees organize evening courses in trades' theory so that the members working with the private crafts-men should round out their knowledge of the trade.[58]

As to the independent trade-institutions of He-Halutz, the Central Committee is called upon to "make them all of one model, with a uniform plan of work and study."[59] These trade institutions are also asked to strive "to become economically independent" but not at the expense of "rational trade hakhshara." Candidates for trade hakhshara should be chosen according to the following directives: that the candidate be physically healthy and ready for hakhshara, and "how suited the candidates are for collective living and creating."[60]

The Second World-Conference of He-Halutz in Berlin, 1923, tried to summarize the trade hakhshara period. In the Polish report it is under-scored that of 1600 Polish halutzim there were 110 in agricultural hakh-shara on six farms, others had organized themselves cooperatively for carpentry, locksmithing, tinsmithing, and blacksmithing, as well as in trade courses in various cities. Most of them had received their trade train-ing from private artisans because of a lack of funds in independent He-Halutz institutions which would also provide a collective communal edu-cation and "which could have saved all the organized halutzim."[61]

The report of the provisional World Central-Committee emphasizes the fact that the hakhshara had developed according to the changing requirements of the Land of Israel. When the Land had required con-struction workers "we began worrying about organizing a course in con-struction theory...geared to place at the disposal of the Histadrut in the Land of Israel a certain number of construction workers and con-struction instructors."[62] But in the discussion about hakhshara at this Conference, there were already voices being heard demanding moderation in its planning, i.e., that it be organized exclusively in their own He-Halutz institutions and only in those trades for which there is a future in the Land of Israel.[63] The point is not to be so influenced by the con-stantly changing requirements of the Land of Israel, which at one time needs trade hakhshara, another time ordinary halutz hakhshara, etc.[64]

The last demand has a very important ideological significance and represents an autonomous tendency of He-Halutz: as for the Land of Israel, the demand is for recognition of the independently evolving lines of the movement in the Diaspora and against its subordination to the

changing circumstances in the Land of Israel, because it only serves to into-
duce chaos into the activity of the movement. David Ben-Gurion came
out sharply against this, demanding that He-Halutz in the Diaspora adapt
itself totally to the requirements of the Land of Israel.[65]

This tendency was to a certain extent reflected in the Conference's
resolutions on trade hakhshara. Generally these are identical to the resolutions of the Third Nationwide Conference of the Polish He-Halutz.[66]
At the same time, however, "the Conference asks the General Histadrut
of the Land of Israel to adapt the activity of its 'Center for Labor and
Aliyah' more closely to the demands of He-Halutz in the Galut and its
activity in the realm of hakhshara. To this end, the Histadrut must create
a special Information Department (which should disseminate information—my note: I. O.) on the state of agriculture, industry, and future
labor plans, so that the Galut hakhshara activity can be adapted accord-
ingly."[67] In the area of relationships with the Land of Israel, the most
that the Conference was ready to do is to demand coordination but not
autonomy or full independence, for that would be contrary to the essence
of He-Halutz which, from its very outself, had felt itself to be an exponent
of the Land of Israel idea and the Land of Israel reality in Galut.

A short time after these two conferences, however, there is another
change in the He-Halutz trend in hakhshara as a result of economic developments in the Land of Israel. In the second half of 1923, an economic
crisis broke out there which lasted into 1924, the beginnng of the Fourth
Aliyah. Every branch of the economy stagnated. Unemployment grew.
At the end of 1923, 2300 workers, i.e., 28% of all wage-earners, were
unemployed.[68] Along with the economic crisis there was also an ideological one. Not a few workers, including some members of He-Halutz,
became disheartened, losing their faith in the Zionist-pioneering values.
The anti-Zionist and pro-Communist wing in the Land of Israel Labor
Movement became stronger and openly preached leaving the country.
"Emigration from the Land of Israel is increasing. The reason: disappointment of the great hopes." So writes the publicist, M. Kushnir.[69] In
that period, in 1922, "about 2000 people have left the Land of Israel,
part of them laborers," writes Sh. Yavnieli in 1924, and the emigration
has not stopped.[70] In 1923, 3480 people leave.[71]

The impact of this development upon He-Halutz was very grave. Its
ranks were depleted, its influence diminished. It became evident that the

trade hakhshara alone was not enough to produce a conscientious member. To achieve that goal, the movement needed an intensive ideological education which would prepare the member to carry out all colonizing tasks. The first signs of this, a new approach to the hakhshara question, are to be found in the He-Halutz Council resolution at the end of 1923 which states: "The Plenum obligates all He-Halutz members to do every sort of productive work—'black' or skilled."[72]

Summing up the trade-hakhshara experiment, Berl Katznelson said at the World Council of He-Halutz in Danzig in 1926 that the trade hakhshara in itself is insufficient; pioneering hakhshara must be given. The artisans who were brought to the Land of Israel were scattered to all the winds. A trade can be mastered: "But first of all we must value the good soldier. The artisan who will be a soldier is important for us."[73] The emphasizes the greater importance of cultural and ideological hakhshara. The He-Halutz members must receive a deep and broad Hebraic cultural education, so that his faith shall not be weakened even in time of crisis."[74]

The full break with the trade-hakhshara and the transition to ideological education and the creation of new collectivist hakhshara forms first occurred during the severe crisis of the Fouth Aliyah.[75]

At the Third He-Halutz World Conference in March 1926, the final accounting of the trade-hakhshara and its failure took place. The point was made that He-Halutz, in the crisis years, had lost all of its trade-hakhshara institutions in Poland and Galicia. At that time, He-Halutz had not a single workshop nor trade. The failure of He-Halutz's own urban trade-hakhshara institutions which had been established on the basis of the requests from the Land of Israel to set up a trade-hakhshara without an economic base or educational values taught the movement to shift its center of gravity to collective educational activity in order to create and strengthen the core of the movement.[76]

CHAPTER 3

THE DEVELOPMENT OF HE-HALUTZ BETWEEN
THE FOURTH AND FIFTH ALIYAH:
1924-1929

A. General Outline of the Characteristics of the Fourth Aliyah

The crisis of the Third Aliyah, which began in 1923, was a result of a few factors: a) a diminished flow of capital into the land of Israel; b) the liquidation of the public government work in which most of the new olim were employed; c) the decrease of the Keren Kayemet (Jewish National Fund) work of drying and draining the lands. This lasted until the second half of 1924, the start of the Fourth Aliyah. In contrast to the previous aliyot, this one has a mass-character with its roots in the developments in the lands of the Diaspora, especially in Poland. The Polish government, in which Grabski was Minister of Finance, had adopted a plan to regulate the Polish economy at the expense of the urban dwellers, i.e., primarily the Jews. In his address to the Polish Parliament on April 7, 1924, at a session dealing with the year's second quarter budget, Yizhak Gruenbaum stresses the fact that the aim of regulating the money-economy has in large measure succeeded "but at whose expense has this regulation been carried out?. . .We cannot rid ourselves of the impression that it was deliberately done in such a way that the main burden be borne by trade and industry, i.e., for the most part, by the Jews. . .77%

of the population have produced 77 million zloty and 23%—33 million. This 23% are urban: merchants, industrialists, artisans, i.e., primarily Jews."[1]

Gruenbaum accuses the government of a tendency to disturb the economy of the Jews by high taxes, forcing them to make way for a Polish middle-class. That the Polish government made the aliyah to the Land of Israel easier by exempting the olim from the high passport fee of 500 zloty can serve as an indication of the validity of this analysis.[2]

Economic edicts against Jews have been nothing new in the history of Eastern Europe. But unlike the 19th century when the declared aim was "to improve" the economic life of the Jews, it was now openly stated that underlying this policy is not the unproductive character of the Jewish economy but the desire to establish a Polish middle-class in order to strengthen the hand of the majority against the Jewish national minority. The Jew was discriminated against for being a Jew. To a great portion of the Jewish middle-class it became clear that it has no future in that land.

The economic situation of the Jews had in any case already been weakened because of the loss of the large Russian market for Polish goods and as a result of the development of the railroad system which made the role of the Jewish town merchants—as brokers between town and city—superfluous. The peasants began to meet their needs for industrial products through cooperatives directly from the city, and marketed their crops similarly. The Grabski-edicts shook the foundations of the weakened Jewish economic life even more. The solution—to save what is left of one's possessions—was, for many of the middle-class, emigration. But since the gates of the United States had been closed with the quota-laws of 1924, and other traditional lands of emigration had limited their immigration, the Land of Israel became the chief destination of Jewish immigration. Not only from Poland, but from all of Eastern Europe, 350,000 Jews left in 1919-1924 and crossed the seas; about 83,000 to the Land of Israel. In 1925, the emigration to Land of Israel came to 36,933, and in the overseas countries, i.e., America, Argentina, and Canada, only 32,000. Polish Jewry constituted over 50% of this emigration overseas and to the Land of Israel.[3]

Characteristic of this aliyah is the nature of its social elements. Unlike the Second and Third Aliyot which bore a primarily ideological character and saw their main goal as the establishment of a Jewish farming and working class, the difference of the Fourth Aliyah is clearly reflected in the composition of its olim. Of 17,740 Polish olim in 1925, 6,063 had capital; 3,317 were invited by mostly middle-class relatives; 6,759 were pioneers and workers; 1,558 were tourists who remained in the country; and the rest were rabbis, etc. By trade, 1,433 were agricultural laborers; 2,369 were skilled and unskilled workers (1,055 in the needle trades); 1,923 were merchants; 1,280 technicians and in the free professions; and 8,185 were without trade or occupation.[4]

This specific character of the Fourth Aliyah made its mark on the development of the land. 80% went to the three cities: Tel-Aviv, Haifa, and Jerusalem. Tel-Aviv alone absorbed 65% of all the olim.[5]

The upswing did not last long. In 1926 the aliyah had already dropped to 13,081 and the emigration rose from 2,151 (of approximately 37,000 immigrants) in 1925, to 7,365. In 1927 the emigration rose even more: 2,713 arrived, 5,071 left. This was the only instance in the modern history of the Land of Israel that more people left than came. In 1928 the change began: 2,178 arrived, 2,168 departed.[6]

After a year of stormy development, a serious crisis erupted, lasting till the end of 1928, and was one of the bitterest periods in the history of the Yishuv (the Jewish Settlement) in Land of Israel. Of the Polish olim, one-half returned to Poland.[7]

The main brunt of the crisis was borne by the city which had absorbed the largest number of new immigrants. The chief investments had been made there. In 1925, 1,436,000 pounds sterling had been invested in Tel-Aviv; in 1926, only 236,000. The decline was a result of the monetary crisis and the inflation in Poland. The capital structure and the manner of its investments aggravated the crisis. The largest part of the middle-class immigrants had brought small capital with them which was not enough to set up rentable and productive branches of industry.[8] This money was chiefly invested in urban land and buildings for speculative purposes. Small enterprises were set up with a capital of 500-1000 pounds sterling, with 4-5 directors who drew high salaries. The lifestyle outdistanced the economic capabilities. A great part of the funds which had flowed in was spent again abroad for unproductive purposes. Of the 8-million-pound expenditure in 1925-1926, only 10% went for productive purposes. The remainder went to import consumer goods. Chaim Arlosoroff characterized this development as follows: "The Jewish city is living a life of leisure in the Jewish land."[9]

At the end of 1925 a shortage of capital was felt. The banks closed off their credit; without enough capital the building activity stopped; and with it, the branches of production which had served it. The number of unemployed continued to grow. In October 1925 it was 1,000; in June 1926, 7.000; and at the beginning of 1928 it was already 8,500, i.e., almost half of all the wage-earners at that time.[10]

As the crisis deepened, a mass exodus begins: not only capitalists or those who have become bankrupt leave, but workers as well, including not a few He-Halutz members who return to their old homeland. The popular and elemental character of the Fourth Aliyah, its ideological indifference and inadequate preparation, brought on a panicky exodus with its concommitant negative phenomena. Only in 1929, with the improvement of the economic situation in the Land of Israel, did the immigration outweigh the emigration by a few thousand. That was the beginning of the Fifth Aliyah, in which the participation of the pioneers was significant.

B. The Growth of He-Halutz

The Polish He-Halutz survived both the rise and fall of the Fourth Aliyah. During that period, certain phenomena crystallized within He-Halutz that influenced the ideological and organizational development of the pioneering movement. At that time, new pioneer movements arose such as the General Zionist He-Halutz and the Mizrachi He-Halutz, that broke the general He-Halutz monopoly on hakhshara and labor aliyah.[11]

As already mentioned, the number of the Polish working element in the Fourth Aliyah was quite significant, despite the dominant middle-class and petit-bourgeois element. The worker count of 1926 showed that 37.6% of all workers came from Poland, a significant number of them He-Halutz members.[12]

Till that period, the Polish He-Halutz had not played a significant role in the communal life of Polish Jewry. Small in number, in 1923 it counted 1700 members,[13] most of them middle-class, and many of them students who came to He-Halutz for ideological reasons. The movement had an avant-garde and somewhat esoteric character. This changed with the start of the Fourth Aliyah. In the second half of 1924 it has 5,060 members; in 1925, 13,000.[14]

This furious growth changed the social structure of He-Halutz. The romantic longings of students were replaced by young workers, unemployed, members of professional unions, Zionist-Socialist and even anti-Zionist parties. This youth, in light of the crisis in Poland and the limitations of emigration opportunities to other lands, saw the Land of Israel as the only escape for its future. With He-Halutz becoming a mass-movement, in a year or two it became a very important factor in the Jewish communal life of Poland.

The pioneer movement was unprepared for the mass influx. Instructors, locations, literature were missing. Nor was there a crystallized ideology. All this was reflected in the nature of its educational activity. The deeper cultural educational process was lost. It did not succeed in controlling the elements.[15] People went to hakhshara who had joined the movement for opportunistic reasons. He-Halutz took on the features of an emigration organization. For many members emigration became the main aim. The ideological premises were forgotten. The pressure from the Land of Israel added to this. In the spring of 1924, the Histadrut asked that He-Halutz send 1000 pioneers to the Land of Israel, whether or not they have undergone hakhshara, because of the country's actual need for labor.[16] Understandably, this group was not prepared to take on pioneering tasks. When they arrived in the Land of Israel, the members were left on their own. No one welcomed them or took an interest in them, and thus their pioneer identity was entirely erased. Many of them remained in the city, cut off from the movement and lost to it. With the outbreak of the crisis at the end of 1925, they were among those who left the country.

The "Aliyah Office" (Immigration Office) of the Histadrut had called upon the pioneer movements to join its ranks in fighting against the negative phenomena. He-Halutz is asked to strengthen the ideological foundations of the pioneer consciousness. The Third Aliyah, which gave up better earnings in the city to go to the village, it set forth as an examplar. But the new pioneers of the Fourth Aliyah function contrariwise. They "avail themselves . . . of all sorts of excuses to go to the city, unconcerned that there is no work there."[17] This call at the first signs of crisis is evidence of the new character of the pioneer aliyah.

The severe crisis in the Land of Israel affected the growth of He-Halutz. The number of pioneers already begins to drop in 1925. In 1926 it falls to 9,500 and in 1927-1928 to 4,000.[18] Branches collapse and members leave the movement by the thousands.[19] The hakshara that had encompassed thousands shrinks to a few hundred. In 1927 its count is about 900 members in all the hakhshara locations, i.e., on its own farms, temporary agricultural hakhshara and other work.[20] Only 23% of the members are on hakhshara; the rest idle at home with their parents. A segment do not believe in hakhshara at all because there is no aliyah.[21] The core of the movement is created by the two hakhshara-kibbutzim, Klosow and Shahariah, that played the main role in the movement's renewal.[22]

Both the failure of the pioneer mass-aliyah which did not go to the villages in the prosperous Land of Israel, and the concommitant drop in the He-Halutz membership as a result of the crisis, produced a certain reaction within the ranks of He-Halutz and outside of it and greatly influenced its later development.

C. The Demand to Abolish the Hakhshara

The opposition in the Zionist movement to pioneer hakhshara in the Diaspora was not new. In 1919, during the Fourth Nationwide Conference of the Polish Zionists, the speaker on the problems of the Land of Israel sharply attacked the agricultural hakhshara. "Most of the so-called farms that the various groups (of—I.O.) He-Halutz have established do not address the serious and noble aim which He-Halutz set for itself. We must put an end to this harmful dilettantism, with this strange new form of 'fakery' which stems from not grasping the full seriousness of the preparatory work."[23]

He-Halutz and the pioneer hakhshara were also attacked by the leftist Poalei-Zion whose ideology was built upon the Borochovist theory of an unorganized aliyah, as a result of objective economic and societal processes which will drive both the Jewish bourgeoisie and proletariat to the Land of Israel in order to build a normal economic structure there that would serve the Jewish working class as a strategic base for its class struggle.

Hakhshara was attacked by the middle-class Zionists because of its radicalism and eschatology and as an answer and reaction to the pioneer critique of opportunism on the part of the Zionist leadership. Poalei-Zion, on the other hand, attacked it because of its "petit-bourgeois utopianism." But these were attacks from outsiders, from opponents. In the

Fourth Aliyah years, the attack upon hakhshara came from within, from those working in the Land of Israel.

The hakhshara opponents doubted its cultural and crafts-training value. Voices were heard claiming that the real hakhshara toward a skill and communal living first begins in the Land of Israel. The suggestion, therefore, was to liquidate hakhshara completely and "concentrate on the urban activity, to create an the Land of Israel atmosphere there . . . the center of gravity should be education in the urban branch, with the physical hakhshara as the last stage.[24] The educational and cultural work should be done there. The practical result: better to have fewer prepared pioneers than many unprepared ones."[25]

The majority of the movement rejected this position and defended the necessity of hakhshara even in the years of free aliyah; all the more so in the crisis years.[26]

Hakhshara is needed for the productivization of the Jewish youth, so that when they reach the Land of Israel they should be prepared to fill the colonizing needs. This revolution in the lives of the youth cannot be achieved by fine words and phrases but only by concrete actions. Hakhshara also has a strong impact upon the entire Jewish youth and public and draws them closer to Zionism: "Every collective labor group which organizes itself in a town and goes out to the village influences all the surrounding towns. Every pioneer farm draws the attention of the Jewish public and wins the hearts of the youth."[27]

Hakhshara spiritually prepares the youth for the Land of Israel. It draws them out of their householder, petit-bourgeois environment and leads them to a life of labor.[28]

The recommendations to liquidate the hakhshara were not implemented. Its vital importance to He-Halutz and the pioneering movement in general became most evident particularly in the critical years of the Fourth Aliyah. Precisely when the movement was suffering a loss of members, new hakhshara forms were developed which, at an opportune moment, turned He-Halutz into a mass movement. At the time of the Fourth Aliyah and the crisis years of 1925-1929, the "kibbutz aliyah" (organized immigration group) and the "permanent kibbutz" (i.e., permanent kibbutz) were established. The latter became the sole hakhshara form in the thirties.

D. The Kibbutz Aliyah

In a circular published in the He-Halutz bi-weekly "He-Atid" of April 30, 1925, there is a proposal to create a new form of pioneering self-realization—the "kibbutz aliyah."[29] The aim of this kibbutz should be to organize the He-Halutz olim within a collective framework so that they should not be lost to the movement when they come to the Land of Israel.

The call came from the Vilna region: "At the initiative of S. Bogdanovsky, the Council of the Vilna He-Halutz has undertaken to solve the dire needs of the He-Halutz movement in the Diaspora, and has decided to organize an aliyah-kibbutz in the Vilna region to be called "Ha-Kovesh" (the Conqueror). The kibbutz wil make aliyah together and put itself at the service of the Histadrut for colonization and work. About 200 members from the Vilna area are preparing for imminent aliyah. The Council has turned to these members in a separate circular and has suggested that they organize the aliyah-kibbutz."[30]

The underlying causes of this call lie in the character of the hitherto individual aliyah. True, Trumpeldor in October 1918 had already demanded that the future He-Halutz should organize its members not only for hakhshara but also for their aliyah. Since the movement will have to carry out colonizing tasks in the Land of Israel in the process of building the country, the members of He-Halutz must "travel to Israel not as individuals but as a well-organized group which will be strong enough to take upon itself varying tasks and carry them out by themselves on their own responsibility."[31] This principle did not find its place in the Polish movement. Until the Fourth Aliyah, one left for the Land of Israel individually or in small, chance groupings—all of this after a short hakhshara period. Upon reaching the Land of Israel, each member of the movement sought to solve his problems in the new reality alone or along with small groups. So long as He-Halutz was a relatively small, ideologically crystallized movement whose members were thoroughly imbued with the avant-garde pioneering spirit, they generally, after reaching the Land of Israel, found their way to the various existing ideological-colonizing labor circles: in "gedud ha-avodah" (an early 20's attempt to establish a collective entity in the whole country), collective labor groups, in building roads, and in the "shomer" (guard)-like and other pioneering groups. Therefore, to organize the aliyah while yet in the Diaspora was not so imperative in the eyes of the He-Halutz leadership.

The situation changed with the massive growth of the movement during the Fourth Aliyah. In the course of a single year it grew from about 2,000 members in 80 branches to 14,000 in 460 branches in 120 hakhshara kibbutzim. It social composition became heterogeneous. Members joined its ranks who wished to emigrate and who, upon reaching the Land of Israel left its ranks for the cities in order to participate in the "prosperity."[32]

The aforementioned call also states: "The last aliyah did not fulfill its task, vis-a-vis neither the pioneering movement nor itself. For years the pioneer swore to be loyal . . . and prepared for . . . any colonizing in order to pave the way for the new aliyah. But not all the members in the Land found their way to organized labor, to the work-kibbutzim in the city, and to the "kibbush" (conquest of labor) groups in the colonies. Part scattered, ran away: some to slave-labor for exploiters, others to a useless life without social responsibilities, without ideals."[33]

The movement was facing a difficult dilemma: its rapid growth was endangering the original character of He-Halutz. That is why voices were being heard calling for a limitation on new members in order to protect its ideological purity and that it not be blinded by the magic of high numbers.[34] On the other hand, the Land of Israel constantly called for new pioneering forces that would enable Jewish labor to make inroads into the colonies, most of whose employees were cheap Arab manpower.[35] But the process in effect till then of individual or chance group aliyah had failed. The news from the Land of Israel told of ships without pioneers, of important positions lost because of a shortage of hands. The pioneering work in the Diaspora came to naught when the pioneer reached the shores of the Land of Israel. At the same time, the movement did not want to close itself to new members because this would be contrary to its folk-character. This produced the answer: an organized aliyah which would place itself under the Histadrut in the Land of Israel.

This initiative which came from below reveals the peculiar and specific character of the He-Halutz movement. More than once did a local, spontaneous initiative create new ideological and organizational values which, in time, became important basic components of the movement.[36] In the pioneer movement, especially in its early periods, the reciprocal influence of the rank and file members on the leadership and vice versa was very constant and evident. It would seem that the reason for this unique situation must be sought in its avant-garde spirit. He-Halutz demanded that its members take an active part in the life and activities of the movement. Unlike a political party, which generally is satisfied with political activities and oftimes even only with its members' declarations of belonging, He-Halutz included all aspects of its members' lives and was total in its demands. In addition, its democratic character, its solidarity, and the radicalism of all its goals—all these together created in the ordinary member a deep sense of responsibility for the fate of the entire movement.

As we have seen above, the "Ha-Kovesh" plan was to organize 200 members who would divide themselves into groups of 50, make aliyah together, place themselves at the disposal of the Histadrut upon reaching the Land of Israel and, together with its representatives, confer about working in partnership within the ranks of labor.[37] After a few months of explanatory work, 100 members enrolled in the aliyah-kibbutz, made aliyah in groups,[38] and later created the kibbutz "Ramat Ha-Kovesh" in the Land of Israel. After this experiment succeeded, new aliyah-kibbutzim were created in 1925-1926: "Avodah" (Labor) in Congress Poland, "Pinsk" in Polesie, and "Achvah" (Friendship) in the Grodno-Bialystok area. At the end of 1926, the aliyah-kibbutzim, including those that had already made aliyah, numbered about 900 members.[39]

The members of the first aliyah-kibbutz, "Ha-Kovesh," had generally not undergone hakhshara together, i.e., they were associated by chance and, despite the organization of the aliyah, there was the danger that upon reaching the Land the group would fall apart. The aliyah-kibbutz was also reproached for accepting members without an hakhshara stage. This introduces demoralization into the He-Halutz ranks, for these new members will make aliyah before those who spend a year or two on hakhshara, i.e., that the aliyah-kibbutz does not encourage going on hakhshara.[40]

Joseph Bankover, one of the initiators of the "Ha-Kovesh" aliyah-kibbutz, in his rebuttal, admits that the "Ha-Kovesh" initiative is not more than a palliative which can succeed if suitable candidates will be selected. At the same time, however, the potential dangers should not delay the aliyah, for the Land of Israel needs pioneers.[41] The reality of the Land of Israel showed that the daring of the new initiative was justified, for the experiment was generally successful. At the same time, aliyah-kibbutzim of the hakhshara members are also organized in certain regions. The genre of regional-aliyah-kibbutzim is coming into being.[42]

He-Halutz throughout all of Poland adopted the aliyah-kibbutsim pattern. The Fourth Nationwide Conference of the Polish He-Halutz in 1925 welcomes the "Ha-Kovesh" experiment. It is regarded, however, as a transitional form for individual aliyah until the time comes that the entire pioneering aliyah will be in collective form.[43] At the plenary session of the He-Halutz Central Committee in 1926 it was decided to organize regional aliyah-kibbutzim of the hakhshara groups and of certain members.[44] After the aliyah-kibbutzim had become an established fact, the world movement decided, at its conferences and councils, to obligate the whole pioneering movement to adopt the aliyah-kibbutzim system.[45]

Analyzing the results of the new aliyah form, E. Dobkin described it as follows: it had become evident that individual pioneers must not be sent to the Land of Israel. As a result of this conviction, two types of aliyah-kibbutzim were created—those that had organized solely for the purpose of making aliyah and doing colonization work together, not deciding in advance their future communal and regulatory patterns, and those that had already in the Diaspora decided that their communal ties were to be with the Kibbutz Ha-Meuhad, the Kibbutz Artzi of the Ha-Shomer Ha-Tza'ir Movement, or the small kevutzah. "Both types organize in their ranks select human material . . . with a serious internship of working and living together closely."[46]

The aliyah-kibbutzim really were a small part of the Fourth Aliyah but were outstanding in quality. Their important achievement was to penetrate the Jewish colonies that had till then employed Arab labor almost exclusively. The effort was successful at a time when pioneers were lightly valued.

For all that, this form of organization was of a palliative nature. The members organized in aliyah-kibbutzim shortly before their aliyah with no period of ideological and communal consolidation behind them. Even the first aliyah-kibbutz, "Ha-Kovesh," concluded after a short time that the best and most fitting form for the movement and the pioneering tasks in the Land of Israel is the hakhshara-kibbutz as an on-going way of life, from hakhshara in the Diaspora to the establishment of kibbutz settlements in the Land of Israel. But the new period in the history of the hakhshara movement in Poland, the setting up of the permanent hakh-shara-kibbutz where the member lives on a collective basis until his aliyah, training himself for kibbutz living in the Land of Israel—that began in the crisis years and the decline of the entire Zionist movement including He-Halutz. It was created by other He-Halutz groups, first in Klosow, and later also through other hakhshara groups and kibbutzim.

E. The He-Halutz in the Crisis Years of the Fourth Aliyah

The crisis of 1925-1929 in the Land of Israel has catastrophic effects upon the Zionist Organization and the pioneering-hakhshara movement within it.

Almost half of the Land of Israel emigrants of those years returned to Poland, bitter and deeply disappointed with the country, spreading depression, hatred and cynicism. The despair in the Zionist ranks increased. Their opposition—the Bund, the Communists, and others—saw this crisis as a sign of the total bankruptcy of the Land of Israel idea. This atmosphere paralyzed every endeavor. Thousands left the Zionist Organization. In 1925, 110,000 *shekalim* (membership dues in the World Zionist Organization) had been sold in Poland, but in 1926 barely 11,000 (10,760), i.e., only 10% of the previous year's quota. Of 430 local Zionist groups there remained only about 200 with a scant 8,000 members.[47]

He-Halutz, too, did not remain unscathed. Its membership dropped drastically, but the movement as such was not broken.[48]

The negative atmosphere for Zionism in the Jewish community influenced the development of He-Halutz.[49] During the prosperity period, people enrolled because emigration to other lands had become very limited. Potentially, this mass was capable of realizing the pioneering goals but the absence of an educating cadre made it difficult. When the crisis erupted, this element was the first to lose its faith in the Land of Israel as a solution to the national and social problem of the Jewish people. Communist or Bundist (anti-Zionist Socialist Party) sentiments were popular among these members, but not only chance members left. Among those who joined the radical anti-Zionist groups were also conscientious and active members.[50] The number fell; many branches collapsed and closed. In 1927, He-Halutz numbered but 4,000 members (in 1925—14,000), of whom a mere 300 were on hakhshara in Klosow in Kibbutz "Shahariah" (Star of Dawn).[51]

The movement's crisis demanded a critical stock-taking of the previous period in order to draw conclusions for the future. In the lively discussion on the causes of the crisis and how to overcome it, a variety of voices and recommendations were heard. But on one point all were agreed: that the main task of the movement is to deepen its ideological content and raise the cultural level of the members.[52]

After the immature youth had not withstood the test of the crisis, He-Halutz turned its attention to the younger youth and organized He-Halutz Ha-Tza'ir (the Young He-Halutz), which educated children and young people from the ages of 11-18.[53]

In the discussion of the causes of the crisis, the old dispute about the character of the movement came to life again among those who wanted to see He-Halutz as an avant-garde, idealistic movement does not seek numbers but emphasizes the individualized education of particular individuals and prepares them to realize the national and social aims. They saw the crisis as a vindication of their opinion.[54]

The supporters of He-Halutz as an open organization for all youth, no only for the select, saw the growth as a positive phenomenon which, despite the crisis, was strengthening the organization: "The thousands have created new forms of mass-hakhshara and aliyah. . . . Many who came because of a certificate, in the course of time became pioneers."[55] Against the charge that the present cultural level is lower than that of the members of the Second and Third Aliyah, the reply was that since the general level was low, so naturally also was the level of the pioneers. He-Halutz, the creator of new, revolutionary values without using revolutionary phraseology, "must ever be ready to accept new camps."[56] Meanwhile, however, the large groups did not come. The enthusiasts of an open, large pioneering movement, also have no field in which to implement their outlook. The pioneering camp was small and isolated. It sought new ways to crystallize and deepen its values, strengthen its ranks, and prepare the movement for new, better times; to be able at that time to accept into its ranks and educate the many who would wish to join. That such a time would come, they very firmly believed. Now the chapter of the permanent hakhshara begins—the hakhshara pattern which in time became dominant for all the pioneering-Zionist groupings.

F. The Crystallization of the Permanent Hakhshara

The He-Halutz crisis of the Fourth Aliyah was in a certain measure the crisis of the vocational training. At the Fourth Nationwide Conference of the Polish He-Halutz in 1925 and at the plenary session of its Central Committee in 1926, it was decided to return to the agricultural hakhshara in both its forms: farms owned by He-Halutz. However, since this possibility was very limited for financial reasons, the Conference obligated the members to go for hakhshara in work-kibbutzim, i.e., the temporary seasonal hakhshara with private farmers. Members went out in the summer in collective groups to do agricultural work and, when the season was over, returned home to their old lifestyle.[57] In the few months of seasonal hakhshara there was also an attempt to provide a certain ideological and cultural education, but it was negligible both because of the expenses of living in the village and its temporary nature: "The members come home for the holidays. From a life of work they return to idleness. The environment has a negative effect. To combat it, winter kibbutzim must be established in the city."[58] This is one of the thoughts which later led to the permanent hakhshara-kibbutzim.

So long as the aliyah was large, the temporary seasonal hakhshara, for all of its limited effectiveness, did not produce great doubts. In the crisis years it was different: those who remained in the movement asked themselves "what lies ahead?" It was difficult to remain in the small town. The brief hakhshara was not satisfactory because of its temporariness. New lifestyles began to be sought which would express the movement's needs in times of crisis and failure. While not abandoning the temporary hakhshara, the new lifestyle developed. At first, the permanent hakhshara form was limited to small groups. Alongside it on a broad scale, as mentioned, was the seasonal agricultural hakhshara, also because in many instances the permanent hakhshara-kibbutz was unable to accept all the candidates for lack of space and work.[59] In time, the permanent hakhshara spreads until, in the 30's, it becomes the main hakhshara form. The temporary hakhshara disappears completely.[60]

In 1929, the beginning of the Fifth Aliyah, the entire hakhshara movement numbered about 1,300 members, of whom about 700 were on permanent hakhshara and the rest in agricultural seasonal hakhshara.[61]

Until the "great migration" into the heavily populated Jewish centers, the hakhshara was primarily concentrated in the eastern part of Poland, far from the centers. The hakhshara members mostly worked in sawmills and other branches of the lumber industry. The kibbutz in Klosow was the exception: there the main work was in quarrying. Jewish youth often found work in the Polish lumber industry, since a large part of it was in the hands of Jews who opened foreign markets for it, especially in Holland and England.[62]

This concentration in the marginal places was not accidental. It was a conscious tendency, somewhat escapist in character, that expressed the desire to leave the Jewish "shtetl" as an act of protest against its abnormal economy, its negative social relations, and its acquired spiritual values, from which the pioneer movement had separated itself and against which it rebelled. This act of going out to a hakhshara-kibbutz, of leaving familiar environs, and entering into new branches of work where there were almost no Jews—this was done with the goal of beginning anew, of building a new lifestyle.[63]

Since it was impossible to create permanent agricultural kibbutz-farms for economic and financial reasons—large investments, low prices for farm products, i.e., low wages—the answer remained lumber and quarrying.

The aims of the permanent hakhshara were much broader than training people to physical or agricultural work. The process of transition to permanent hakhshara was tied to the ideological premise that it must raise a new person who is thoroughly imbued with collective-communal values. During this process of separation, a kind of Land of Isreal reality was created. The strength of its new values enabled it to withstand the difficult years of the crisis in Zionism. When there was no aliyah, the members had to remain on hakhshara from two to four-five years and continue to believe in their future.

The process of building the permanent hakhshara was a gradual one. Already in the time of the broad aliyah there were voices heard demanding a more intensive, longer hakhshara, because the short hakhshara had made for a panicked rush to the Land of Israel. The belief that a three-month seasonal hakhshara was enough to produce a pioneer was proven false; therefore the deamnd that the member be in a hakhshara for a year or two. Only then would he be prepared for kibbutz life in the Land of Israel.[64]

The first values of the lengthy hakhshara were already established in 1924 by its predecessors. The first were a few tens of young people in the town of Sarny, not far from the Russian border, who were disappointed with the individual trade hakhshara and sought to realize their dreams of a collective creative life. After unsuccessful attempts to settle into the lumber work, they made their way to Klosow, to one of Poland's largest quarries. With some effort, they managed to make their way into this work.[65] The kibbutz, whose name was "Kibbutz Hotzvei Avanim Al Shem Yosef Trumpeldor" (The Joseph Trumpeldor Quarrey-Workers' Kibbutz), at first had as its goal the concentration of the aliyah from Volhynia and its preparation for colonizing work in the Land of Israel. The first group, all told, consisted of ten people; later the number grew. In its finest hours it had over 200 members.

This group issued a new challenge: to create a collective life in the Diaspora, a totally new form that would include all aspects of life. Very quickly Klosow became a symbol. There, new hakhshara values were forged. In conditions of need and poverty Klosow laid the foundation of the permanent kibbutz. It was decided that the kibbutz is a permanent form of life, not a transit station. Therefore: a full life in the kibbutz, which means no long furloughs home; no sending a sick person to the parents; trying to solve all of the member's life-problems on the spot— and all of this in spite of the frightfully difficult conditions of hard, twelve-hour work and the low pay (which often was not given in cash but in scrip for the company store where the prices were higher, making the pay even lower), and their bad living conditions. They implemented these aims with ruthless fanaticism. The kibbutz slogan was: "He-halutziut ha-ivrit akhzarit bi-metziutah ve-niflaah be-mahutah." (Hebrew pioneering is brutal in its reality but wonderful in its essence.)

In Klosow a new type of life was created for Jewish youth, suffused with proletarian pride, wearing tattered clothes, rubber sneakers, cut off from home, proud of its life of small earnings, of its independence. Its life-motto: "We have nothing here; we need no one."[66]

Klosow's zealousness in realizing its aims, its maximalism that did not consider the real needs, its wish to live a fully collective life as in the Land of Israel kibbutz, aroused certain criticism, but its role in the formation of the permanent hakhshara was great.

The second permanent kibbutz, Shahariah, created in 1924 at the initiative of the He-Halutz members in the town of Siemiatycze, took a somewhat different, less maximalist, course. The began with agriculture, renting an abandoned 60-acre property. Since they did not have means of their own for rebuilding, they went out to work in the surrounding sawmills and invested their earnings in the property. The members remained at the kibbutz until their aliyah. Shahariah created another type of permanent hakhshara: the center was the farm, with outside groups scattered in the neighborhood that worked for the most part in the sawmills and other lumber-related work. Thus a synthesis was established between agriculture and wage-earning, with a common treasury. People exchanged places: from the farm to the sawmill and vice versa. Shahariah quickly became attractive not only for its surroundings. Young people came from distances: from Grodno, Warsaw, Vilna, etc. in order to live there.

Shahariah had also developed the bases for a permanent kibbutz lifestyle, but with less fanaticism than Klosow. Both had a common treasury, a concern for the sick, a striving to grow, etc. Shahariah, however, unlike Klosow, was against declaring for a predetermined, specific form of colonization while still in the Diaspora. Shahariah, in its early years, had supporters of various colonization forms such as the large kibbutz; the small, intimate kevutzah; the moshav (individual farm settlements); as well as some who planned to live as wage-earners.[67]

In the first period, the permanent hakhshara was but a tiny part of the general pioneer hakhshara, but the more severe the Fourth Aliyah crisis became, the more important was the role played by this hakhshara form. This development was a gradual one.

A year after the creation of Klosow and Shahariah, in 1926, the Fourth Nationwide Conference of He-Halutz greeted the strengthening of hakhshara through "work-kibbutzim . . . and sees them as the most appropriate was to expand the pioneering camp for the Land of Israel."[68] The Conference made hakhshara incumbent upon all the members as a condition of aliyah but also recognized the provisional seasonal hakhshara as sufficient.[69]

At the same time, in the pioneering camp, there were increasing voices demanding that the seasonal hakhshara not be deemed inadequate because, thereafter, the members return home to their secure life and the pioneering values are obliterated by the negative influence of the "street."[70] Meanwhile, though, the crisis within the movement was increasing. In 1926 there were only 306 members on hakhshara in 26 locations, of whom only 70 were living on a collective basis.[71]

An important stage in the permanent hakhshara development was the pioneers-convention of Volhynia in January 1927. It convened with Zionism at its lowest and disappointment with the Land of Israel. They decided that members who do not go on kibbutz hakhshara shall be excluded from the movement. It is also resolved that: a) the He-Halutz of Volhynia associates itself with Klosow which is recognized as the regional-kibbutz; b) since aliyah has been stopped by the British government, all the members who have undergone the provisional seasonal hakhshara are urged to return to hakhshara on the kibbutz and remain till their aliyah.[72]

A further step in bolstering the values of permanent hakhshara was taken at the August 1927 He-Halutz convention at kibbutz Shahariah in its Kajanka setting. There it was decided "to spread the values of the permanent hakhshara in the movement" and see the provisional hakhshara as a reserve for the ongoing hakhshara which is considered the threshold of the Land of Israel.[73]

1927 signals a new break in the history of the hakhshara in times of crisis: a slow growth begins. In 1928 the permanent hakhshara numbers about 700 members. The kibbutz-hakhshara offered a solution for many young people who had lived in hope for the morrow. The kibbutz became their rescue vehicle and an alternative for the movement.

The concept of an on-going hakhshara also influenced other pioneering movements. "Gordoniah" (a youth organization based on the ideology of A. D. Gordon) also demands that its members give up the temporary hakhshara and go over to a permanent hakhshara.[74]

The Fifth Nationwide Conference of the Polish He-Halutz in January 1929 continued to assess the nadir period and decided that it "sees the permanent hakhshara-kibbutz as the main way of pioneering hakhshara, asks the movement to expand and strengthen hakhshara through a mass entry into agricultural work, into factories, and into other crafts." The movement obliges each He-Halutz member "to go on hakhshara on a kibbutz or kevutza (a small collective entity)."[75] The decisions of this conference signal the arrival of a new period in the evolution of He-Halutz, from concentration to expansion. The Fifth Aliyah, in which the movement played a meaningful role, begins in mid-year. Preparations are made to receive thousands of new members but, meanwhile, in mid-1930, the aliyah stops once more.

In July 1930, in Dombrowice, the convention of the hakhshara-kibbutzim in Polesie and Volhynia takes place. Participating are representatives of the 700 members in Klosow and its sections, Shahariah and its divisions, the Rovno kevutza, and the Ha-Shomer Ha-Tza'ir kibbutzim.

The mood of the discussions is generally optimistic. Hakhshara has begun to expand. But the local reports reveal the complex realities: of difficult labor conditions in the sawmills and quarries; low salaries which barely suffice for food but not for rent, clothing, or healing for the many ill as a result of the difficult living conditions. On this subject, a major discussion developed about the place of the hakhshara-kibbutz in the Diaspora. Two opposing stands emerged:

One, the maximalist, represented by Klosow, which defends the opinion that hakhshara must not be looked upon as a mere transit form which prepares for life in the Land of Israel. To the Klosow members, the hakhshara-kibbutz is a permanent way of life beginning in the Diaspora, with its natural continuation inthe kibbutz in the Land of Israel. Therefore all of the member's life must be encompassed by it and all of his problems solved within it, i.e., the sick member must be healed in the kibbutz; he must not be sent home.

The radical Klosow position is a result of its ideological attitude, an expression of the proletarian pride of petit-bourgeois youth that has decided to divorce itself from its environment and live on its own earnings. If the Jewish "shtetl" is a symbol of the rot which is being opposed, it would be hypocritical of the pioneers to return home if sick. This would be admitting failure. "In the opinion of the Klosow members it is a patter of compromise that could lead to the destruction of the hakhshara work, discrediting it in the eyes of the youth for whom the attraction of hakhshara lies in its radicalism, even when it demands sacrifice."

The second, more moderate position, held that the kibbutz in the Diaspora cannot be considered the value-equivalent of the kibbutz in the Land of Israel. The difficult reality does not permit it to solve all the problems of the members. Therefore, sick members must be sent home for healing. Also, those members who have been on hakhshara for years, must be given the opportunity to go on home leave so that new members can be taken into the kibbutzim. These differences of opinion were not solved at this meeting.[76]

The decisions taken at this convention talk of strengthening the collective trend in the hakhshara education. It should prepare the members to continue their lives on kibbutz in the Land of Israel.[77]

Decisions of two plenary sessions of the He-Halutz Central Committee stressed the importance of educating toward kibbutz life in the Land of Israel even more.[78] These decisions to educate exclusively for kibbutz are, in a certain measure, antithetical to the He-Halutz tradition till that time. Until then, the movement had been careful to identify with any form of colonizing in the Land of Israel whatsoever. Theoretically, there could by hakhshara-kibbutzim whose members were preparing to establish private-economy moshavim in the Land of Israel, or go to the city, to the colony, as wage-earners.[79]

Already by the end of the twenties, and even more so in the thirties, the education becomes exclusively kibbutz-collectivist, and the pioneer movement aligns itself solidly and completely with the kibbutz forms in the Land of Israel: "Kibbutz Ha-Meuhad," "Kibbutz Ha-Artzi," "Ha-Shomer Ha-Tza'ir," "Hever Ha-Kevutzot" (organization of small collectives), except for the He-Halutz; the General Zionists with its kibbutzim in the Land of Israel; the "He-Halutz Ha-Mizrahi" (Religious Pioneers) mainly with "Ha-Kibbutz Ha-Dati" (Religious Kibbutz movement).[80]

He-Halutz's path to achieving permanent hakhshara met major opposition from Ha-Shomer Ha-Tza'ir.[81] In a series of articles during the thirties, that organization had developed theoretical and pragmatic arguments against permanent hakhshara. In the article, "Our Position in He-Halutz," one of the Ha-Shomer Ha-Tza'ir leaders writes that he sees a certain significance in hakhshara as the culmination point of the pioneering enterprise's training to be able to withstand physical suffering and steeling the character of the hakhshara members—but all of this can also be achieved by temporary hakhshara. "People do not have to lose their physical health in the Diaspora."[82] At the He-Halutz March 1931 plenary session, the Ha-Shomer Ha-Tza'ir strongly fought the decision which obligated the entire movement to implement permanent hakhshara. Its representatives call for limiting it to six months, for the longer one remains on hakhshara, the less its value. It is senseless to compare hakhshara in the Diaspora to the kibbutz in the Land of Israel. The plenum discussion was conducted in a pause in the aliyah. He-Halutz at that time had 12,000 members, of whom only 700 were on hakhshara. The youth movements—Ha-Shomer Ha-Tza'ir and Gordoniah—who were a minority, proved the permanent hakhshara incapable of handling all the members who wish to participate in it. Therefore they propose increasing the rotation by shortening the hakhshara period to the barest necessary minimum, i.e., minimum hakhshara for maximum members. The minority also opposes the proposal that the hakhshara stage should be right educate for aliyah and demands that educational work in the youth movemnt should also be recognized as a stage in certification for aliyah.

The majority rejected all of these arguments. It claimed that the minority considers hakhshara as a "major nuisance" to be gotten rid of as soon as possible; that this approach empties He-Halutz of its ideological and educational values and transforms it into a technical hakhshara and aliyah bureau. Without the permanent hakhshara, the branch faces the danger of falling apart. The majority decides that "the movement sees the kibbutz here as the permanent locus of the member's life until his aliyah to the Land of Israel.[83]

The "great wandering" and influx into the urban centers of Jewish life in Poland[84] also brought the youth movements to change their position on the permanent hakhshara. At the session of the Supreme Council of Ha-Shomer Ha-Tza'ir in September 1932 it became clear that, in light of the new tasks facing the movement both in educating the individual members to work and to collective living, as well as preparing the entire hakhshara-kibbutz to live as a collective in the Land of Israel, "the Council decides that permanent hakhshara is our way."[85] Thus, when the Plenum of the He-Halutz Central Committee convened in October 1932, the speaker on the condition of the branch, Mr. Braslavsky, could sum up as follows: "At the last Plenary Session, the central question under discussion was permanent hakhshara. Today that debate is behind us. Permanent hakhshara has become part of the entire movement in all of its sectors. The values of this hakhshara are also spreading to all the pioneering movements outside Poland."[86]

At the aforementioned session of the Plenum in 1931, the majority underscored the important function of the hakhshara as an instrumentality for productivization of all Jewish youth in the Diaspora. "He-Halutz is the most important productivizing movement in Jewish life," says Herschel Pinsky, in the discussion of hakhshara at the March 1931 plenum.[87] Or: "We see He-Halutz as a movement with certain social goals, important functions vis-a-vis both the Land of Israel and the Diaspora. It is not our practice to divide our work into different areas: education is the youth-movement's realm; productivization is ORT's domain, etc. He-Halutz encompasses all areas relating to the training of Jewish youth and moving them into a renewed life of labor."[88] From this point of view, the general objective—the important productivization function of the hakhshara in the Diaspora—lies in the fact that it had the daring to "leave the traditional Jewish professions" and move into new areas of labor.[89] And this was done at a time wehen the Jewish Labor movement was fighting with its last ounces of strength to defend the weak positions of the traditional Jewish work "without leaving its narrow confines."[90] The majority in He-Halutz of that opinion did not mean hakhshara directly to undertake the task of educating to labor that Jewish youth who did not intend to go to the Land of Israel. The intent was that the objective influence of the hakhshara extend beyond the borders of the movement. The accomplishment of the hakhshara work, though it is primarily the Land of Israel directed, has a great impact upon the general productivization process of the declassed Jewish youth, showing how to leave a life of uselessness for new work opportunities even in times of economic crisis.[91]

The prevalent belief was that the process of the dynamic spread of the hakhshara would encompass all of Poland and become a factor whose impact would revolutionize Jewish life. It was hoped that thanks to this influence of the hakhshara, the Jewish working class—whose majority was anti-Zionist due to Bund or Communist influence—would alter its position and that the labor movement hegemony would pass to the Zionist-Socialist parties. There were even circles that dreamed of a collectivist labor movement in the Diaspora.[92]

Ha-Shomer Ha-Tza'ir saw this approach as an hakhshara retreat from the primacy of the Land of Israel and a danger for itself. The hakhshara's influence upon the productivization of the Jewish masses is understandable, says an Ha-Shomer Ha-Tza'ir discussant at the session, "but this is not the purpose of He-halutz has not task in the Diaspora. Its sole aim is

to get people to the Land of Israel and provide them with hakhshara so
that they should be able to work in that country."[93] This approach is at
the root of the conception that the hakhshara must serve only the needs
of the Land of Israel and the aimsof the kibbutz movement there. Every
other aim weakens the movement's exclusively the Land of Israel character and negates it. The feeling it that there is a danger that the realities
of life can erase the main goal so that the center of gravity might shift
from the Land of Israel to the Diaspora.

In summary: the chief values of the hakhshara-kibbutz lay in the establishment of permanent communal ranks. Instead of the temporariness of
the seasonal hakhshara and its main aims of agricultural or trade preparation, its place is now taken by communal, ideological, and psychological
education aimed at preparing the member for a collective lifestyle and
physical labor. The emphasis is placed upon every physical work. This is
elevated to an educational and moral chief principle upon the assumption
that the kibbutz member must be prepared to fulfill every colonizing task
demanded of him.

The aims of the permanent kibbutz are far-reaching—the desire is to
totally revolutionize man's life by tearing him from his surroundings and
its influence, building a collective form of living as a transitional step
between the Diaspora and the Land of Israel, and creating Land of Israel
islands in the Diaspora whose influence upon the entire movement will
strengthen it in time of crisis.

The permanent hakhshara was an answer to the crisis of Zionism and
He-Halutz during the Fourth Aliyah. At the same time, however, it drew
upon deep, inner spiritual sources, upon the yearning for a new, better,
and more just social order built upon collectivist foundations of a non-
hierarchical, equalitarian, and direct democracy.

The hakhshara set itself the goal of encompassing all areas of the member's life-needs and of fulfilling, as far as possible, all of his material and
intellectual requirements, i.e., making the hakhshara-kibbutz into a permanent home and freeing him of dependence upon family. Diaspora conditions permitted fulfillment of these maximal goals only to a limited
extent. Despite this, there did emerge a new form of collective living
which bore a character of permanence. The values of the permanent
hakhshara, crystallized during the difficult crisis years of the Fourth
Aliyah, did become the chief instrumentality of the great achievements

of the hakhshara in the thirities, when it left the eastern border areas, moved into the centers of Poland, and grew from 700 members to a camp of 9,000 people.

CHAPTER 4

THE "GREAT MIGRATION" AND THE
ENTRY INTO THE CITIES

The transfer from the marginal areas into the densely-populated Jewish centers and the Fifth Aliyah were simultaneous processes of varied origin. As parallel phenomena, both strongly influenced the development of the entire hakhshara movement—of He-Halutz especially, but of the other pioneer organizations as well.

Between 1929 and 1935 hakhshara became a mass venture in the life of Polish Jewry and assumed an important place in its communal development. Before the beginning of the '30's, the development of the pioneer movement was of little interest beyond its own ranks,[1] first of all because of its small numbers. In the eyes of the leftist, anti-Zionist parties, the pioneer movement had spent itself in the crisis of Zionism in 1925-1929. Secondly, because of its geographic isolation, its withdrawal to the areas far from the centers of active Jewish life weakened the general interest in its internal development processes.

In the thirites, however, it was different. The entry into the cities in and of itself might not have transformed He-Halutz into a mass movement had not, at the same time, the general situation of Polish Jewry become catastrophically worse because of the overtly anti-Jewish politics of the Polish regime; and had not the doors of the traditional lands of emigration been closed as a result of the world crisis. The Land of Israel thus became the main emigration goal of Polish Jewry.[2] All of these simultaneous factors made the pioneering movement in Poland very attractive to Jewish youth and placed it in the center of the Jewish Polish reality. In 1928 the hakhshara in Poland had 879 members; in December 1935, 8,500 members. Including pioneering organizations outside of He-Halutz, the hakhshara movement numbered 12,317 members. Even more imposing is the membership growth of the entire movement. In October 1929, He-Halutz has about 4,000 members; according to the February 1935 count, its membership stood at 29,000.[3]

The direct cause that forced hakhshara from its isolation and drove it to wander was the general economic crisis which reached its height in Poland in 1931-1932.[4] Since the lumber industry was mostly for export, it was most affected. The winter of 1931-32 was very difficult for the hundreds of hakhshara-members. The low standard of living fell even lower. The daily wage in the sawmills fell from 1 zloty a day (7-8- zloty /$1) to 50 grosz, and even these pennies were not paid in cash but in scrip, chits, etc. so that the actual wage was even lower. The hakhshara kibbutzim were constantly in deficit; hunger and cold spread illness. The situation in the Land of Israel, too, was difficult and did not bode well for the future. After the unrest of 1929, the British Government sent two investigating commissions: the so-called Shaw and Simpson Commissions. These cast doubt upon the future of Zionism in the Land of Israel, asserting that the land is incapable of accepting new Jewish immigrants except at the cost of the Arab population. Even the certificates which had already been approved were withdrawn. The Zionist organizations, due to lack of funds, had almost entirely stopped their investment activities. The Land of Isreal reality was a very difficult one.[5] Despair and resignation enter the halutz movement ranks. It seemed that in the prevailing circumstances the hakhshara must be completely liquidated—and it is then that the hakhshara kibbutzim set out on their wanderings.

Its success is a direct result of the values which had crystallized in the earlier years of the permanent hakhshara.

The "great wandering" has elements of an epic of endurance, suffering, and audacity. First, two or three "kibbush-niks" (job-finding vanguard) from every kibbutz would set out. They went on foot, by wagon, by train—boys and girls without a penny in their pockets—in the frost and cold, sleeping on benches and tables in the He-Halutz branches, seeking work for themselves and their members who had sent them. "In the winter of 1931-32 there began . . . the great wandering from the kibbutzim. As born workers demanding their right to work, the members of the hakhshara kibbutzim wandered through the towns and gradually entered various branches of work, finding their way in the struggle to survive."[6]

A short fragment of an actual report illustrates the atmosphere which prevailed at that time: "Anyone who takes a train through Polesie and Volhynia will be overwhelmed and amazed. He will be able to get an inkling of an idea of the struggle of the halutz camp . . . to find new job opportunities in its constant wandering.

"On that long rail line from Rovno to Sarna, which goes all the way to Baranovichi and Lida—there are young Jewish vagabonds, the 'kibbutznikim' of the surrounding area, looking for work for themselves and their members . . .

"There is not a stop on that 'line' where they have not been, worked a bit, left the job . . . looking for new places again . . . . The chapter of job-getting is rich and very full of incidents, meetings, and tales of help proferred, and also of estrangement, sanguinity, of being turned away at the threshold of Jewish institutions, homes, communities, apart from the internal squabbling and differences of opinion among their own members."[7]

The first to set out were the kibbutzim Shahariah, Klosow, and Tel-Hai.[8] At first the wandering is limited to the surroundings near the base of departure. Then, when no work was found there, the wanderings spread to the borders of Lithuania in the north and Galicia and Roumania in the west, i.e., throughout all of Poland.

The wandering was chaotic, not organized by any central body. Therefore there were some negative phenomena as, for example, competition by different hakhshara kibbutzim for the same place. Often representatives of various kibbutzim, unbeknown to one another, appeard at one and the same place and "took it over." Then it became apparent that there is no room in that same city for two kibbutzim. The quarrels often required the intervention of the He-Halutz Central Committee, until it was decided that there be "only one kibbutz in any one place." Furthermore: since the aim was to reserve as many places as possible for one's own movement, it often turned out that places were "preempted" which could not provide minimal survival and had to be abandoned."[9]

By the end of 1934, hakhshara had made its way into almost all the places that offered at least a minimal possibility of survival. It then became evident that the front must be shortened and certain places abandoned, especially the smaller ones where the job possibilities were less than minimal. The members left these places for the larger cities, and despite the fact that 40% of the locations were liquidated, the number of hakhshara members did not diminish.

During this wandering period, five "gushim" (blocs) were created—part of the general "gush" in He-Halutz. Each bloc had its territorial boundaries in order to avoid internal competition.

The blocs were the following:

1) Klosow in Volhynia, which had about 32 branches with 1,526 members. It later spread and its territory reached the borders of Galicia.

2) Shahariah spread over an area of hundreds of kilometers in the neighborhood of Baranovichi, Vilna, Brisk, and numbered about thirty groups with 1,500 members.

3) Kibbutz Tel-Hai, around Bialystok-Grodno, had 15 groups with 708 members.

4) Kibbutz Borochov, spread over the industrial centers of Congress Poland, numbered about 29 groups with 1,353 members.

5) Kibbutz Grochow, centered on its agricultural farm, with sections in the Warsaw area—13 sections and 602 members.

Heading each bloc was its central kibbutz and a secretariat which handled its various affairs, transferred people from place to place as needed, organized their communal and cultural life, the mutual assistance, aliyah, etc.

In addition to the "blocs," there were youth movements associated with He-Halutz on an autonomous basis: the Ha-Shomer Ha-Tza'ir hakhshara kibbutzim in the "Brit Ha-Kibbutzim" (Kibbutz Association) and those of Gordoniah in "Hever Ha-Kevutzot" (Small Collectives Association). These were less centralized. Each kibbutz was an autonomous societal and economic unit, and they did not create bloc divisions. The central bodies really enjoyed little power.[10]

The move into the cities opened new perspectives for hakhshara. It shifted from the economically backward areas of Poland to the industrial centers which offered the opportunity to enter new fields of employment hitherto closed to Jewish labor. At that time the hakhshara kibbutzim also developed their own workshops which met their own needs and also produced for the market.[11]

Until the hakhshara kibbutzim stablized their lives in the urban labor pool, they confronted two types of difficulty: a) the severe unemployment in Poland at that time; there were a few candidates fighting for each job. b) The Jewish occupational and trade tradition. As we know, Jews concentrated in special fields of work, in small or medium-sized shops. Their share in large heavy-or-middle-industry plants or in mining was minimal, even where Jews were the owners of these plants.[12] The hakhshara kibbutzim expended a great deal of energy in the struggle against this discrimination and the deeply rooted prejudices about the Jewish worker. Even after they had somewhat succeeded in making inroads into the Jewish establishments, they often suffered hostility and anti-Semitism on the part of the Polish workers who were often "enlightened" by the Bund and the Communists who portrayed the pioneers as strike-breakers and agents of the employers. Despite it all, the battle of the pioneers succeeded to a certain degree and they became acclimated in their new jobs.[13]

Coming to the city, to new better-paying branches of employment, did more than make possible a rise in the standard of living. The needs of a multi-branched, urban economic unit, especially in the large kibbutzim in the industrial centers, served the members as schools for democratic self-management and economic behavior.

On the other hand, establishing itself in the city, in the centers of Jewish life, at a time of massive growth, the hakhshara was faced with significant problems with which it wrestled mightily.

So long as the hakhshara had kept itself in the peripheral areas, far from the mainstream of Jewish life, its problems were primarily internal. Now its members had to contend with a new and complex reality without having ready answers at hand.

Coming to the city had a deep psychological effect upon the hakhshara members. First of all, the gap between the real and the ideal became greater. The first and main aim of the movement was to draw Jewish youth closer to nature and agriculture. But the urban reality often forced the members to remain at their traditional skills, even on hakhshara.

Therefore there were in fact members who argued that, since they already were skilled, they had no need to become "productivized" on hakhshara and could make aliyah without it. The answer was: hakhshara trains for collective living and these values are paramount. One can acquire a skill, but to kibbutz life one must be educated.

Life in the city created dialectical tensions which were part of hakhshara in the thirties. On the one hand, pressed by reality, strict relationships were created between the hakhshara and the society around it in various areas such as employment, housing, political party education, and other practical, spiritual, and communal matters. That is, the prevailing atmosphere of the Jewish "street" influenced the hakhshara. On the other hand, the hakhshara embodied a lifestyle which stook in sharp, conscious contrast to the surroundings. The hakhshara movement's educational goal was to call forth an uprising against Diaspora life and all its manifestations. The tension between these two tendencies created a contradiction and an ambivalent attitude toward the Jewish community and its activities. The hakhshara members lived, as it were, on two planes—one which they shared with the environment and whence stemmed the feeling of closeness and solidarity with their surroundings. The other plane was that of the Land of Israel, of the ideal with which one was spiritually and emotionally identified—as a picture of the future—already here in the Diaspora. This, in turn, created a tendency to withdraw from the surrounding reality and isolate oneself as much as possible against its influences. But the situation of the Jews in Poland in the thirties allowed no isolation. Their very difficult situation pushed them to more active general Jewish undertakings and in the pioneering circles there actually were calls for more intensive participation in the "'avodat ha-hoveh" (the local struggle for civil and political rights). The main articulators of this demand were hakhshara members who had been raised in "Freiheit" (Freedom), the youth movement of the Poalei-Zion (Right Z. S.) Party, which saw the political work in the Diaspora as an organic and fully equal part of the Land of Israel work.[14]

Most of He-Halutz, however, preached "negation of the Diaspora" and was skeptical of the effectiveness of the political and communal battles of the Jewish minority. Extreme in its opposition to any activity whatever which bore no direct connection with the Land of Israel was the Ha-Shomer Ha-Tza'ir. The other pioneer groups recognized the relative importance of the Jewish struggle in the Diaspora, provided it did not hinder the main activity—preparation for the Land of Israel, operating on the assumption that the very existence of hakhshara has a significant influence upon the Jewish community in its struggle for the right to work. The fact that this youth movement—part of the majority—were connected with the Poalei-Tzion Z. S. Party, undoubtedly worked toward their more positive approach to the "'avodat ha-hoveh," while Ha-Shomer Ha-Tza'ir, which as an exclusively youth movement vetoed any political party activity of its members, especially vetoed any Diaspora activity which had no direct relationship to the Land of Israel.[15]

The transition to the city and the rapid growth, to a certain extent changed the sociological composition of the hakhshara movement. Young people from circles which till then had been far from the pioneer ideology, including former Bund members, Communists, Left Poalei-Zion began to enter its ranks. In general, however, the sociological structure of He-Halutz and the hakhshara effort did not change. It still consisted mainly of the pauperized and declassed youth of the petit and middle bourgeoisie, mostly from the small towns of eastern Poland, and economically backward section of the country.[16]

In our opinion, the reasons for this social structure are the following: the loosening of the traditional forms of living, as a result of the decay of the Jewish shtetl which had lost its specific economic role as broker between city and village. The gap was deepened by the official anti-Semitic economic policy of the Polish regime. The impact of this development is more severe in the backward regions of Poland than in the more developed ones. The closing off of the lands of emigration plus the small expectations of changing one's employment, aggravated the situation even more. In this situation, one can understand that the feelings of despondency had "no choice" were stronger there than in the large cities. Despite the severe crisis, there were more opportunities open to Jewish youth in the city than in the small town.

For all that the condition was critical, the traditional communal life and family ties were stronger in the shtetl than in the large city and could potentially to a certain extent diminish the leftist radicalization of the Jewish youth. In any case, this was more so there than in the city where these ties were weakened.

The small city also did not enable the Jewish youth to attempt to be assimilated by the environment because: a) the cultural level of the surrounding non-Jewish population in the outlying areas was lower than the Jewish and therefore had no attraction for the Jewish youth; b) in eastern Poland the Jews did not live among a single dominant ruling people but among many nationalistic groups (Ukrainians, Poles, White Russians, Lithuanians). Their bitter inter-group conflicts made assimilation impossible. On the contrary, it influenced the Jews in strengthening their own national consciousness.

The answer for Jewish youth which could possibly solve both its economic and national problems and, at the same time, not create an absolute conflict with the environment, was in many cases the Zionist-pioneering hakhshara movement. What is more: this area, more than others in Poland, was notable for its strong, solidly anchored, Zionist tradition, even among the youth. The large-city working youth participation in hakhshara was a relatively small one.

During the years of entry into the cities and the period of mass growth, the hope was that the situation would improve "so that if the wall of hatred toward the Land of Israel, which has from way back been characteristic of Jewish workers in Galut, will ever be broken down . . . it will be the city hakhshara-kibbutz which will make the hole in this wall of enmity. "May I behold it and not from afar."[17] But the expectations were not fulfilled. In 1935 it is said of the He-Halutz social structure: "Those who come to us in the process of the pioneer rebirth, to prepare themselves for a life of labor, mostly come from the small shtetl where the distance between different social classes is not too great, from homes where the warmth and comfort of the householder life still remains.[18] The social homogeneity was even stronger in the other pioneering organizations not within He-Halutz, established by the bourgeois and religious Zionist parties.[19] The university youth participation in hakhshara was very small. It was in great measure under radical influence, rightist Revisionist, and leftist Communist even more.

This social configuration became even firmer after the massive growth of the hakhshara movement stopped. In 1936-1939, He-Halutz consists primarily of youth, members of the pioneer youth movements, i.e., chiefly the middle class and petit-bourgeois elements.

The relationships between the hakhshara and the Jewish public such as the *kehillot* (organized religious communities), parties, etc., intensified during that period. The analysis of these relationships requires a detailed treatment which we shall undertake after describing the internal developments of He-Halutz and the organization of other pioneering movements outside of it.

CHAPTER 5

THE INTERNAL DEVELOPMENT OF
HE-HALUTZ IN THE THIRTIES[1]

He-Halutz in the thirites was a mass movement with ideologically heterogeneous societal and psychological groups, some with centrifugal and others with centripetal tendencies. The latter aspired to complete unity in the movement. The former defended their particular ranks and their specific interests. They were prepared for only that degree of cooperation that would not endanger their own autonomous existence.

Schematically there were two large non-homogeneous blocs in He-Halutz:

1) Ha-Gush Ha-Klali (the general bloc) to which belonged He-Halutz Ha-Tza'ir,[2] the He-Halutz youth movement which had come into being in the crisis years of He-Halutz during the Fourth Aliyah, along with "Freiheit," the youth movement of the Poalei-Zion Z. S. Party, and ordinary pioneers, i.e., members of He-Halutz who belonged to no other movement and had joined He-Halutz at the age of 18 or older.

This bloc, which was the majority in He-Halutz, aspired to unite the entire pioneering movement, establish a single youth organization of He-Halutz, and set up a general mixed hakhshara kibbutz that would accommodate advocates of all sorts of colonization, leaving each member the option of deciding where he wants to live when he reaches the Land of Israel: in a kibbutz, moshav, or even as a lone wage-earner in the city or colony. The education in these kibbutzim would emphasize the kibbutz form of life as the most outstanding way of national and social progress.

2) The minority of 30-40% consisted of Ha-Shomer Ha-Tza'ir, Gordoniah, Akiva,[3] and other small groups.[4] This segment consequently refused to accept the centralizing concept of the majority, demanded continuing to allow each group its freedom to educate in the Diaspora toward a specific kibbutz colonizing form in the Land of Israel. The minority saw the demand for unity as an attempt to swallow it up through the Kibbutz Ha-Me-uhad and the Mapai Party. Ha-Shomer Ha-Tza'ir, in particular, opposed this since Gordoniah was part of Mapai but did not accept the colonizing-communal path of the Kibbutz Ha-Me-uhad.

The conflicts between the camps were partially ideological-political, along the party divisions of the Land of Israel labor force, but also in part mental-psychological.

Especially bitter was the difference between the Gush and Ha-Shomer Ha-Tza'ir. The He-Halutz organization, mainly in Russia, was from its start an organization of mature youth, influenced by various populist-revolutionary, mostly Russian traditions. The "youth-culture" concept as a separate, independent social and psychological category developing an independent, immanent dynamic, was strange to it. This also accounts for its unconcern with the younger youth in its early phases. In 1924, under the pressure of reality, it first created its own youth movement which developed its own educational methods.[5]

Ha-Shomer Ha-Tza'ir's course was different. Unlike the other segments of He-Halutz, it was a free youth movement from its inception, i.e., organized, developed and led by the youth, with emphasis on the sociological and psychological specificity of the adolescent age not as a transitional period between childhood and maturity but as a separate stage of life. This also accounts for its sharp opposition to the parties' youth organizations whose ideological foundations and political goals were worked out by grown-ups and not by the youth itself.

Ha-Shomer Ha-Tza'ir was a bitter foe of party activity by the youth. This opposition was an expression of the youth rebellion against the adult world and its values.

This movement developed specific values, its own forms of expression, feeling, and thought, and zealously guarded its uniqueness and elitist feeling. Though in the thirties, it in great measure freed itself from its individualistic, aesthetic-moralistic ideals that had characterized it in its early years, it still continued to stress its uniqueness now in "scientific-objective" economic-societal categories, as a separate avant-garde force in the Zionist-Socialist labor movement, and the only independent youth movement.[6]

Why did Ha-Shomer Ha-Tza'ir, however, join He-Halutz? It was, we believe, a result of its evolution from a free, individualistic, ideologically indifferent, youth movement into a pioneering "one hundred per cent" self-fulfilling movement which ejects from its ranks members who are not prepared to go on hakhshara and then to a kibbutz in the Land of Israel. The decision came in the crisis years of the Fourth Aliyah and the establishment of the Kibbutz Artzi, Ha-Shomer Ha-Tza'ir's kibbutz movement in the Land of Israel. Then the older level (the "Bogrim") decided that, "wishing to link the lot of the 'Bogrim' with that of the Land of Israel working class," we have approached He-Halutz." Ha-Shomer Ha-Tza'ir, on its part, also felt that it had something to offer He-Halutz. The emphasis on the general character of He-Halutz which had recognized within its ranks the legitimacy of various ideational and educational streams, just as the Histadrut had done in the Land of Israel, made it easier for Ha-Shomer Ha-Tza'ir to join.[7]

In the unification contract of 1925 both sides agreed that the Ha-Shomer Ha-Tza'ir hakhshara kibbutzim (and those of the youth movements that subsequently affiliated with He-Halutz) become the property of He-Halutz. The Keren Ha-Shomer, Ha-Shomer Ha-Tza'ir's financial arm for hakhshara, will cease to operate. All aliyah questions of the shomrim (members of Ha-Shomer Ha-Tza'ir) also are to come under the jurisdiction of He-Halutz.

The older level of the Shomrim, the Bogrim, join the local pioneering branches with the equal rights and obligations of the other members, taking an active part in their activities, but not at the expense of their educational work in Ha-Shomer Ha-Tza'ir.

Ha-Shomer Ha-Tza'ir was recognized as having full autonomy in the establishment of its hakhshara kibbutzim, in the composition of their members, and in their organizational structure communally and culturally, and in the educational work there. All of this is on condition that its foundations do not contradict the general principles of He-Halutz. As for the certificates of aliyah, it was decided that at first the head leadership of

Ha-Shomer Ha-Tza'ir will certify its members in each given country, but the decisive certificate will be issued with the consent of the He-Halutz Central Committee in that country.[8]

This agreement was meant to lay the foundations for cooperation between Ha-Shomer Ha-Tza'ir and He-Halutz, but its different interpretations caused quarrels which shocked the halutz movement in the thirties and brought it to the brink of a split. The reason, we feel, lies in the fact that each side saw something else in the agreement: according to Ha-Shomer Ha-Tza'ir, and the other minority youth organizations as well, it meant the final legitimization of its independent existence within the ranks of He-Halutz. To the majority it was no more than a first step to a full and complete merger. The summary of the Polish He-Halutz Council in 1927 states: "a) The Council sees in the full unification of the youth within a single united pioneer youth movement directly linked with He-Halutz in the Diaspora and the Histadrut in the Land of Israel, the complete solution of the youth problem. . . c) The great tasks before the pioneer youth movement and the condition of the various youth organizations, make the unification actual and necessary. The Council fully empowers the delegates of Ha-Shomer Ha-Tza'ir in Poland to the convention of "Brit Ha-No'ar" (a loose federation of Zionist youth organizations of a few European countries) and the delegates to the World He-Halutz Council, to propose the unification of all pioneer youth movements. d) The Council fully empowers the Central Committee to work out basics for unification which will enable the admission (to He-Halutz—I. O.) of all segments."[9]

The various implications of this agreement aroused differences of interpretation almost from the start. In Poland, the very tiring and complicated negotiations lasted more than three years, until the Bogrim of Ha-Shomer Ha-Tza'ir, in December 1928, came into He-Halutz on the basis of autonomy.[10] At the He-Halutz World Conference in Berlin in 1930 the admission of Gordoniah was approved on the basis of the existing autonomy agreement.

The differences reached their peak in the discussion about the 6th Nationwide Conference of the Polish He-Halutz which was twice postponed and finally not held because the minority threatened to boycott it and even to split the movement, arguing that the majority, by bureaucratic pressure, wishes to force unification upon it against its will. The negotiations and discussion about the Conference reveal the real relationships between the various sectors of He-Halutz.

A. The Differences of Opinion about the Relationships between He-Halutz Ha-Tza'ir and He-Halutz

The direct cause of the flare-up of the bitter debate was the decision of the 4th World Conference of He-Halutz, October 1930 in Berlin, to rescind the decision of the previous March 1926 Conference about the separate relationships between He-Halutz and He-Halutz Ha-Tza'ir which took place, as aforementioned, in the low years. He-Halutz had then concluded that it could not limit its activities only to the 18-year-old and older young people, because a large part of these had left the movement in its difficult days. It is then that He-Halutz began to organize and educate children. Formally, He-Halutz Ha-Tza'ir was organizationally independent, but it ignored the existence of a third, older level of He-Halutz Ha-Tza'ir members. Upon reaching the age of 17-18 they were obliged to move into the adult He-Halutz. There they constituted the ideational and leadership core. The relationships between the younger and older He-Halutz were very fragile. Its main center was in the eastern sections of Poland, its members the children of the folk classes, pupils, and working children.

The decision of the 3rd World Conference of He-Halutz about separate organizational relationships between He-Halutz and He-Halutz Ha-Tza'ir merely gave formal recognition to the actual situation. However, it enabled He-Halutz Ha-Tza'ir to make use of the organizational and financial help of the world organization and of the Polish He-Halutz. In the early years of its He-Halutz affiliation, Ha-Shomer Ha-Tza'ir was not strong enough to change that situation. But at the 4th World Conference, after Gordoniah joined, a new constellation was created. The youth movements constituted a slim majority which rescinded those separate relationships. The resolution which was passed by a 51-49 vote states: "The World Conference decides that all the pioneer youth movements have equal rights and rescinds He-Halutz Ha-Tza'ir's separate organizational relationship with He-Halutz."[11]

This decision is indicative of the strength of the autonomistic youth movements and their desire to assert the organizational and ideological foundations of He-Halutz as they see them. In a series of articles, Ya'akov Hazan, one of the outstanding leaders of Ha-Shomer Ha-Tza'ir, expresses the attitude of the youth movements to the place of He-Halutz Ha-Tza'ir in He-Halutz.

According to him, the 4th World Congress decision is for the good of all the sectors of He-Halutz as well as for the "Gush Ha-Klali," because it will serve to assure good relationships among all. He charges that the "Gush," in the guise of generality, sought to use He-Halutz for its own particular party purposes. He-Halutz Ha-Tza'ir has the same character as the autonomistic youth movements. Therefore it also has no right to use the financial and organizational help of the entire He-Halutz. As for the argument that He-Halutz Ha-Tza'ir educates only for He-Halutz while the others are only concerned for their own interests, Hazan replies:

a) The youth movements are devoted to He-Halutz no less than He-Halutz Ha-Tza'ir which exists only in Poland and developed only thanks to the support of the Poalei-Zion Z. S. Party. In truth, it is devoted not to He-Halutz but to its majority, i.e., to the Poalei-Zion Party in Galut and the Ahdut Ha-'Avodah (later Mapai) in the Land of Israel. In the countries that have no He-Halutz Ha-Tza'ir, He-Halutz did not suffer from this.

b) He-Halutz Ha-Tza'ir closed its ranks to members who did not identify with the course of Ha-Kibbutz Ha-Me-uhad.

c) The real aim of He-Halutz Ha-Tza'ir is to absorb the other youth movements. If it so wants unity, why, asks Hazan, does it not unite with Freiheit which is ideologically close to it?

In sum, Hazan feels that the World Conference decision thwarted the tendency of He-Halutz Ha-Tza'ir to take over the other youth movements.[12]

These decisions jolted He-Halutz Ha-Tza'ir which reacted strongly, seeing them as a betrayal of the Polish He-Halutz tradition which, at its 5th Nationwide Conference in 1929, had already decided: "The Conference obligates He-Halutz to protect the separate, long-standing organizational relationships with He-Halutz Ha-Tza'ir."[13]

In its first release immediately after the World Conference, He-Halutz Ha-Tza'ir protests its decision, sees it as an historic injustice, stresses its general-pioneering character in contrast to the particularity of the autonomistic youth movements, and demands a return to the status quo ante.[14]

The Nationwide Conference of He-Halutz Ha-Tza'ir also sharply protested the Berlin decision and solemnly decided to follow its traditional course. This decision was taken against the will of a small group of members that demanded that He-Halutz Ha-Tza'ir also become an autonomous youth movement and not transfer its older age group to He-Halutz. The decision-making majority rejected this course.[15]

The Berlin decisions also provoked widespread discussion in He-Halutz in Poland. The majority—in Gush—saw them as a minority attempt to deny He-Halutz its right to educate youth, emptying it of its ideational and educational content and transforming it into a federalistic technical bureau solely for aliyah and hakhshara matters. Therefore the Plenum of the He-Halutz Central Committee in March 1931 decided, with the votes of the majority: "to refer the question of the relationships between He-Halutz and He-Halutz Ha-Tza'ir, in connection with the decisions of Berlin, to the Nationwide Conference of He-Halutz in Poland."[16]

The minority saw in this resolution an attack upon the democratic principles of the movement because, according to the legislation of He-Halutz, no Nationwide Conference is empowered to rescind the decisions of the World Conference.[17]

At this Plenum and the next, of October 1932, the majority decided, over the strong protest of the minority, also to place on the agenda of the next Nationwide He-Halutz Conference the matter of establishing mixed hakhshara, i.e., demanding that the members of the autonomistic youth movements should also give up their independent hakhshara kibbutzim and join the general hakhshara of He-Halutz.[18]

The minority saw in this decision intentions of the majority to liquidate its autonomous existence and force its unification, clearly an attack upon the spirit of the 1925 agreement.

The discussion of these issues lasted three years and publicly revealed the different conflicting ideational tendencies of He-Halutz. It was conducted in harsh, loud tones accompanied by threats of secession, and the intervention of the Histadrut in the Land of Israel prevented the split.

B. Unity or Autonomy

The main issue was that of unification, and we shall deal briefly with the tradition of unity and the myth which had grown up around it.

The desire for unity indicates the rich universal socialist tradition which emphasized the fact that unity is a precondition for the political success of the labor movement. Yet there has seldom been a movement in which the divisions have been so numerous as in the socialist.

The unity motif is also deeply rooted in the pioneering tradition from its beginning in Russia and Poland.[19] In the history of the Russian He-Halutz, outstanding are the efforts of Joseph Trumpeldor and his comrades, as well as those who preceded him, to unite scattered pioneer groups in a general organization on the basis of a few fundamental principles upon which a broad, mass-based organization could be built. The basic premise from which the rest followed was that united action is more meaningful than the most lofty theories which in their very nature even come between close friends, often creating artificial contradictions which paralyze constructive activity. This is in our opinion the soil from which the unity myth evolved as a prescription for all the chronic weaknesses of the pioneering movement.

In consonance with this tradition, the majority supporters of unity urged that the energy expended on empty debate be shifted to constructive ways to broaden the movement, introducing the pioneer idea to circles hitherto closed to it. The majority sees the given situation as a unique historical opportunity not to be missed. The mass flow into the ranks of He-Halutz makes one painfully aware of the absence of a leadership cadre. Despite this, however, the older youth of the youth movements do join the narrow confines of their movement without evidencing any concern for the new youth masses, always placing their particular interests about the general ones of the entire He-Halutz. As a result, many young people who would be able to find their way in the ranks of the pioneering movement are estranged.[20]

The majority's pressure for unification grew stronger with the creation of the Mapai in the Land of Israel. The minority bemoans the fact that this pressure has more than once assumed an administrative guise, such as discrimination in sending people to hakhshara or in certifying for aliyah.[21] As the Nationwide Conference came closer, the discussion became sharper.

One of the claims of the minority was that hidden beneath the cloak of generality was the fact of the desire of (Mapai and) Kibbutz Ha-Meuhad to force Hashomer Ha-Tza'ir and Gordoniah to unite with them by

administrative means, after having been unable to achieve it by negotia-
tion. The minority accuses the majority of wishing to cut off the Kibbutz Ha-Artzi and the Hever Ha-Kevutzot in the Land of Israel from their
natural manpower reserves, i.e., from the Diaspora youth movements
associated with them, in order to force unification upon them in the
Land of Israel.[22]

To this charge the Gush replied that its ideological solidarity with
Kibbutz Ha-Me-uhad in the Land of Israel does not contradict its general character since Kibbutz Ha-Me-uhad is in essence an open, non-
party kibbutz. It does not force any obligations upon its members as far
as party outlook, in spite of its ties with Mapai. That its members join
the party is certainly to be desired, but the kibbutz is also open to other
political persuasions so long as they do not contradict the fundamentals
of the Histradut and the Zionist-Socialist world view.[23]

The majority also accused the minority, especially Ha-Shomer Ha-
Tza'ir, of "aristocratism" and being afraid to belong to a broad class
category. Furthermore: Ha-Shomer Ha-Tza'ir is losing because of its
fanaticism, for its isolation also hinders it in spreading its influence in
those circles hitherto closed to it. Admittedly, it has not a few positive
values and therefore it is a pity not to exploit them. The Jewish reality
in the Diaspora and the Land of Israel demands that Ha-Shomer Ha-Tza'ir
not lock itself in and unite.[24]

The Gush stressed that its battle for unification will not brook turning
He-Halutz into a federation of independent bodies more concerned with
their own interests than with those of He-Halutz in general.

According to the Gush, He-Halutz has its own specific ideational,
educational, and social values based upon the Zionist-Socialist world outlook. But the tendency to stress its own specific Zionist-Socialist He-
Halutz point of view and its special place in the labor movement contradicts its other tendency: to take into its ranks all pioneering organizations,
even non-socialist ones, that arose in the 20's and 30's, such as He-Halutz
Ha-Klal-Tzioni (The General-Zionist Pioneer), He-Halutz Ha-Mizrahi (The
Religious Pioneer).

To achieve that goal, the majority agreed to make further ideological
and organizational concessions and limit itself to a few generally-binding
principles such as: self-labor; not exploiting any outside labor; Hebrew
culture; recognition of the Histadrut as the only legitimate representative

of labor; activities for the Keren Kayemet and Keren Ha-Yesod (Zionist National Funds). The majority position was characterized thus: "As has been stated at Conferences more than once, He-Halutz still has room for and is prepared to take in all segments of Jewish youth that recognize the pioneering principle and the strivings for aliyah to the Land of Israel. This enables all pioneer youth segments, independent of their political convictions and party affiliations to unite in He-Halutz. Even religious youth can also find its place in He-Halutz."[25]

This citation reveals the tension between the two tendencies: one, to create a homogeneous, independent movement with its own specific world view; the second, to take the maximum number of pioneer groups into its ranks even at the cost of becoming heterogeneous. It appears that the myth of an unbecoming unity dialectically gained the upper hand over the tendency toward ideological crystallization.

On the one hand, the will for an ill-suited organizational unity to a certain degree weakened the majority demand that the minority liquidate its independent existence. And, on the other hand, it strengthened the federalistic tendency of the autonomous youth movements. Ha-Shomer Ha-Tza'ir complains that the majority is conducting negotiations wit the General-Zionist Ha-Shomer Ha-Le-umi and is prepared to guarantee it very broad autonomy; but, at the same time, demands that Ha-Shomer Ha-Tza'ir surrender its legal rights.[26]

Ha-Shomer Ha-Tza'ir is also for taking the ordinary Zionist pioneer youth into He-Halutz in order to prevent the emergence from within of competing pioneer organizations.[27] But, this is on condition that those who join recognize the fundamentals of He-Halutz.[28] Ha-Shomer Ha-Tza'ir's support for broadening the ranks is understandable: it is strengthening its positions and the autonomistic tendency. Within the majority, however, there is a contradiction between two opposing tendencies.

In a memorandum sent to the Executive Committee of the Histadrut in the Land of Israel by the autonomistic youth groups, they expand upon their arguments against the majority's desire to convene the 6th Nationwide Conference in order to decide upon the mixed hakhshara. They recall that their entry into He-Halutz was based upon the autonomy principle which recognizes the youth movements' authority over their members and their right to determine the character of their hakhshara kibbutzim, to organize their members' aliyah, and their freedom independently to conduct cultural, educational, and ideological activities among their mature members, the oldest (bogrim) group in the hakhshara kibbutzim.

They strongly condemn certain tendencies among the majority that are of the opinion that the time of the youth movements as such has passed. They underscore the fact that not only in the time of the depression, when the number of ordinary pioneers was non-existent, did they save the pioneering movement, but that they and their autonomy are not superfluous in the time of massive growth either. It is precisely now that the pioneer movement is in need of an avant-garde core to carry on when He-Halutz is liable to be flooded by the mass elements.

They reject the accusation that because of their particular egoism He-Halutz was unsuccessful in establishing a general youth movement. In their opinion it is simply not possible. They use as an example the fate of He-Halutz Ha-Tza'ir: it began as a general youth movement and ended up by identifying itself with a particular ideological camp. According to the minority, this was an inevitable development because there is no such thing as ordinary general education.

It is noted that the ideological differentiation in He-Halutz is no mere caprice. It reflects the true reality in the Land of Israel and the Diaspora. Every attempt at levelling and uniformity must, in their opinion, fail because one cannot forcibly impose abstract formulae upon reality in order to rape it.[29]

For the youth organizations, autonomy was a life or death matter for which it would "rather be killed than transgress." In the discussion about the condition of the movement at the 4th World Conference of Ha-Shomer Ha-Tza'ir, Meier Ya'ari authoritatively spelled out his movement's stand: "For us there are three sacred areas in which we live and work: the Zionist Organization, the Histadrut Ha-'Ovdim, and Ha-Shomer Ha-Tza'ir. Beyond these, we belong and are active in a few other areas which are no more than adjuncts to our activities in the three sacred areas whose completeness are (for us—I. O.) unconditional. If the adjunct areas endanger one of them (sacred—I. O.) areas, we will not be able to relate to them. This also means He-Halutz. The moment that our belonging to it raises a question about the existence of Ha-Shomer Ha-Tza'ir, we will not belong to it . . . if the hostile decrees, the intrigues . . . will not cease, it is better that we part."[30] He does give assurances that before leaving He-Halutz, Ha-Shomer Ha-Tza'ir will exhaust every possibility of reaching an understanding, but should these attempts fail, Ha-Shomer Ha-Tza'ir will indeed leave.[31]

This declaration undoubtedly strengthened the argumentation of the majority, that the youth organizations relate to He-Halutz as an area of secondary importance. And in the case of a conflict of interest between He-Halutz and their movement, their concern will be the latter, i.e., that their particular interests come before the general ones.

In rebuttal, the minority replied that it functions exactly as does the majority, only it says so openly and does not hide behind slogans about unity as the majority does.

For the majority in He-Halutz there were two clear possibilities: to continue to respect the autonomy of the youth movements or by the power of their numbers to take over the organization even at the cost of a split. This however was avoided in no small measure due to the pressure of the Histadrut.

The discussion over unification and autonomy involved two other issues: a) the way in which He-Halutz is structured: as an avant-garde or mass movement; b) the matter of mixed hakhshara.

C. The Question of the Structure of He-Halutz (Avant-Garde or Mass Movement)

The differences of opinion between the advocates of a mass movement or an avantogardist one were, from 1917 to 1919, differences between the "idealistic" avant-gardists and the "materialistic" mass movement supporters.[32] Of course, in Poland in the 30's the quarrel was carried on under other conditions, nurtured in the womb of the Jewish-Polish reality of that period when the influence of the kibbutz movements in the Land of Israel upon all segments of He-Halutz was very strong. On the one hand there was the open and massive Kibbutz Ha-Me-uhad and, on the other, the Kibbutz Artzi of Ha-Shomer Ha-Tza'ir and Hever Ha-Kevutzot that evolved an organic avant-gardist ideology. Despite the great difference between the two periods, the arguments of both sides in both periods have a certain similarity.

Now that the Land of Israel has become a country that is absorbing masses of emigrants; and as a result of the destruction of Jewish life in Empire; most of those in He-Halutz became convinced that the dominant historic-objective trend points to an ever more intensive rapprochement between the mass workers and the youth in He-Halutz, which along the way has itself become a mass movement which will realize the goals of the labor community.[33] From this it follows that everyone wh comes into a pioneer branch is, after a certain period of education, objectively fit for kibbutz life so that the national and colonizing tasks be fulfilled in him.[34]

This outlook was vetoed by the supporters of avant-gardism. They emphasized that preparation for kibbutz life is dependent upon a lengthy process of education and selection. The majority opposed this, stressing that an intellectually aware adult is preferable to youth groups members whose motivations are entirely emotionally based. Not only the select are fit for kibbutz life.[35]

The youth movements are accused of aristocratic and elitist conduct rooted in a lack of faith in the power of the people to be the carriers of their own national and social liberation. True, such derogatory remarks were heard in certain Ha-Shomer Ha-Tza'ir circles. "Many of our young people (members—I. O.) have no contact with Jewish reality and are alienated from it."[36] This is explained by their having exchanged the legitimate hatred of Diaspora-life with the erroneous hatred of Diaspora Jews. In spite of this, the writer feels that these inclinations should not dilute the avant-gardist ideology which is the only correct one. But this is only on condition that the avant-garde is really the vanguard of the people and does not tear itself away from it.[37]

The counter to the elitist Ha-Shomer Ha-Tza'ir was the mass-accepting Gush and its faith in the potential power which will be revealed under the pressure of reality. The national and social need will strengthen the will of the masses and especially of the youth to assume colonizing chores and join the kibbutz movement in the Diaspora and in the Land of Israel.[38]

The continued membership growth strengthened this point of view. It seemed that He-Halutz was entering a new phase in its history that would fulfill the old dream of the movement's founders who saw before their spiritual eyes a mass pioneering movement of tens of thousands of young people preparing themselves to do their duty in the Land of Israel.

The youth movements, as well, could not close themselves to this development and welcome the streaming masses of ordinary pioneers. In their view, however, these members should not be given any duties which they will not be qualified to fulfill, i.e., they should not be educated to an ex-clusive-obligatory kibbutz commitment. Better that they should be given a general-Zionist pioneering and socialist-Histadrut education, learning Hebrew, educating to labor etc.; and only for those who show a desire to live in a kibbutz should it be made possible. Kibbutz life is in essence voluntary and requires a lengthy education within the ranks of the youth movements. To force all indiscriminately to declare themselves and iden-tify with kibbutz life creates situations of lies, falsity, and pretence, that contradict the true character of He-Halutz. The loss in such education is great because many of the ordinary pioneers who declare for the kibbutz, completely distance themselves from the movement when they reach the Land of Israel.

Therefore the youth movement proposes two patterns of education in He-Halutz: one, for the ordinary pioneers, which will educate in the general values of the labor movement and the Histadrut; the second, for the members of the youth movements. The avant-garde "which is the movement's core of strength, maintains the ideological tension even in the nadir years. . . . The Hashomer Ha-Tza'ir has an avant-gardist tradition which synthesizes the subjective element (the individual's striv-ing to work for the group—I. O.) and the objective" (i.e., the general his-toric needs—I. O.).[39]

It seems that the viewpoints of the majority also produced a certain echo in Hashomer Ha-Tza'ir. This is the reason for the refrain that avant-gardism is an objective-historic necessity: "Our course is the course of an avant-gardist movement. . . . For a long time to come our strength will lie in quality, not in quantity. We wish in the course of time to transform the high quality into a meaningful quantity." Meanwhile, Ha-Shomer Ha-Tza'ir must continue to educate cadres of pioneers even at the cost of quantity "for we are an avant-garde which must never, especially in the time of general upswing,[40] go against the general direction."[41]

It may be that the above quotations obliquely reflect the disappoint-ment of Ha-Shomer Ha-Tza'ir and the other youth movements with the result of the voting at the 6th Nationwide Conference of He-Halutz which gave the Gush Ha-Klali (the General Bloc) a decisive majority. Of 30,323 votes from 502 branches and 167 hakhshara kibbutzim, the re-sults were:

1) Gush Ha-Klali—65.5%
2) Ha-Shomer Ha-Tza'ir—23.1%
3) Gordoniah—8.1%
4) The Witkin Coalition[42]—2.9%
5) Religion and Labor—0.4%[43]

The majority explained this victory as an objective expression of deterministic-historic processes among the Jewish people which confirm their basic convictions. It also, therefore, saw in avant-gardism an anachronism whose time has passed. The result of the balloting strengthened it all the more in its striving for unity and the building of a single youth movement of the entire He-Halutz.[44]

The minority, and especially Ha-Shomer Ha-Tza'ir, again stressed the fact that the mass-character of He-Halutz had brought it to a blurring of its values and a bureaucratic-centralist regime in the movement. The individual has been lost in the mass. It is true that the avant-garde is really small in number, but it is radical in its outlook, the true heir of the original pioneering. Its loneliness is transitory and its victory assured, for it alone represents the historic future. When the number of those disappointed with the mass-ideology will increase, it will emerge from its isolation and take over the leadership of the movement.[45]

After the outbreak of the unrest in the Land of Israel (1936-1939), when mass aliyah ceased and the ordinary pioneers left He-Halutz in great numbers, the youth movements saw this process as a confirmation of their avant-gardist concept. To the contrary the majority. In its opinion, it is not the concept which is responsible for the crisis in the movement. That was and remains correct. A great share of the blame in the difficulties of the crisis lies with the youth movements that isolated themselves and were not sufficiently active. Had the decisive element of the youth movements been more active, it would have been possible to curb the mass defection even if not to stop it completely because of objective circumstances.[46]

D. Problems of the Mixed Hakhshara

Formally, the majority did not arrogate unto itself the right to abrogate the autonomy agreement, but the Plenum of the He-Halutz Central Committee at which, inter alia, the matter of hakhshara had been discussed, did adopt the following resolution over the votes of the minority:

"Whereas there were members of the Central Committee who saw no other proper way to organize the hakhshara to harmonize with the needs of the He-Halutz movement except jointly, with a mixed hakhshara of all He-Halutz members in the locations, in the regions and in all of Poland;

"And, on the other hand, there were members of the Central Committee, who as members of the autonomous movements decisively opposed the establishment of this hakhshara because it impinges upon the autonomous rights of Ha-Shomer Ha-Tza'ir and Gordoniah within He-Halutz;

"And since the Central Committee has no right on its own to decide on the problem of mixed hakhshara (so that the decision—I. O.) should bind the autonomous youth movements;

"Therefore the Plenum is submitting the question of mixed hakhshara for discussion within the movement in all of its segments until conferences. . . will work out the authoritative and binding position of He-Halutz."[47]

Before analyzing the arguments of those for and against mixed hakhshara, it must be stressed that Gordoniah and Ha-Shomer Ha-Tza'ir denied the legitimacy of any Conference whatever to decide the matter against their will. Therefore they saw the resolution of the Plenum as an attempt to undermine their right to exist and as a very good reason to secede from He-Halutz.

The reasons which led the majority to place the mixed hakhshara question on the movement's agenda were partly principled, partly pragmatic: a result of negative developments in the life of the hakhshara kibbutzim as, for example, certain vulgar manifestations in inter-personal relationships, the decline in cultural level, etc. In the mixed hakhshara the Gush saw a remedy for the situation. It hoped that sending members of the youth movements, who were on a higher culture and ideological level, into those kibbutzim where most members were ordinary pioneers, would raise the general level there. They were certain that the members educated in the youth movement for many years would be qualified to solidly establish an ideational atmosphere in the hakhshara kibbutzim.[48]

As weighty as the practical reasons were those of principle which flowed from the ideology about a unified mass-He-Halutz in which the mixed hakhshara is an important, organic part, its highest phase. The mixed hakhshara was, in fact, not a new concept. The first lasting hakhshara in Klosow was, for a certain period, mixed: "Shomrin also lived and worked here for a long time. . . . The day that 'higher strategy . . . withdrew' the Shomrim from Klosow was a dark day for those forcibly withdrawn and a painful day from Klosow. It seems to me to have been the first great disappointment in the power of labor and the labor community to unite people with different ideologies."[49]

The Gush, at different times, had proposed an open hakhshara for the advocates of all sorts of patterns in the kibbutz colonization, leaving each member free to choose while on hakhshara or after arrival in the Land of Israel.[50]

In the eyes of the Gush, the detailed debate at the Plenum was a natural continuation of tendencies within He-Halutz. To them it seemed that now was the time for decision.

In that discussion, the following arguments were presented for the majority:

The establishment of a mixed hakhshara is a natural continuation of the permanent hakhshara-kibbutz. Since hakhshara stands for mass growth, it is vital that there be found in each kibbutz an ideational core capable of absorbing and educating the newly arrived members. The young movements, isolating themselves, are losing an opportunity to meet with the working folk youth which has its own merits. Such a meeting together would fructify both; it could result in a new synthesis that would be a blessing for all.

The mixed hakhshara is especially important in these times when hakhshara is becoming acclimated to the city, losing its romantic-agricultural character, and striving to penetrate the labor community. The sealed, homogeneous hakhshara-kibbutz closes itself off from the community and creates a rift between its members and the general Jewish surroundings.

It is a fact, emphasized the Gush members, that all of the new and renewed initiatives in the pioneer movement in Poland came from the open kibbutz. It built and strengthened the permanent hakhshara and set out on the "great migration." The open kibbutz is dynamic in character, ready to cope with the changing circumstances. But the member of a closed hakhshara-kibbutz does not possess the pathos of conquest, of the turmoil and striving. Had the closed kibbutzim not freed themselves of their dogmatic conduct and become more open, they would have entirely disappeared.[51]

The majority also rejected the youth movement's arguments that the division reflects the Land of Israel reality, claiming that there are various realities and one must not automatically transfer the situations of one reality to another. In the Diaspora, in the open hakhshara kibbutz, the member will be educated to the general concept of kibbutz, and to the Histadrut only by living in a hakhshara kibbutz and not before. Only then, when the member becomes acquainted with the complex reality, does he first become capable of deciding upon a specific kibbutz form.

The open kibbutz is also more economical. The division causes duplication. Unification will release resources that can better be used for constructive purposes as, for example, to expand the movement, deepen its ideological, societal, and cultural values. All arguments are for the mixed hakhshara-kibbutz, which is also for the entire He-Halutz with all of its segments.[52]

The minority dismissed both the theoretical and practical arguments, because it began with other, opposing basic premises.

Its starting point was the comparison of the organic kevutzah and kibbutz. To it, the difference between the open and the organic hakhshara-kibbutz is that conceptually the latter is considered as an intermediate stage in the organic educational process. The hakhshara-kibbutz is not a chance heterogeneous group of individuals who have joined it from various circles and environments. The hakhshara kibbutz of the youth movements is the result of a gradual, lengthy, process of education and development that starts in the children's group as the first stage, and its goal is the kibbutz in the Land of Israel. The Diaspora hakhshara, therefore, is on the one hand connected with the youth movement educational process and, on the other, with specific kibbutz living in the Land of Israel. Therefore, it is not desirable to interrupt the organic process in the very middle, at the most important stage of hakhshara, in order, at that point, to take the members who, from childhood, have been trained toward a specific kibbutz form in their youth movement, and move them for a specified time into a mixed, heterogeneous hakhshara and place before him anew the matter of deciding where he will live in the Land of Israel. "I believe," said one of the participants at that Plenum discussion, "that a member who will live in an open kibbutz will not be educated to life (in the Land of Israel—I. O.) in a small kevutzah. It would not be a proper education for that."[53] The minority is therefore of the opinion that the youth must be educated early toward a specific form of kibbutz life. An ordinary general education does not answer the emotional needs of the youth. The miniroty agress that one must educate toward the general values of the Histadrut in the Land of Israel and He-Halutz, but not to that alone because it is inadequate. Each kibbutz form has its original values and the differences must not be blurred. The education toward various kibbutz lifestyles is not a result of spiteful schisms but a result of objective needs.

The open hakhshara kibbutz is not progress but a retreat. There are dangers of crumbling in its heterogeneous social and ideational composition: as a result of the sharp ideological differences between members within one kibbutz, tensions will be created which are bound to destroy the hakhshara kibbutz.

The organic kibbutz is linked to another principle: the autonomy of each and every kibbutz and hakhshara cell in matters of economy and social structure. The structure of the open kibbutz, which is close to the Kibbutz Ha-Me-uhad, is characterized by the minority as collectivist statism which stems from Russian centralist influences and regards the individual kibbutz as an instrumentality at the disposal of the central authorities, with very limited local authority. There is no effort to create a synthesis between the general national demands and the will of the individual. The open mass-kibbutz is faced with the danger of a bureaucratic take-over and the development of a mechanical relationship between the individual and the group. Thus, indirectly, that kibbutz must also have failures in fulfilling the national and social goals. The kibbutz, by its very essence, can not be an instrument for influencing the masses. For that there exists a political party. As for rentability, the organic kibbutz is economically no less rentable than the open one.

The minority is ready to continue to live as partners within the ranks of He-Halutz on conditin that its autonomous rights not be reduced. It also presents a list of complaints about the discrimination and bureaucratic domination in the movement. On behalf of the entire body, the Gush workers act for the good of their particular interests. An ordinary pioneer who wishes to declare for one of the youth movements' hakhshara kibbutzim is forced to join an open hakhshara kibbutz or most likely not go on hakhshara, i.e., they close the doors of the Land of Israel to him. It is no wonder that many of these ordinary pioneers, upon coming to the Land of Israel, generally have nothing to do with the movement.

Furthermore: on the one hand there are complaints that the members of the youth organizations are neglecting the branch, but when they are active they are accused of having party concerns.[54]

The youth movements saw the Gush's desire to create a mixed hakhshara as an intention to liquidate them and unequivocally declared that a decision in that vein adopted by the majority without their consent would automatically cause a split in He-Halutz. This caused the majority to pull back a bit and declare only its kibbutzim as open mixed hakhshara kibbutzim. At the same time, however, it futher disseminated its opinions throughout the entire movement and continued the discussion about general, open hakhshara kibbutzim in all segments of the pioneer movement.

The closer the time came to vote for the 6th Nationwide Conference the worse the internal relationships became. As mentioned above, the Gush received a clear majority. The Conference was to have opened in May 1934, but the youth movements turned to the Histadrut in the Land of Israel stating that if the Conference takes place they will not participate, i.e., the split will become a fact. Under pressure from the Land of Israel it was postponed. The attempt to convene it in May 1935 failed again due to the youth movements' pressure.

In the Land of Israel meanwhile, the disturbances began which were to last until the outbreak of the war in 1939. The pioneer movement came upon difficult, low days. Ordinary pioneers left it when the doors to the country were shut. The youth movements strengthened their position in He-Halutz. The general political situation of Polish Jewry also worsened catastrophically. All of these things made it no longer possible to convene a new Nationwide Conference before the outbreak of the war.

CHAPTER 6

THE HAKHSHARA MOVEMENT OUTSIDE HE-HALUTZ

In great measure thanks to the entry of He-Halutz hakhshara into the cities of Poland, new perspectives also opened for the other hakhshara organizations: of the General Zionists, the Religious, the Revisionists, etc. The He-Halutz efforts to unite all the organizations into one body were unsuccessful. These hakhshara movements remained as independent groups: one of them only till 1936-1937; others till the outbreak of World War II, and even then continued their activity. In the following chapter we will briefly characterize these hakhshara movements and their place in the general hakhshara in Poland.[1]

1. The General-Zionist He-Halutz (He-Halutz Ha-Klal Tzioni)[2]

The General-Zionist He-Halutz, in its last organizational form, was a roof organization of various General-Zionist formations. Like the general He-Halutz, it united various movements: regular General-Zionist pioneers, the youth movements Ha-No'ar Ha-Tzioni (Zionist Youth) and Akiva (General Zionist Youth with a religious tendency). The latter broke away in 1934 and joined the general He-Halutz.

The General-Zionist He-Halutz was formed in the stormy years of the Fourth Aliyah. Like the general He-Halutz, its beginnings were spontaneous, not organized from above.

The movement took its first steps in 1925-1926 in the Lithuanian city of Brisk and other Polish cities such as: Lodz, Pinsk, Kalish, etc. The groups organized under various names: He-Halutz Tekhelet-Lavan (The Blue-White Pioneer), He-Halutz Ha-Tzioni Ha-Klali (The General-Zionist Pioneer), etc., with no contact between them. The initiative to organize on a country-wide basis came from Brisk and Lodz. The first Conference took place in Warsaw in 1926. Despite the opposition of part of Poland's Zionist leadership, Yitzhak Gruenbaum, for example, greeted the establishment of a General-Zionist youth movement but called upon it to join He-Halutz in order to be a General-Zionist counter-influence to the socialistic tendencies which were growing stronger there. The organizers of the new movement rejected the proposal.[3] The Warsaw Conference decided to create a national organization called He-Halutz Ha-Merkazi (The Central Pioneer) as an organic part of the General-Zionist movement in Poland.

The He-Halutz Ha-Merkazi immediately began to establish various hakhshara locations which prepared its members for aliyah and work in the Land of Israel. With the crisis of the Fourth Aliyah, this organization almost disappeared and only revived in the upswing period of the Fifth Aliyah in the thirties. In the crisis years Ha-Shomer Ha-Leumi (The National Scouts) remained, the future Ha-No'ar Ha-Tzioni (The Zionist Youth).[4]

The reasons for the establishment of this new hakhshara endeavor, to our mind, lay in the ideological evolution of the general He-Halutz from a General-Zionist group without an expressly ideological character into a movement with clearly crystallized Zionist-Socialist aims.[5]

This development provoked the opposition of certain General-Zionist circles that decided not to condone this and to create an address for that segment of the pioneering youth which does not identify with the Socialist ideology.[6]

The legalization of the new hakhshara organization by the World Zionist Movement was made possible after the 14th Zionist Congress of 18-31 August 1925 had legitimized the hakhshara activities of pioneer organizations outside of He-Halutz, i.e., had decided to also support them financially and organizationally.[7] This resolution called forth a strong protest from the general He-Halutz because this was contrary to the decision of the 13th Congress of 6-18 August 1923 which had recognized it as the sole legitimate hakhshara and aliyah organization: "Concerned with the unified management of hakshara, the Congress decides to place all hakhshara work in the hands of the He-Halutz World Organization. It will conduct its activities under the control of the Zionist Executive."[8]

Later, also, He-Halutz continually tried to nullify that decree, trying to prove that there is room in its ranks for all pioneers regardless of their political and ideological world-view, but without success,[9] because the creation of different hakhshara ranks was an expression of the objective antagonistic, ideological, social, and political reality within the World Zionist Organization.

The crisis of the Fourth Aliyah hit the General-Zionist He-Halutz hard. At the same time, however, the General-Zionist youth movement developed and, in the thirties, became an important adjunct segment of the renewed He-Halutz Ha-Klal-Tzioni, as its avant-gardist-exclusive pioneering force.

A. Ha-No'ar Ha-Tzioni

The beginnings of the General-Zionist youth movement are linked to the developments within Ha-Shomer Ha-Tza'ir, the first and oldest independent Jewish youth movement which began as a general Zionist organization with unclear socialistic leanings. The ideological crystallization process was halted in 1924-1926. Then the Shomer Ha-Tza'ir took on an explicitly Zionist-Socialist Borochovist-Marxist character. The youth circles that had opposed this new tendency, seeing it as a betrayal of the exclusively national ideals, reacted to these developments. Considering that these were difficult crisis years in Zionism with the strengthening of the Communist and the Bundist tendencies among the youth, these circles saw a danger to integral Zionism in Ha-Shomer Ha-Tza'ir's new course.[10]

This Ha-Shomer Ha-Tza'ir decision drew their members, without exception, to the kibbutz life. The negation of the work of the older Zionist generation to achieve Jewish civil and national minority rights in the Diaspora played a part in the establishment of the new movement: "These decisions of Ha-Shomer Ha-Tza'ir totally tore the pioneering-Zionist youth movement from the Zionist sphere and from its partnership in thought and act with the great majority of the Zionist movement in Poland and East Europe."[11] The opposition to the right, radical, Revisionist Betar with its militaristic leanings also played a certain part in the creation of Ha-No'ar Ha-Tzioni.[12] The youth of this organization came from middle-class circles and had national-democratic leanings.

Organizationally the movement consisted of four currents that subsequently united: Ha-Shomer Ha-Leumi and Herzliah in Poland, and Ahvah and Akiva in Galicia. The merger took place in Bistri in 1932 and called itself Ha-No'ar Ha-Tzioni.[13]

This movement's opposition to the Zionist-Socialist class ideology flowed from the basic premise that the nation is an organic, natural whole with an eternal character, not an historic-temporary one according to the Marxist ideology. Zionism contains social centent and therefore the negation of the divisive class-ideology.

Ideologically the movement felt close to the Tze'irei-Tzion, whose motto was integral nationalism, negation of the Marxist class division of the Jewish people, becuase in the Diaspora it has no economic base nor any means of production that could enable a class struggle as is the case with other peoples. They were convinced that the Marxist analysis of the Jewish reality is no more than an aping of the abstract societal models, foreign to the specifically Jewish situation and falsifying it.[14] The conclusion of this analysis was that in the Jewish people the national solidarity is dominant over class conflicts because all suffer in the Diaspora. Therefore the realization of Zionism demands complete national cooperation.

The ideational-societal goal of Ha-No'ar Ha-Tzioni was to create a Jewish labor people and productivize it, identical to the general He-Halutz but critical of its Socialist-internationalist leanings.[15]

In contrast to Ha-Shomer Ha-Tza'ir, Ha-No'ar Ha-Tzioni characterized itself as an exponent of General Zionism, rejecting the Shomer avant-gardism and the rebellion against the political parties. On the contrary, its aim was ideationally to revive the original General Zionism as the supra-party body that it was when it began.[16] But despite its harmonizing tendencies, it was not long before the antagonism between the radical pioneer youth and the moderate older leaders erupted here as well, not as a result of political differences but as a result of the dynamics of psychological generational cnnflicts such as happened between the general He-Halutz and the Zionist-Socialist parties.

With productivizing the youth as a goal, the movement faced the quession of its relationship with the Histadrut, the class struggle in the Land of Israel, and the problems of private and national capital, private initiative in the upbuilding of the Land of Israel, as well as the concept of pioneering.

Though the productivization of the Jewish people in general and of the youth in particular was one of the main principles of the General-Zionist pioneering, it maintains however, unlike the left He-Halutz, that a householder who liquidates his holdings and makes aliyah to the Land of Israel is also a pioneer. Furthermore: also "a person who for various reasons cannot make aliyah and remains in the Diaspora working most devotedly for Zion . . . is also a pioneer,"[17] i.e., this ideology does not consider only the shift to physical labor as pioneering. The concept is broadened still further: "What increases the economic or spiritual national potential" is pioneering.[18] This broader definition of pioneering which was later also rejected by Ha-No'ar Ha-Tzioni itself[19] is rooted in the General-Zionist ideology in which the purely national concept is dominant that "the pioneers of Ha-No'ar Ha-Tzioni do not come to the Land of Israel to prepare the liberation of the world working class."[20] This is the source of the opposition to the Socialist class categories and the striving for a liberal regime of "personal freedom, true democracy, and a synthesis between freedom of the individual . . . and the general aims."[21]

At the unification conference of the General-Zionist youth movement in Lwow in 1931 the following principles were adopted:

"A. The national element in Zionism is the most important, both in building the Land and in the outlook about the essence and existence of Jewry in the Diaspora.

"B. Therefore, in the process of realizing the building up of the Land, its non-party character must be protected and every *intensification* (underlined there—I. O.) of class contradictions must be opposed.

"C. . . . The youth must be raised in the pioneering spirit in its broadest sense," i.e., "the members who, for justifiable reasons cannot make aliyah are not to be excluded from the movement. . . ."[22] This paragraph is in agreement with the opposition to the exclusive, kibbutz self-realization as Ha-Shomer Ha-Tza'ir conceived of it.

Ha-No'ar Ha-Tzioni also opposed the negation of the adult society toward which Ha-Shomer Ha-Tza'ir was educating: "We relate positively to the adult community: to teachers and parents, seeing in the youth the natural continuation of the tradition of generations"[23] i.e., a sharp negation of the "youth-culture" category.

Opposing every sort of class education, the movement faced the question of its relationship to He-Halutz. In the first period it had sent its members to He-Halutz as autonomous groups but quickly concluded that it was not the right place because Ha-No'ar Ha-Tzioni is educating toward class cooperation and He-Halutz to class separatism. Therefore this Conference, in the paragraph on He-Halutz, decides that:

"a) pioneering education, hakhshara, and aliyah must be conducted in an impartial spirit;

b) unfortunately, today the attitude of He-Halutz to non-Socialist organizations is not correct and objective;

c) therefore, if our demands are not met by He-Halutz, we authorize the top leadership to take steps to organize the General-Zionist He-Halutz . . . ."[24]

He-Halutz did not change its character, arguing that General Zionist hakhshara kibbutzim can also find their place in its ranks because its basic principles are broad enough. Ha-No'ar Ha-Tzioni, however, thought otherwise. It felt strange in He-Halutz becuase of the close He-Halutz ties to the leftist labor wing and therefore it was one of the initiators of the renewed He-Halutz Ha-Klal-Tzioni.[25]

In the Diaspora the different hakhshara movements conducted their separate activities, but in the Land of Israel there was the matter of relationships with the Histadrut. The Progressive wing of the Ha-No'ar Ha-Tzioni, ideologically close to Yitzhak Gruenbaum, wanted its members in the Land of Israel to join the Histadrut and yet retain their ideological autonomy, criticizing the Socialist leanings there as against integral, organic nationalism. The other wing, more conservative and closer to the Dr. Gottlieb group, was for setting up a separate General-Zionist labor movement in the Land of Israel.[26]

Beyond the pragmatic-tactical strictures about the relationship to the Histadrut, the principle attitudes of both wings to the labor movement, to the relationships between private and national capital, and to their place in the building of the Land of Israel, can be summed up briefly.

The labor movement is fulfilling important national objectives but clothes them in a foreign class-phraseology unsuited to the real Land of Israel or the Jewish reality throughout the world because the private sector also has a large role in creating sources of employment. Therefore there must be a national armistice, class peace. At the same time, the Histadrut must be enabled to conduct a free professional struggle if it forgoes its Socialistic goals such as nationalizing the economy, international proletarian solidarity, etc. The aim of the General-Zionist hakhshara movement is to create a synthesis between national and private capital, united in the work of building the Land of Israel.[27]

Ha-No'ar Ha-Tzioni's road to hakhshara as each member's obligation without which one could not emigrate to the Land of Israel, and the establishment of collective settlements in the country, was not a direct one. At first, after its withdrawal from Ha-Shomer Ha-Tza'ir in protest over its Socialist development and its decision of 100% collective self-fulfillment, going to hakhshara was a voluntary matter in the movement. Even those who did not go through hakhshara were, in contrast to Ha-Shomer Ha-Tza'ir, not excluded from its ranks.[28] But the immanent dynamic of radical pioneering development brought it as well, after a few years of evolution, to pioneering maximalism, i.e., to the obligation of every member to go through hakhshara and oppose the tendency "to dilute" the pioneering concept, demanding the non-recognition as a pioneer of those who make do with reading a Hebrew newspaper, educate their children in a Hebrew school, are active in the Jewish National Fund, etc. Without denigrating those activities, Ha-No'ar Ha-Tzioni came to the conclusion that its main goal is "to educate for pioneering, to self-fulfillment, to a productive life, and to a renewed contact with the earth."[29] Consequently, therefore, in the middle of the educational work, a kevutzah (small group) was established to enable the creation of "a synthesis between the individual will of a member and the pioneering demands." The collective hakhshara is characterized as a form of life which best reflects "the Jewish way of life" and answers the requirements of Zionism.[30]

These lines are an attempt to provide a non-Socialist argument for the collective form of life from the General-Zionist youth movement point of view. For, at the beginning, the collectivist idea was strange and repugnant to these circles. To them it was connected with the socialist ideology of the other pioneer youth movements such as Ha-Shomer Ha-Tza'ir, He-Halutz Ha-Tza'ir, Gordoniah, and He-Halutz.[31]

Giving it a monastic, Zionistic, ideological background as an original Jewish-Zionist form of life that is a result of the immanent development

of the Land of Israel independent of foreign influences, Ha-No'ar Ha-
Tzioni came to the conclusion, as did the other pioneer youth organizations, that the kibbutz is at one and the same time a means of realizing
Zionism and an aim in itself, a lifestyle, i.e., that it is not a temporary
form which disappears after doing its job but is a place where the member
lives out his life and lays foundations for the future generations.[32]

A logical consequence of this development was the demand to obligate
each member to self-fulfillment and exclude those who do not go to
hakhshara.[33]

This movement underwent the same development with the question of
the member's course in the Land of Israel. At first each member was free
to choose: to go to the city or to the kibbutz as a worker. But, as noted
above, its inner radical dynamic as a pioneer self-fulfilling movement
brought it, like it did the general He-Halutz and Ha-Shomer Ha-Tza'ir,
to an exclusively collectivisit education. This tendency received its prominent expression at the Nationwide Conference in September 1933.[34]
Thus the circle was closed. Having come into existence as an expression
of protest against the collectivist-socialist tendencies of Ha-Shomer Ha-
Tza'ir, Ha-No'ar Ha-Tzioni came around to kibbutz-collectivism as a conclusion of purely national reasoning.

Its older members Ha-No'ar Ha-Tzioni sent for hakhshara in the thirties
to He-Halutz Ha-Klal-Tzioni which had served as the roof organization for
all the General Zionist pioneering formations. Its position there was similar
to that of Ha-Shomer Ha-Tza'ir in the general He-Halutz, i.e., it enjoyed
a separate autonomy.[35]

B. He-Halutz Ha-Klal-Tzioni in the 30's

Just as Ha-No'ar Ha-Tzioni arose as a reaction to the socialistic development of Ha-Shomer Ha-Tza'ir, He-Halutz Ha-Klal-Tzioni arose as a negation of the general He-Halutz whose identification with the Zionist-Socialist ideology and movements evoked the opposition of those circles that
wished to continue to protect the organization's General-Zionist character of its early years.[36]

The ideological principles of this movement were as follows: a) broad
national unity; b) practical, devoted Zionism; c) pioneering and self-realization; d) idealistic traditional Zionism; e) productivization and a productive life in the Land of Israel.[37]

These principles illustrate the difference between this movement and the general He-Halutz. They underscore the demand for Zionist hegemony and national unity as a monistic ideology with no socialistic content.

During the years of the Fourth Aliyah which had a mass character, this movement went through a certain period of upswing, but with the eruption of the 1926-1928 crisis it almost fell apart entirely.[38] Only with the new perspectives of emigration to the Land of Israel in the Fifth Aliyah years does it begin a new period of activity. Analogous to the stormy development of the general He-Halutz, He-Halutz Ha-Klal-Tzioni also moves into the city. Its chief base was Lodz and its general area. There it can record a series of successes, including penetration of the textile industry.[39]

The economic, social, and political reasons that made for the growth of the general He-Halutz also influenced the development of He-Halutz Ha-Klal-Tzioni, and 1932-1935 was a period of strong growth. According to the statistics of the Palestine Office of August 1935, its hakhshara kibbutzim had 1,395 members in 56 hakhshara locations in various places in Poland.[40]

Until 1935, Ha-No'ar Ha-Tzioni and He-Halutz Ha-Klal-Tzioni had separate hakhshara and aliyah activity. Only then did the two organizations unite, after negotiating for two years despite the fact that they had no ideological differences. The reasons were mental and psychological. On the one hand you have a radical democratic youth organization; on the other, an organization of older members part of whom is moderate in their demands. Ha-No'ar Ha-Tzioni had educated exclusively toward collective life in the Land of Israel; He-Halutz Ha-Klal-Tzioni also toward an individual life of labor but as an artisan in the city. The hakhshara kibbutzim of Ha-No'ar Ha-Tzioni were communally more homogeneous. Their members had grown up together from earliest childhood. The others were together by chance.[41] Therefore, the document of unification contains certain privileges for Ha-No'ar Ha-Tzioni:

a) All Bogrim (the grown-ups—I. O.), members of Ha-No'ar Ha-Tzioni 18 and over are to join the sections of He-Halutz Ha-Klal Tzioni . . . with all duties and privileges . . .

b) Ha-No'ar Ha-Tzioni is forbidden to accept members over 18. He-Halutz Ha-Klal-Tzioni is again forbidden to accept members 17 and younger.

c) All hakhsharas of Ha-No'ar Ha-Tzioni are absorbed by He-Halutz Ha-Klal-Tzioni.

d) From the day this agreement is concluded, He-Halutz Ha-Klal-Tzioni is the only legitimate insstitution for pioneer activity in general and for hakhshara and aliyah in particular.

Considering the situation, the central body will still continue with the separate hakhshara: He-Halutz Ha-Klal-Tzioni members will be sent to General Zionist hakhshara kibbutzim, and the members of Ha-No'ar Ha-Tzioni to the hakhshara kibbutzim of Ha-No'ar Ha-Tzioni.[42]

The organization's bright period lasted until 1935. Thereafter there is a sharp decline. The 1937 tally shows a decline in membership of 50% in only 20 hakhshara sites concentrated in the large cities. As was the case with the general He-Halutz, this development changes the character of He-Halutz Ha-Klal-Tzioni.[43]

2. The Religious Hakhshara—The Torah Va-'Avodah Movement

A. The beginnings

The first information about the organization of religious pioneering stems from May 1918, i.e., along with the first stages of the development of the general He-Halutz. A convention in Lodz in which 46 delegates from 20 places participated[44] passed resolutions in which the young Mizrahi people demand that the Mizrahi Central Committee establish, as soon as possible, hakhshara colonies to enable the religious pioneers to learn agriculture.[45] The plenary session of the Mizrahi Central Committee welcomes this demand "to establish a colony this coming spring."[46] That same year, a religious pioneer group organizes in Lodz and begins two work in a vegetable garden near the city. Soon similar hakhshara groups are organized in other cities.[47]

Typologically they were no different from the general pioneer groups, i.e, they were based upon temporariness linked with the romanticism of working the land,[48] except for the fact that these groups consisted of religious members only.

Ideologically, as well, the religious pioneers see themselves close to the general He-Halutz, identical in aims, but different in their motives and ideational sources. Still, in 1925, when both movements had already crystallized their specific ideological values and outlooks, one of the leaders of He-Halutz Ha-Mizrahi writes about the identical aims of both movements: both are suffused with universal, messianic goals and strive to create a more just society, not by words but by deeds of self-fulfill- ment. Both have as their goal the realization of "the full revitalization of the Jewish people that should become a 'light unto the nations.'" Both wish to create an egalitarian, free, cooperative, skilled society. The general He-Halutz, however, seeks the road to fulfillment through its own free-thinking and life tendency, whereas He-Halutz Ha-Mizrahi's path is clear and its lifestyle firmly set: "The age-old tradition of Israel, the vision of the Prophets and the exalted ethic of Judaism." This difference, however, need not hamper the close cooperation of both movements.[49]

Actually, however, the paths of the two movements parted. Over the years the barrier between them grew. New antagonisms came along. Some were ideological, like the relationship to the Histadrut in the Land of Israel. The general He-Halutz had indeed always called for the unification of all the pioneer movements on a broad ideational platform. But one of the conditions was recognition of the Histadrut as the only labor representative. The religious pioneer movements, however, had created Ha-Poel Ha-Mizrahi (The Mizrahi Worker) in the Land of Israel as an inde- pendent professional movement for the religious worker. And some antagonisms were practical, e.g., the struggle over certificates, etc. All these things not only prevented unification but even widened the gap between them.[50]

The rapid growth of the religious hakhshara led to attempts at a central organization. As in He-Halutz, the initiative was taken by the Warsaw Tze'irei Mizrahi (The Mizrahi Young People) who "with the agreement of the national Tze'irei Mizrahi formed . . . an information bureau which took it upon itself to establish contact with all the Tze'irei Mizrahi and Mizrahi youth groups.[51]

In the first period of their activity, the Tze'irei Mizrahi was an organic part of the Mizrahi Party. Very soon, however, the radicalism of the youth led to a split: first, in the area of a certain autonomy, and later as an inde- pendent organization. At a conference in 1921, the movement adopted the name of Torah Va-'Avodah (Torah and Labor).[52]

In the Fourth Aliyah years this movement, too, experienced a period of growth but, when the crisis came, it also suffered greatly. Only small groups remained.[53]

Because of this negative development, in the 1926-1930 years there takes place within the movement, as in He-Halutz, an intensive self-critical discussion about the character of the hakhshara system used till then. This results in the crystallization of new thoughts and recommendations about this area in order to strengthen, intensify, and deepen its values so that it be able to withstand the tests of crisis and retreat and not fall apart. The aim was to make it more ideological and more permanent.

There are complaints that not all the members who came to the Land of Israel were ready to undertake pioneering chores. One of the most important reasons for that was seen to be the temporariness of the hakhshara. Ha-Poel Ha-Mizrahi is urged "to critically delve into and criticize its hakhshara methods to see if they are in keeping with the needs of Ha-Poel Ha-Mizrahi in the Land of Israel and if the members are being sent too soon, before they are ready."[54] An identical discussion was taking place in those same years within He-Halutz. There, as a result of the crisis, the permanent hakhshara crystallized, organically tied to kibbutz life in the Land of Israel.[55] Ha-Poel Ha-Mizrahi was not yet ready for such a radical step. The recommendations are more moderate. What is demanded is more preparation of the members for self-fulfillment through deepening the spiritual and practical hakhshara values, with special attention to be given to agricultural preparation so that the member become used to living with nature naturally and to a collective lifestyle as the more desired mode but not as the only obligation toward which the movement is educating.

The conference and conventions of the movement in 1928-1932 expresses this trend to intensify hakhshara. The conference of the movement in East-Galicia in 1928 firmly insists that "a three-month agricultural season hakhshara is insufficient. The pioneers in the Diaspora also must work all the time. They must be organized in groups and the leadership must find them work.[57]

In the period of the movement's renewed growth, in 1932-1935, when masses of religious youth joined it from the same motives which brought the non-religious youth to He-Halutz, the organization, learning from the past, intensified its demands of the hakhshara members as a condition of hakhshara and aliyah. To avoid a new Fourth Aliyah-like crisis as much as possible, the 6th Conference of the Tze'irei Mizrahi-Torah Va-'Avodah decided that "a member can be sent to hakhshara only after having been in the movement at least a year."[58]

As a broad mass roof organization it had various currents, some close to the Mizrahi Party who saw the hakhshara as only a partial deviation from the entire party-political activity and devoted their energies to the home front, even at the expense of the exclusively Land of Israel activity. The World Council of the Mizrahi Youth in Danzig in 1928 regretfully asserted that the weakening of the movement in the area of religious hakhshara in Poland is also a result of "the national political activity: elections for the Sejm, city councils and kehillot (the organized Jewish communities)." This activity "occupied the full time and energy of our young members so necessary for strengthening our movement."[59] This provoked a sharp response from certain circles "whom the experiences of the Fourth Aliyah had radicalized in the direction of more pioneering and exclusively Land of Israel activity as an expression of the negation of the Diaspora and the home front work." This development gave birth to certain avant-gardist voluntaristic tendencies in which one detects a certain reflection of the currents within Ha-Shomer Ha-Tza'ir bu tailored to the religious structure of the movement and as an expression of Jewish religious Socialism.

Starting from this point of view, it is asserted that Ha-Poel Ha-Mizrahi must not be satisfied with only a religious youth mass movement which sets as its goal the solution of the problems of that youth that wishes to emigrate to the Land of Israel in order to be productive there. "Its task is to establish a camp of religious youth with the will to pioneer, that aspires to a life of labor as a result of wishing to live a life of Torah, and whose social tendency is to create such a community on the basis of the Torah ethic, whose communal laws are the Torah and the mitzvot (the religious commandants)."[60]

To implement these progressive tendencies the movement must be active in two directions: one, in creating an elective permanent hakhshara, i.e., "in creating work kibbutzim. While still in the Diaspora, the members will organize their communal life . . . in order to become used to the ethical life of source-based Judaism (that is—I. O.) aware pioneernng, for the Torah is not the property of any individual but the foundation of every communal regime."[61] And here the second direction is expressed: "We must not limit our activity to the religious working youth only. We must also awaken all of religious Jewry . . . and we bring the message of labor and building in the Land of Israel so that religious Jewry should know that . . . Ha-Poel Ha-Mizrahi has undertaken the responsibility of being its avant-garde."[62] This article, in our opinion, expresses this movement's avant-gardist, pioneering tendencies which stood in opposition to religious Jewry which, while being Zionistic, was less radical and anti-pioneering. During that time, out of these radical youth circles, there developed Ha-Shomer Ha-Dati (The Religious Scouts), which occupied a special place in the Torah Va-'Avodah movement as an exclusively kibbutz organization.

B. Ha-Shomer Ha-Dati

The process of the coming into being of Ha-Shomer Ha-Dati bears a certain similarity to that of the creation of He-Halutz Ha-Tza'ir in He-Halutz,[63] as a youth movement to serve as a reserve for pioneering. A like development was also evident within the General-Zionist pioneering: the emergence of Ha-No'ar Ha-Tzioni and Akiva.

In the Torah Va-'Avodah movement as well, it was a result of the disappointment and crisis of the elemental and inadequate hakhshara at the time of the Fourth Aliyah. The conclusion drawn from those negative developments was that the preparation of a reserve of pioneers prepared to weather the tests, crises, and setbacks, requires a lengthy, intensive, and selective education from childhood on.

The educational structure of Ha-Shomer Ha-Tza'ir with its scounting, colonies, mixed youth groups, education for work, etc. and their specific values also served as a model for Ha-Shomer Ha-Dati with the adaptations necessary for religious youth.[64]

The reasons for setting up its own youth group is explained by there being no existing youth group suited to the needs of "the national-religious youth whose aim is to merge nationalism with religion and tradition. This youth could not find its place in the existing youth organizations and therefore Ha-Shomer Ha-Dati was founded."[65] To the charge that the new organization further widens the split in Zionism, the answer is that it is the result of objective needs: that in the days of Zionism's despair and decline only the religious-Zionist ideals are able to keep the immigrant from doubt. The new organization is undertaking to create a new type of pioneer who will build the Land on the basis of Torah, turning his back on the rotting European civilization in order to establish a just society on the basis of Torah.[66] This romantic anti-European attitude was expressed at the First Nationwide Conference of the movement and carries a voluntaristic, evangelical character.

The first Ha-Shomer Ha-Dati groups organized at the end of the twenties in Galicia and later spread throughout Poland.[67]

At the 1931 Hol Ha-Moed Pesah (the intermediate days of the Passover festival) convention in Crakow in which 150 delegates participated,[68] the religious and educational foundations of Ha-Shomer Ha-Dati were laid that characterized it as an avant-gardist, radical, pioneer youth organization. Thirteen binding principles were adopted.[69] The member of Ha-Shomer Ha-Dati is duty-bound, among other things, to be true to the Torah, the people, and the Land; to love labor and detest idleness; to see the nation's future as being in the Land of Israel; to love nature, etc.[70] About hakhshara the decision was: "The period of hakhshara must be not less than a year." Ha-Shomer Ha-Dati also obligates its members to immigrate to the Land of Israel by age twenty-five at the latest. Those who do not do so "automatically become ex-members of Ha-Shomer Ha-Dati and move into the Tze'irei Mizrahi (The Mizrahi Youth),"[71] i.e., the Party's youth movement.

The avant-garde character of the Ha-Shomer Ha-Dati movement stands out in its demands that as a member of He-Halutz Ha-Mizrahi it have autonomy in hakhshara, i.e., the right to organize its own hakhshara locations that will have its members only.[72]

At the first Conference in 1931, Ha-Shomer Ha-Dati was not yet an exclusive collectivist movement. Going to a kibbutz was posited as a desired educational goal but not as an absolute obligation. "We must work hard to see to it that a large number of religious youth find its place in our movement, be educated in it and, after hakhshara in kibbutzim, strengthen the religious settlement in the Land of Israel. We take into account the fact that in the future we will have to create hakhshara kibbutzim in which our young people will receive their physical and spiritual education."[73]

But the developmental dynamic of Ha-Shomer Ha-Dati as a radical wing with religiously-colored socialistic tendencies also led to the kibbutz becoming its only educational goal. A few years after the permanent kibbutz became the dominant form in the general He-Halutz, the Second Ha-Shomer Ha-Dati Conference in west Galicia and Silesia, decides to see in the standing kibbutz "the pioneering cell for a life of Torah and labor and as a communal instrument for establishing a community of justice and righteousness."[74] The movement describes itself as a "religious, educational, scout organization. . .which educates toward religious pioneering and the religious kibbutz. . . . The member of the movement fulfills its aims only by personal self-fulfillment in the Land of Israel. The wish to completely realize the ideal of Torah Va-'Avodah leads us to a kibbutz (collective) life which is its fullest expression."[75]

After the Second Conference, the movement develops on a broad mass scale. It organizes summer colonies and seminars. Its membership reaches 15,000 in 250 local units. But already at the Third Conference in 1936 echoes were heard of the general crisis in the entire hakhshara movement. In Ha-Shomer Ha-Dati, as well, units collapse and hakhshara groups shrink.[76] Under the crisis pressure, the radical, exclusive kibbutz tendencies become even more prominent. They are seen as the only way of overcoming the crisis.[77]

The more Ha-Shomer Ha-Dati developed and crystallized its specific character, emphasizing the total radicalism of the religious youth also as the messengers and avant-garde of national and social self-fulfillment based upon the Torah, the more strongly was the difference underscored; and even the antagonism between it and the Mizrahi Party. Unlike the party member who is satisfied with empty declarations which demand no actions, the religious pioneer is a man of action who feels himself obligated by the criterion that "study is not the most important thing but practice" to fulfill both the communal-religious and the pioneering duties in daily life.[78] Furthermore: in the religious camp the commandments between man and God and even more those between man and man had been emptied of their concrete content, had become hollow phrases. The religious pioneers undertook the task "of realizing the Torah in daily life through self-fulfillment, through returning to the land, and through productivization."[79] The consciousness of mission also created elitist feelings: "Since the Party is a mass (phenomenon—I. O.). . .it is clear that the (youth—I. O.) movement has ambitions to be the top level in religious Jewry. It is its duty to work out the differences between it and the religious party" in various areas as, for example, the absolute negation of the Diaspora. This is also the case even when the Party conducts a ramified activity about current national matters in the Diaspora and actively educates the individual, nevertheless the individual as party member remains passive, and especially in the obligation of self-realization. Ha-Shomer Ha-Dati's situation in the religious pioneering camp is dialectical: on the one hand it is an integral part of the Torah Va-'Avodah movement while, on the other, "we are a special, current within it . . . educating to full self-realization of the Torah Va-'Avodah aims."[80]

C. The Torah Va-'Avodah Hakhshara in the 30's

The opening of the doors of the Land of Israel to mass immigration and the catastrophic plight of Polish Jewry also affected the religious hakhshara which, like the other hakhshara movements, also went into the Jewish urban centers and set up its hakhshara points. In 1933 a chapter of strong development in the history of Ha-Halutz Ha-Mizrahi begins. It sets up tens of new locations. In 1933 it had 450 members at 14 hakhshara sites; at the beginning of 1936, 1,779 at 109 sites.[81]

The internal structure of the work division in these hakshara kibbutzim is similar to that of He-Halutz. The largest group of members, 89%, worked in the city, 35% of them in skilled work. But only 11% were in agriculture, and the rest in various menial labor. When the hakhshara becomes permanent, the number in agriculture declines. The reasons are familiar: the low wage in the Polish village did not allow for survival as village proletarian wage-earners. But to maintain their own farms was too expensive because of the large investments and the low prices of farm products. Therefore the movement had but two farms and an agricultural yeshiva (school of higher Jewish learning) where half a day was spent in the field and the other half in study. Workshops were also established for carpentry, tailoring, etc., and cooperatives were even established in the Land of Israel.[82]

The inner developmental tendencies go from the temporary, brief hakhshara to the permanent one. First in that direction were the members of Ha-Shomer Ha-Dati who were in any case educating themselves for the kibbutz collectivist lifestyle, unlike the mass members of He-Halutz Ha-Mizrahi. In the Diaspora they actually lived in the collective hakhshara but without obligating themselves to live in a kibbutz in the Land of Israel as well. The movement as such made do with educating toward a life of labor in general, not specifically in a village of kibbutz. This hakhshara form is severely criticized by Ha-Shomer Ha-Dati. It charges that though Torah Va-'Avodah is already in existence for twelve years and thousands of members have passed through its ranks, it has not yet managed to set up a single kibbutz in the Land of Israel. Nor are the members skilled in any sort of colonizing work. The conclusion of this critique was that the movement has eschewed this area. The exception is Ha-Shomer Ha-Dati, that has undertaken the task of educating "the youth . . . so that when they immigrate to the Land of Israel they should continue to live on a kibbutz."[83] As a result of this critique and after aliyah was curtailed, in 1935, four years after the general He-Halutz, the Torah Va-'Avodah movement decides to institute the principle of permanent hakhshara throughout the entire movement in all of its divisions, not only in Ha-Shomer Ha-Dati as heretofore.[84] It was also hoped that this decision would help avoid the process of leaving the collective ranks and help the individual member settle in when he comes to the Land of Israel. In order to deepen the collectivist tendencies, i.e., to bring the optimal number of member immigrants into the kibbutzim, it was also decided to form aliyah kibbutzim on the He-Halutz model, but without a single success. In 1933 the further attempts did not succeed. In spite of this, the movement decides again, in 1937, to create an aliyah kibbutz but, to make sure that it is successful this time, members are to be admitted only after strict selection.[85]

In conclusion, we wish to briefly touch upon the matter of the female member in the religious hakhshara. For various reasons, it was difficult enough. Parents opposed sending their daughters away from home. It was hard to find work for a woman who generally was unskilled. And there were psychological difficulties of adjustment to the difficult (and complex) life of the kibbutz.

But this problem was even more difficult in Orthodox circles. As mentioned above, the girls' organization, Beruriah, was formed in 1930 as an organic and active part of the Torah Va-'Avodah movement.[86] The organization set as its goal the education of its members to a life of labor nurtured on the foundations of social justice in the spirit of the Torah and the Prophets.[87]

It is to be assumed that the more extreme religious circles demanded a separate hakhshara for men and women. Ha-Shomer Ha-Dati from the outset, in the spirit of co-education in the youth movement, set up mixed hakhshara groups. He-Halutz Ha-Mizrahi also took that course, but later went over to setting up separate hakhsharot (Heb. pl. of hakhshara) for the female members because no work was found for them in the mixed hakhsharot except in housekeeping and the kitchen. This caused the girls suffering and unhappiness. It was therefore decided to establish female groups that worked in various productive branches including gardening and agriculture.[83]

D. The Agudat Israel Hakhshara

The organization of hakhshara kibbutzim by the Agudat Israel is an exceptional phenomenon in the history of pioneering. Till now we have dealt with various hakhshara formations that, despite the political and ideological differences, were linked as partners in the Zionist world-view. The Agudat Israel, however—a party that arose on the eve of the First World War and one of whose principle goals was to combat Zionism in general and religious Zionism in particular—had as its main base the Hasidic dynasties headed by the masses of Gur, whose Tzaddikim (religious leaders) had all the years used every means to combat Zionism and its constructive work as contradicting the Jewish faith. Zionism was considered a rebellion against the Divine will.

Therefore the establishment of hakhsharot by the Po'alei Agudat Israel (Agudat Israel Workers) is nothing short of a revolutionary act. It reflects the bitter controversies between the older conservative generation and the young radical one even in those circles that based themselves upon a strong traditional lifestyle.

This antagonism appeared in a principle article by Benjamin Mintz, a leader of the Agudah (short for Agudat Israel) youth, in which he stresses the fact that the Land of Israel has become the only salvation even in the eyes of those who have till recently not wished to hear of it. He sees the reason for Agudat Israel's estrangement from the work of building the Land in the oligarchic leadership of the wealthy Hasidim in the movement and in the Orthodox community. He demands that this be ended because they are responsible for the petrification of cultural life and the estrangement of the youth. "We have not established a single settlement in the Land of Israel. . .because even there we have waited for the wealthy man . . . . Our tragedy is that we dance around him and place him at the head of everything." It is high time to set up our own settlements. But this can only happen if the party will turn to the masses and the youth, teach them productive work, strengthen the ties with the Land of Israel, and stop depending upon the rich. There is nothing to hope for from them. The only ones who have in the meantime created a crisis in the Agudah are the young people of the Po'alei Agudat Israel who are characterized as "the Agudah vanguard in the land of Israel."[89]

The tension between the older and younger avant-gardist generation reflects the influence of the pioneering idea even in neighborhoods far removed in lifestyle, in beliefs and opinions. The hakhshara kibbutz is also popular at that time in circles that had till then been far from Zionism in general and pioneering in particular.

One must admit however that not only principle ideological reasons brought the movement to hakhshara. There were other practical reasons as well, secondary but important. After the Agudat Israel demanded that the Mandate Government not distribute its certificates through the Zionist Organization, the Jewish Agency obligated itself to distribute a portion to the Agudah on condition that it not break the national solidarity. Since according to the decision of the Zionist Congress young workers could make aliyah only after going through hakhshara, the Agudah also set up its own hakhshara locations.[90] But, as we said above, the main reason was ideological: no longer wishing to be satisfied with the passive word and the striving toward deeds and productivization. After the prospects for the future of Jewish life in Poland became hopeless, the fact of the establishment of kibbutzim in the Land of Israel by the Po'alei Agudat Israel, with Hafetz Hayyim the first, is proof that the ideological stimulus was more important than the tactical-practical emigration experiences.

The first hakhshara location was established in Barzel, near Slawa, on a run-down piece of land of a Jewish estate which the Agudah lads by hard work converted into a fruit-bearing terrain. It is worth emphasizing that they had worked for nothing because the landowner had not wanted to pay them a wage, for he did not believe that "yeshiva boys" could work the soil so well that it could become rentable even from an economic standpoint in view of the low prices for agricultural products.

The successful experiment had an important psychological impact upon the Orthodox youth. In 1933-1934, the Agudah already has about 16 hakhshara locations. All except the single farm are in the cities where the lads busied themselves with various crafts and menial labor such as construction work, gardening, the wood industry, etc. Of course the movement supervised the division of the sexes and set up a separate hakhshara for the girls.

The religious young people had a very difficult time getting into productive labor, perhaps even harder than the others. Their natural course was to turn to religious employers. Here they ran into strong resistance. Orthodox manufacturers, often members of Agudah, Hasidim, simply boycotted the Agudah pioneer. The well-known publicist Noah Prilutzki characterizes it as a joint economic boycott of the Jews and the Polish antisemites aginst the Jewish religious worker and, when they do employ an Orthodox pioneer, they exploit him more than do the non-religious employers. The Agudah youth had organized a month of propaganda for Jewish labor's right to work. Noah Prilutzki calls for support of this campaign and demands that the Agudah employers who do not want to engage a pioneer should be publicly branded.[91]

In the reports published by the Orthodox press about this hakhshara there is a sense of pride that the Orthodox hakhshara has eliminated the disparaging attitude toward students of Torah as agriculturalists, that "the stigma of parasitism has been removed from them."[92]

This hakhshara was no more than an episode in the history of the pioneering movement in Poland, because in the crisis years of 1936-1939 it lost its communal importance since its numbers were almost nil. Yet the fragment is significant because it reflects the spread of radical trends and the impetus of the shift to labor even in circles that hitherto had been far from this way of thinking. The hakhshara as a means of solving the national and social problems of Jewish youth is in great measure also a reaction to the Polish Jewish youth's opposition to the growing antisemitism and the suppressive politics of the Polish government which had intensified even more the already existing pauperizing processes within Polish Jewry.

3. The Revisionist Hakhshara[93]

The following lines reflect only a fragmentary aspect of the history of the Revisionist youth movement Betar (Brit Trumpeldor—the Trumpeldor Covenant) and its hakhshara activity which began a few years after its formation.

Betar was formed in 1924 after Jabotinsky came out with a sharp attack upon the official Zionist politics. On a Baltic visit in 1924, a few of the youth bodies, especially those from Riga, rallied around him and formed Betar. At the 1927 (December) Conference in which Jabotinsky participated, the ideological and organizational course of Betar was crystallized. In 1928 he became the head of World Betar. He is called "Our Leader." Betar characterized itself as "a scout-legionnaire organization."[94]

The organization is built on combat-legionnaire principles modeled after the Polish and at a certain time the Italian legionnaire ideology.[95] Organizationally and structurally it is an authoritarian movement. In Betar "there is no election system. All the leading figures are determined by the higher echelons. . . ."[96]

Its ideological bases draw upon Herzlian Zionism which is interpreted as state monism, upon a legionnaire ideology, pioneering as represented by BILU (an earlier pioneering group) and Trumpeldor, and upon unconditional obedience to Jabotinsky.[97]

Both the organizational structure and the ideological principles created a specific mentality that emphasized a para-military education, external appearances, an authoritarian spirit, and obedience to orders from above. All of these qualities stood in very sharp contrast to the character sketch of the pioneering hakhshara which is at its core a democratic cell, built on foundations of unmediated democracy that requires the active participation of all members in the life of the community. Not only that: the communal and political aims of Betar, on the one hand, and the pioneering hakhshara on the other, were antagonistic. The former oriented itself on a free middle-class ideology with a certain liberal tendency of laissez-faire and political maximalism that looked with scorn upon constructive deeds as a basis for the future Jewish autonomy in the Land of Israel. It placed its main emphasis upon military action and independent political realms which, at a later stage, would enable constructive work. The pioneering hakhshara movement drew its nourishment from other sources entirely.

The Revisionists scoffed at the slogan of "another dunam and another cow." Pioneering saw the concrete, constructive, also essentially ethical, act as the chief basis for the national, and the also no less important social, renaissance of the Jewish people. Pioneering developed its ethos based upon foundations of Socialism (Marxist and non-Marxist), populism, Russian "Narodnik" traditions, and other communal utopian ideas. Its goal was not another state like the rest, not another Middle-Eastern "Albania," but to build a model community on foundations of productivization and social justice, wishing to avoid the faults of Europe which it had left. Therefore Betar's path to hakhshara was not understandable as a matter of course or smooth, and it first began to organize hakhshara in 1929, five years after its formation.[98]

The motives for this step are different from those of the pioneer movements. There hakhshara was considered as a preparatory vehicle for collective living in the Land of Israel. These motives were not an organic part of the Betar ideology. To the contrary. It was mentally and ideologically foreign to it.

The hakhshara concept of Betar contradicts that of the other pioneer movements. The revisionism underscored in a programmatic article admires Ra'ananah, i.e., a colonly on a private basis exactly like Ein Harod, a large kibbutz open to all,[99] "because from a purely national standpoint the kibbutz is not preferable to the Jewish city or colony. The Zionist management, instead of being concerned with solving the problem of all Jews, was concerned with quality, i.e., it supported Socialist-collectivist experiments of a class character instead of developing pioneering in the spirit of Trumpeldor as an instrument in the hands of the nation for the quickest building of its state."[100]

The Hakhshara Conference in Volhynia emphasizes the instrumental character of the Betar hakhshara:

"1) The hakhshara council in Volhynia asserts that vocational hakhshara is not an end in itself but only a means of educating the Betari (the Betar member) to his tasks in the Diaspora and in the Land of Israel. Our entire position on the problems of hakhshara in our squads derives from this assertion.

"2) The council asserts the necessity of hakhshara as follows:

a. The hakhshara units serve as a test-point for the Betaris and for the front-line immigrants to see if they are ready and suited for enlistment;

b. as a place where the next Betari perfects his Betar hakhshara and prepares himself psychologically for his enlistment;

c. as a place where the Betar immigrant accustoms himself to the working and living conditions that will await him in fulfilling the Betar tasks in the Land of Israel.[101]

Missing in these decisions are the social motives which occupy such an important place in the other hakhshara movements. The deduction is that the establishment of the hakhshara kibbutzim was only a happenstance and, had it been possible to prepare the Betaris for their national tasks in the Land of Israel otherwise, they would have done it. In other words, if hakhshara for the other pioneer organizations is at one and the same time both a means and an end, for the Revisionists it is only a temporary means, and its collective form has no ideational significance for them whatsoever.

For Betar, the establishment of the hakhshara is only a tactical matter, a temporary necessity, since according to the decisions of the Zionist establishment no youth could receive a certificate who did not successfull undergo hakhshara. Therefore it also does not occupy a central place in the educational activity of this movement and is constantly criticized in the hope that it might be possible to replace it with other instrumentalities more befitting its nationalist ideology.[102]

The concern with agricultural hakhshara is also sharply attacked. It is seen as an anachronism and as an aping of the "leftist He-Halutz." To the Betar ideology the issue of productivization was practical rather than ideological. The main Betar aim is not the establishment of a Jewish peasantry but preparation to receive millions of Jews. The conclusion is that the Betar people must prepare to be laborers, artisans, and even merchants. One must rid oneself of the incorrect, anti-merchant ideology and the peasant exclusively especially in its collectivist forms.[103]

However, the influence of the pioneering hakhshara and its ideological values also reach Betar. Two principle articles attempt to contend with these influences and reveal how deeply these foreign "baneful" influences had penetrated Betar.[104]

Eliezer Shostak, author of "A Confusion of Categories and Contents" and "On the Brink of a Serious Debate," admits that at the beginning "we considered hakhshara as an evil decree of the 'left' or of the Palestine Office of the Jewish Agency in the Diaspora . . . in order to get a certificate." But later on the means became an end in itself. There are even voices in the movement demanding that Betar shift to obligatory self-fulfillment. The author sees in this position influences of the leftist He-Halutz and a retreat from original Betarism. The chief aim of the Betar hakhshara was not collectivisit self-fulfillment but vocational hakhshara. "We must not permit today's hakhshara to be the Betar member's main avenue to aliyah." There are other ways to serve the movement.[105]

How deeply the concepts of pioneering self-fulfillment as the main route penetrated even the ranks of the most bitter opponents is indicated by this article. What is more, the author admits that "the course we followed with hakhshara was crooked from the start and till now . . . without a solid foundation. The thought (of hakhshara—I. O.) had no educational Betar value or content. From the day it began it was no more than an imitation of files in the Palestine Office.[106]

The fact that hakshara did not become an organic part of Betar's educational values evoked the principle opposition within its ranks.[107] The author proposes adopting various methods of improving the hakhshara so that it become an important part of Betar's educational system.[108]

This ambivalent attitude of Betar to its hakhshara work is present from the very start. It is a mixture resulting from submitting to external coercion: the demands of the Palestine Office to be able to make aliyah. Hence the endless criticism that accompanies the history of the Betar hakhshara and the desire to shunt it aside or at least, in the long run, to reform it, i.e., if it cannot be gotten rid of, to try to shape it in such a way as to suit the goals of the movement.

Another reason made hakhshara popular even in Betar: the situation of Jewish youth in Poland. "At every Betar conference, at all Betar councils, the problems of hakhshara occupy the most important place, and it is no wonder. In Poland at this time one feels a fantastic striving for hakhshara in connection with the certificates being 'thrown' them. But there are other reasons also that are in great measure a cause of this striving, namely, the material crisis, the horrible poverty, that in a most intensive way attacked the declassed Jewish masses in Poland."[109]

It began in Klosow in the summer of 1929.[110] At first the group numbered only 28 members. In less than a year the Betar hakhshara includes 450 members at 12 locations.[111]

At the beginning of 1933, the Betar hakhshara includes 60 locations and the pressure keeps mounting to expand it.[112] The growth is so chaotic that already in June of that year the leadership is constrained to shut down 20 locations because they were not at a satisfactory level. It was also decided that members will go to hakhshara only after examination. At that time Betar had 70 locations with 2,000 members. The trend was to close the temporary locations and create permanent farms and workshops.[113]

A report of activities in the period from October 1933 to May 1936 illustrates the course of the Betar hakhshara. The report breaks the period into three subdivisions: a) October 1933 to February 1935; b) February to October 1935; c) October 1935 to May 1936.[114]

The extent to which this hakhshara was temporary and of no real Betar substance is evidenced by its decline as early as the end of 1933 when other hakhshara movements were in the midst of blooming. Only a few Betar hakshara points, particularly in Lodz, remained. And even these were inconsequential for no one of them had any ideational content.[115] The Betar explanation for this decline is the Agency's refusal to allot certificates to the movement.[116] Even were this claim true and the chief reason for the crumbling process of the Betar hakhshara, it indicates that its hakhshara was a circumstantial phenomenon and when the circumstances changed, the hakhshara disappeared.

A new period begins in February 1935 after issuance of the order to set up new hakhsharot in various areas. The mobilization is successful in only a few sectors, chiefly in Volhynia. In June 1936 there are again 60 locations throughout Poland but because of the disorder, inner conflicts, and the generally difficult situation, 30 points are dissolved. The intense internal crisis forces the leadership to reform the hakhshara. The hakhshara Solelet is established.

In the October 1935 to April 1936 period the Betar hakhshara consists of 39 locations and 620 members. This was totally disbanded and the shift was made to an exclusively vocational preparation—"hakhshara Solelet" in limited format.[117]

During the entire hakhshara period there was bitter internal criticism. In the following paragraphs we shall deal with its main points because they reveal Betar's ambivalent attitude toward its hakhshara.

In the first year of the Betar hakhshara there are already accusations that the people in it are not compatible, therefore they cannot manage to fraternize, the members are embittered, and there is no communal harmony.[118]

The reasons for this difficult situation, in our opinion, are varied: first of all is the tactical-programmatic approach to hakhshara rather than one of principle. As we saw above, Betar considered hakhshara as an outer-motivated striving, as a means to emigration. This also influenced the members' attitude to hakhshara living. Unlike in the other pioneering movements, in Betar it was considered as unavoidable but undesirable. It lacks the social ethos, the egalitarianism, the attitude to the hakhshara kibbutz as an organic step of permanent kibbutz life in the Land of Israel. The fact is that the collectivist hakhshara and its cooperative living was a foreign body in the Revisionist ideology. Thus, as a means, it was doomed to failure.

People were put together haphazardly, heterogeneously. It is true that similar problems were not absent in the general He-Halutz either, but that movement made intensive efforts to overcome and solve them, to create an atmosphere of organic symbiosis in the hakhshara.

Unlike the situation in the other pioneering youth movements where self-fulfillment was everyone's duty and hakhshara was considered a higher state, the crown of the entire educational process, its non-obligatory character in Betar resulted in the fact that not the right members but "those whose material situation at home was difficult, saw hakhshara as the only end-goal for themselves."[119]

After spending a period of time at this demoralizing hakhshara, the members would return home demanding the right to make aliyah first, not recognizing that other members who had not undergone hakhshara also had the right, according to the Betar ideology, to emigrate to the Land of Israel. Thus, indirectly, they demoralized and poisoned the atmosphere of the local groups.

At a meeting of the region commanders in March 1933, the hakhshara was the center of a broad self-critique. It was stressed that the hakhshara as developed by He-Halutz, with its political and ideological content, is unsuited to Betar. In spite of this, the criticism is that "today there is no difference between our hakhshara and that of the leftist kibbutzim. The only difference is psychological: in the attitude of the youth to it. A member of Ha-Shomer Ha-Tza'ir attends hakhshara because the kibbutz will be his future lifestyle and in his Diaspora kibbutz he learns to adapt to his future living conditions. . . . A member of Ha-Shomer Ha-Tza'ir attends hakhshara not in order to receive a certificate. . . . Therefore he can live in a Diaspora kibbutz for years and no only for a few months. Not so the Betarist. He does not go to hakhshara to prepare himself *but because of a cold calculation: because under the present conditions it makes it easier for him to obtain a certificate*" (underlined in the original— I. O.).[120] The call is to reorganize, to pull back to the first position, i.e., to transform it into a vocatinal hakhshara and not tie it to the right to make aliyah.[121]

The decisions of this meeting reflect the new tendencies of the Betar hakhshara: "The Council meeting. . . decides a) that the vocational hakhshara is not an end in itself but one of the means for Betar education. b) . . . hakhshara is important however because: 1) it is the touchstone of the Betarists. . . whether they are ready for enlistment."[122] 2) Hakhshara makes possible the "improvement of his Betar awareness his psychological preparation for enlistment. c) As a place where the Betarist immigrant prepares himself to working according to the needs of the land."[123]

The decisions indicate that in the meantime all had remained the same as before despite the desire to make changes.

The internal structure and relationships of the Betar hakhshara is a chapter in itself. There was a dichotomy between the democratic immanent essence of the collectivist hakhshara and its para-military modus operandi.

The hakhshara kibbutz is egalitarian in its essence but the Betar lifestyle was built upon military principles, i.e, the hakhshara site was not conducted by democratically elected bodies but by "commandants" nominated by the highest bodies of the movement.

This regime created difficult divergences: "The commandments of the hakhshara locations also related to the members as if to 'submissive serfs,' and the servile brethren were thankful and 'kissed the whip' for at least receiving their dry crust of bread. Being on hakhshara and hoping to receive a certificate afterward, strengthened them not to leave and to surrender to their bitter lot."[124]

That these were not isolated instances can be seen from other correspondence and articles. For example, "And end must be put once and for all to the inconsiderate treatment by some of the commandants . . . . Every-one must know that it is his great privilege to fulfill the maximum duties; to be an example in behavior and speech; to be first on the job; the first to get up and the last to eat, to sleep, and to take a furlough. Public opin-ion must be the most important factor in the nomination of a command-ant. The command structure must be chosen in the short time of 3-4 months. Then the lack of consideration in completing the work will dis-appear."[125] It is also reported that the commandants abuse their authority: "When the members are confined to the base" by order of the command-ant "he is in another city with his friends."[126]

To improve the internal relationships, the leaders of the movement were compelled to adopt pseudo-democratic devices which they held in rather low regard. It was decided to have the members elect bodies of the hakhshara points but that the commandant continue to be nominated by the leadership.[127]

This palliative did not sideline the essential conflict. The crisis became even deeper and more intense. Therefore the 2nd World Conference of Betar, January 6-9, 1935, decided to completely reorganize the entire hakhshara. Betar education was divided into three phases: cultural, self-fulfillment, i.e., paramilitary training, and vocational hakhshara, i.e., the so-called hakhshara Solelet. About this the decisions state as follows: "1) It is every Betarist's duty to learn a trade but not through the move-ment. The movement has the duty to teach only those skills that have a colonizing and mobilizing significance. 2) Every Betarist must be able to fulfill the pioneering tasks. Therefore Betar will organize the "hakhshara Solelet" as part of the legionnaire hakhshara in which the members will receive a) basic knowledge in important work . . . the leadership, with the help of specialists, will prepare a plan of hakhshara Solelet for selected members in which they will learn various skills . . . 3) The hakhshara Solelet will again be able to consist of groups, as in the past, but will learn according to a plan worked out by the leadership . . . 4) Betar will also establish special trade-schools. Their graduates will be exempt from hakhshara Solelet. 5) The conference rejects the former vocational hakh-shara system which does not assure knowledge of any trade . . . 6) Con-sidering the difficulties in quickly chaning the form of hakhshara prevail-ing till then, the conference decides that the extant groups should not be disbanded but gradually transformed into vocational groups."[128]

These decisions signal the end of the hakhshara fragment of Betar history. They confirm our earlier comment that the pioneering hakhshara was forced upon Betar, that its internal essense remained alien to Betar, and that, as soon as feasible, Betar freed itself of it.

4. The Jewish-State Party Hakhshara (The Grossman Group)

This party arose after the Revisionists led by Jabotinsky decided to secede from the World Zionist Organization after "the Kattowitz putsch" in 1933. A group led by Meir Grossman remained in the Zionist movement and also created a hakhshara organization named He-Halutz Ha-Medina (The State Pioneer). The Grossman group's aim was to protect "the pure Herzlian idea" in the realm of hakhshara as well at a time when Communist influences are rampant in He-Halutz.[129]

Here to, as with the Revisionists, the attitude toward hakhshara was mixed at first, but the external drive for certificates forced it to establish He-Halutz Ha-Medina which, unlike He-Halutz, has no collectivist communal goals: "it wants to impart a skill—and a productive hakhshara."[130] It also stands opposed to the militaristic spirit of Betar which belittles productivization and creates a military-barracks atmosphere in its hakhsharot. But precisely like Betar it also declares "that He-Halutz Ha-Medina has come to renew the pioneer type as dreamed of by Trumpeldor."[131] According to this interpretation, it means national-monistic rather than class pioneering but, unlike Betar, He-Halutz Ha-Medina also has positive opinions about the kibbutz both as a national colonizing instrumentality, on the one hand, and as a lifestyle allowing the individual a satisfying life, on the other.[132]

The He-Halutz Ha-Medina hakhshara was limited in numbers. At its height it had 20 locations with 600 members.[133] When the aliyah was restricted, the hakhshara experience almost totally disappeared.

CHAPTER 7

THE ZIONIST ORGANIZATION AND PIONEERING

The ideational values of self-realization, aliyah, and the establishment of a Jewish peasant class are an organic concommitant of Zionist history from its beginnings, as an integral part of its ideology. Every generation had its small groups that implemented these pioneering demands, but for the largest part of the movement these aims remained stated but not obligatory. A contradiction was created between creed and deed. This led to an alienation between the national-radical youth and the Zionist leadership.

The first pioneer groups that had already organized themselves before World War I fought to eliminate the contradiction, to restore the word to its full weight and seriousness. As a result, the tension between the generations was bitter and accompanied the history of the hakhshara movement from its inception till World War II.

Berl Katznelson characterized the difference between pioneering and Zionism as follows: "There were times in the Diaspora that Zionism meant: shekel, chairman, delegate and 'heritage.' And there were times of unrest and disruption when the middle-class Zionism was broken, the maskil was tired of his Hebraism and, seeking tangible results for his children, sent them to a good secondary school. And out of nowhere, somehow, these wild ones grew up: "Off to the village, to physical labor, in hakhshara and kevutzah. . . and quarrying and wood-chopping. . . ."[1]

In the realm of theory the pioneering movement did not add much. Its goals were the same as those of the entire movement, drawn from the treasure of Zionist ideology. The revolutionary innovation is the act of self-realization. The youth negated and fought the passivity of the adult leadership, which in turn regarded the young people's radicalism with suspicion. When the first Tze'irei Tzion groups sent their representatives to the 11th Zionist Congress in Vienna in 1913, they were met with distrust. "Our situation," writes one of the delegates in his memoirs, "was not comfortable in the Russian Zionist organization of which we were part. Its leaders related to us with a certain disdain and fear, afraid to take the wrong path (of Zionism—I. O.), and not even once supported the trying attempt to start a democratic youth movement in Zionism upon whose banner the ideal of labor was inscribed. It ended with the severing of relationships between the youth and Zionism in general, because it turned to outside and opposing movements. The fear was put upon us especially by Jabotinsky and Gruenbaum."[2]

This description reveals the roots of the leadership's distrust of every attempt at an independent youth organization. It also attests to the fact that the reasons for the failure in the relationships between the Zionist establishment and the pioneers lay not in that they were antagonistic opponents, since their bases and aims were shared, but in their disagreement over how to realize them. Both sides knew that they needed each other. The Zionist Organization needed a movement of fulfillment that could consolidate its political gains, since without the constructive deed these would lose their meaning. The pioneering endeavor, for its part, could not manage without the backing of a political stratum with influence among the Jewish people and without its financial support. When Zionism found itself at a critical stage, pioneering was its mainstay and was marvelled at but was still regarded with some suspicion. In the upswing period, however, it was often considered a superfluous and sometimes anachronistic phenomenon.[3] The history of the adversary relationships between the hakhshara movement and the Zionist Organization and its leadership develops within these parameters.

Unlike Russia, where the tensions existed almost from the start of He-Halutz's history,[4] the conditions in Poland were different. The Polish He-Halutz in its beginnings was an organic part of the General Zionist movement[5] and had its full support. In a call from the Zionist Organization's

Central Committee at the beginning of 1918, the youth is strongly request-ed to create pioneer groups. The goal is parallel to the political work: *"to set up a strong, active freedom army to exploit to the full the conditions achieved by our political body for our revitalization work in the Land of Israel."* (underscored in the sources—I. O.).[6]

In order to rationalize the activity of these groups, the Palestine Office was established with a He-Halutz Department as the public relations organ for hakhshara and subsequent aliyah.

These Zionist committees are strongly called upon to agitate among the young that they join pioneer groups. Young members of the Zionist Organization are urged "to be the first to build the He-Halutz vanguard in Poland." The call is directed to the youth of all classes and outlooks."[7]

The idyll did not last long however. The latent contradiction between the leadership and the youth soon became acute. It centered on a few key problems such as, for example, the character of the Zionist activity for implementation of the Minorities Treaty of the Versailles Peace Con-ference of Land of Israel exclusivity; the position of He-Halutz as a limited autonomy movement within the Zionist Organization ranks or total inde-pendence of it;[8] the place of the pioneers in the Zionist aliyah, etc.

Leafing through the eleven issues of the first He-Halutz organ in 1919-1920, one can uncover from the very outset the increasingly bitter de-bates and differences of opinion between He-Halutz and the Zionist Organization.

In the very first article, a difference in principle is already drawn be-tween pioneering and Zionism. The former is characterized as "an out-standing expression of national will," as an avant-garde for whom the main role is not abstract idealism but the embodied will to act. Zionism, on the other hand, "has nurtured the ideal more but done little to streng-then the will of the people." The conclusion is that "not the theory but the practice is the main thing."[9]

From this standpoint, the Zionist leadership is criticized for not recog-nizing the revolutionary renewal activity of pioneering and for relating to it negatively or, at best, as it routinely "relates to any regular Zionist non-pioneer groups such as Bnai Zion (Sons of Zion) or Tifereth Zion (Glory of Zion), etc. It was not the relationship to a vanguard . . . there was no appreciation of the value of the He-Halutz achievements and the great potential that it has."[10] This is also the source of the negative attitude toward the pioneers' striving for aliyah. For the immigrants, "the Jewish young people, they had a few bitter words about their haste."[11] The question of aliyah and especially of the pioneer aliyah, over the years becomes one of the main matters of contention between the cautious Zionist leadership and the pioneer movement which was gripped by a sense of "an exceptional situation," that the Jewish people is facing a catastrophe and must be saved. This is possible only through mass aliyah which is not cowed by difficulties and will not let itself be stopped by objective difficulties in the Land of Israel.

In a commentary on the London and Paris peace conferences, He-Halutz criticizes the Zionist representation for not appearing aggressively enough in its philanthropic West European Jewry character. It showed "a lot of calm and a fear of too hasty emigration. Here in the East we have other ideas. We here do not talk about emigrations but about a question of to be or not to be."[12]

This criticism, though it is still quite moderate, characterizes the radical character of the pioneering movement which is without doubt influenced by the generally prevalent revolutionary atmosphere, and therefore has no patience for gradual, evolutionary solutions and no understanding of salon-diplomacy and cautious tactics. In its hastening the day of redemption there are also worldly-eschatological elements.

A few months later the result was a bitter clash between the two camps. In July 1919, in the name of the Zionist leadership, Chaim Weizmann, Menahem Ussishkin, and Simon published a call against a mass, unplanned emigration to the Land of Israel. This call, bearing the heading "Toward a Clarification of the Situation," states among other things:

"Let no one set about disrupting his home and business before knowing for sure that he can settle in the Land of Israel. An unprepared, unorganized mass aliyah would be the greatest misfortune both for the emigrants and for the revitalization of the Land . . . . We understand that the closer we get to the goal the more impatient we become and a day is like years. Still we appeal to you, comrades. Calm yourselves. We are steadily moving closer to our goal. A giant but organized job is necessary. You do your duty and we will do ours. Redemption is already near."[13]

The call goes on to list the kinds of emigrants who can immediately leave for the Land of Israel: 1) those who have already been there or have family or possessions there; 2) emissaries of groups for the upbuilding of the Land of Israel; 3) specialists in certain skills; 4) people with much capital who can set themselves up immediately. The call ends with a second warning: "We repeat: *the folk en masse should not dare to make aliyah. Do not try to hasten the final date of redemption.*"[14] (underlined in the original–I. O.).

The call appeared at a time when hundreds of pioneers were roaming the roads under frightful conditions. It therefore called forth a wave of sharp protests from the labor community in the Land of Israel[15] and the pioneer movement in the Diaspora. At the 4th Conference of the Zionist Organization in Poland in 1919, the He-Halutz representative harshly criticized this policy: "We get one answer from the Land of Israel Office to all of our demands: the time for emigration is not yet ripe. We must in the meantime make do with preparations. What sort of preparations no one knows.

"Perhaps it is logical that instead of raising a voice against the pioneers' emigration it would be better to protest . . . to the Zionist leadership in London, that it shove aside the hindrances to emigration of the productive elements so necessary to the Land of Israel . . . .

"They argue that one cannot come to the Land so long as there are no homes built. Who will build them if we remain sitting here? . . .

"We understand that preparation and patience are necessary but we demand immediate preparations in the Land of Israel and in the Diaspora."[16]

How great the mental and psychological estrangement was between the radical youth and the moderate Zionist leadership can be seen from the following episode. A group of pioneers from Bendin, among the first of the Third Aliyah, reached Odessa in its wanderings and there turned to M. Ussishkin to help them make aliyah because they had heard that he had been nominated as a Jewish Minister. The dialogue between them is recorded as follows: "One of the pioneers naively recounts that he received us truly as a Minister . . . looked at us with startled eyes and asked: How did you manage to get here? Where do you want to go? To the Land of Israel? Are you of sound mind? Through where? It's out of the question. There are no possibilities."[17] The pioneers did find a way, however, and reached the Land.

On the matter of the tempo of the aliyah there is a quarrel throughout the period of the Third Aliyah between the pioneer movement which is demanding that an energetic, dynamic emigration policy be conducted and that the British regime's restrictions be fought, and the Zionist leadership which restrains the striving and must consider various objective factors such as the economic absorptive capacity, the general political situation, Arab opposition, etc. He-Halutz accuses the management of "exchanging great hopes for petty pennies."[18]

Another aspect of the relationship between the pioneer movement in Poland and the Zionist Organization in that country was the attitude to the work of here and now, i.e., to the political and communal battle for civil and national rights for Polish Jewry.

In general, the pioneer movement related with a certain skepticism to these efforts. The Zionist organization, on the other hand, having great hopes of realizing it through the minority-treaties which would supposedly guarantee the Jewish minority in Poland broad national rights, threw itself with great enthusiasm and zeal into the daily political work such as elections for the Jewish community, city-councils, parliament, etc. This activity absorbed their full energies and pushed the direct Land of Israel action aside for future planning. The Zionist leadership's call against a panicky mass emigration—whose motivation stemmed from a fear of false messianic hopes and illusions a la Shabbetai Zevi (17th century) and which could end in doubt and despair—to a certain extent became an alibi for those circles in Zionism who saw it only as a declaratory matter with no obligation to concrete action. Against this obfuscation of the issues and placing Zionism on a level of empty words, the pioneer movement came out with a bitter critique. It set itself the goal "of taking the word 'work' out of the lexicon used at party leaders' and program planners' meetings: not 'civil, national rights work' nor political 'work' and not even 'general work,' but simply put, physical work . . . that is how we understand the word and this is how we wish to implement it."[19] Pioneering tried hard to realize this program with the greatest consistency. Before the 4th Nationwide Conference of the Zionist Organization in Poland, the He-Halutz organ sharply and directly attacked the dualism of the Zionist work which inevitably leads to an abandonment of direct Zionist fulfillment.

With caustic sarcasm it deals with the Zionists' elation and enthusiasm over their election victories, sees them as hollow, and demands: "Everything is fine, but give us, for God's sake, give us genuine Zionist activities;

give us work in the Land of Israel; give us work for the Land of Israel right here, and really only for the Land of Israel."[20]

The rebuttal is that the time is not yet ripe. The pioneering efforts made under the most trying conditions should serve as an example for the Zionist activity. The article makes a clear separation between He-Halutz and the Zionist Organization and parties: "We are moving farther and farther from the Zionist credo which makes do, at a moment of need, with pinning a metal or paper Star of David to one's lapel."[21]

The more the optimistic illusions of the post-World War I period vanished and the limitations upon the Jewish minority increased, the whole pioneer movement in all of its shades saw this development as a vindication of its exclusive Land of Israel prognosis, and related all the more negatively to the dissipation of Zionist energy on the local Jewish civil-national rights struggle at the expense of the Land of Israel activity; but they did not totally negate the Jewish rights struggle for limited specific goals, but as a palliative solution only, second in importance to the national, Land of Israel solution of the problem. And except for exceptional cases, especially in the thirties in self-defense against pogroms, in professional groups and similar activities, the pioneer movement took no active part in the political actions of Polish Jewry. The Zionist Organization and party leaders again for a long time were satisfied with declarative Zionism. Thus the mental and psychological gap between the two did not become smaller. Just the opposite.

Until the Fourth Aliyah, the quarrel between the pioneering movement and the Zionist leadership bore a more fragmentary character, i.e., even when the Zionist leadership did not meet the demands of He-Halutz, it was not because of issues of principle but for practical reasons such as unemployment in the Land of Israel, lack of funds, etc. On the contrary. At all the post-war congresses, starting with the 12th Congress in Carlsbad in 1921, the necessity of the pioneering hakhshara was emphasized. At the 13th Congress in 1923 it was even decided "to give the management of the hakhshara work to He-Halutz."[22] The 14th Congress in Vienna in 1925 recognized the hakhsharot established by the various parties. The 15th, in Basel in 1927, convened during the critical times of the Fourth Aliyah, decided to make aliyah possible for some of the pioneers who were on hakhshara.[23]

At the start of the mass emigration in the years of the Fourth Aliyah, a new sort of criticism of pioneering, more in the nature of a matter of principle, came to be expressed in the staid Zionist circles. It distinguished between the past, when pioneering was necessary, and the present, when the emigration to the Land of Israel has become a mass phenomenon and the Land no longer needs a voluntaristic, avant-gardist element because, henceforth, it will be able to develop according to the natural economic laws like every other country in the world. On the contrary, it was charged that pioneering was conducting a deficit operation and using Jewish funds for utopian, socialistic experiments. Therefore the demand was to stop supporting it and to transfer the Zionist activity to the urban economy because the pioneering phase has already ended.[24]

After the outbreak of the severe economic crisis in the Land of Israel in 1925-1927 and the great exodus from the country, this argument was no longer heard. The pioneer movement's wrangle over greater pioneer aliyah also did not cease in those years. At that time, too, when the number leaving was greater than the number arriving, the hakshara movement demanded that the aliyah of its members not be stopped. In those years of despair and depression, the pioneer movement, though also shrunken, did not stop sending its members to hakhshara and demanding aliyah possibilities for them.[25]

After the beginning of the Fifth Aliyah, the relationship between the pioneers and the Zionist Organization entered a new phase. Though the items of contention remained almost the same, they assumed a greater gravity due to objective developments in Poland and in the Land of Israel.

In all the years of its existence the hakhshara received very limited financial support from the Zionist management. These sums only in small measure covered the hakhshara budget and the on-going demands for increases did not bring the desired results.[26] The situation was difficult when the hakhshara activity was being conducted on a small scale, and precisely in the years when it broadened out and took on a mass character, the support became relatively and absolutely smaller. The hakhshara had to cover its expenses out of its own labor and since the wages were next to nothing, its living standard was very low.[27]

In 1930, when the hakhshara gradually recovered after the serious crisis of the Fourth Aliyah, and youth, reacting to the bloody events of

1929, began to come into the movement and to hakhshara, He-Halutz bemoans the fact that despite all its efforts it has not managed to receive any support from the Jewish Agency for hakhshara in general or agricultural hakhshara in particular, especially because the latter requires large investments which He-Halutz cannot muster. The American Agency members are blamed for the fact that their concern for a balanced budget even at the expense of varied activities has cancelled the hakhshara support in spite of all the nice talk about its importance.[28]

The reason for this indifference, according to the hakhshara activists, is because the Zionist management sees the hakhshara as a mechanical function of the actual and changing development of the Land of Israel. It does not understand that the hakhshara has become independent, with its own autonomous rules of life, "the first and major expression of the nation being reborn and fulfilling itself."[29] The demands are in the direction of recognizing the hakhshara as a broad framework which needs constant support because without it the Zionist propaganda has no future.

The agency did in fact recognize the great Zionist importance of the hakhshara and insisted that the workers' aliyah be composed only of hakhshara members as the suitable colonizing element,[30] but drew no conclusions therefrom. It continues to support the hakhshara meagerly even when hakhshara moved into the cities, and despite the fact that at the Agency's head were representatives of the Labor parties. In a memorandum to the 19th Zionist Congress, it is underscored that despite all efforts to support itself by its own labor, the hakshara very strongly needs financial support for investments to establish itself in the new places: housing, kitchen, etc. The catastrophic plight of the hakhshara is emphasized in light of the difficult economic situation in Eastern Europe.[31]

The 19th Zionist Congress actually did debate about hakhshara, recognized its national importance, the need to expand "the agricultural hakhshara, improve the living-conditions. . . assist in establishing supportive systems for the urban hakhshara and broaden the cultural work and the learning of Hebrew." It even obligated the "Jewish Agency to fix a suitable budget for the hakhshara needs and to utilize it only for the purposes listed."[32] But the financial picture of the hakhshara kibbutzim did not change radically as a result of these decisions.

In the years of mass emigration to the Land of Israel between 1932-1935 and the massive growth of the hakhshara, the discussion about the place of the hakhshara members and the emigration to the Land of Israel flared up anew, often assuming a tenser, more dramatic character because of the catastrophic situation of Polish Jewry as a result both of the world economic crisis, the official state anti-Jewish policy of the regime, the strengthened antisemitic propaganda wave involving pogroms, and of the closing of the doors of all the traditional lands of immigration except for the Land of Israel. It becomes the main emigration goal of Polish Jewry. In 1932, of all the Jewish emigrants from Poland, 39.9% went to the Land of Israel. In 1935, the Land of Israel received 80.6% of all the Jewish emigrants from Poland. In 1937, with the restriction of aliyah, again only 32.2%.[33]

During this period, the certificate more than once becomes the only chance for the pauperized and oppressed Jew and his family.

The demands of the pioneer organizations between 1930-1932 to increase the aliyah of the hakhshara members bear the same character as in the prior years. The Agency is urged to fight the immigration restrictions of the Labour Government and to continue to maintain the pioneer share of the labor aliyah at 89%, just as in the 1928-1929 years.[34] This request had good chances of being accepted. Even the pioneer press admits "that the time is irreversibly past that the existence of He-Halutz was negated because the pioneer period of building the Land of Israel is over;" that certainly the rules of a capitalist economy will develop there. The press emphasizes that it has been shown that without the strenuous pioneering efforts the Zionist work cannot be developed: "Unlike the Fourth Aliyah,[35] He-Halutz comprises the majority of the labor aliyah in the Fifth."[36]

The hope that the recognition of the primacy of the pioneering aliyah would be a lasting one, frittered away in 1932 after the doors of the Land of Israel were re-opened to mass aliyah. Once again, almost with the same arguments as during the Fourth Aliyah but with an eye upon the critical condition of Polish Jewry, a battle begins against the primacy of pioneering. This time the wrangling is much more extreme on both sides because the pressure to emigrate had become stronger in the pioneer camp as well, as a result of the growth of the hakhshara.

At a session of the secretariat of He-Kibbut Ha-Meuhad in November 1932, Yitzhak Tabenkin analyzes the new situation after it seemed "that the criticism of the permanent hakhshara was no longer on the agenda because it had passed the colonizing, avant-gardist, self-realization test in the Land of Israel."[37]

The reason for the new anti-hakhshara tendency lies not in the failure of the colonizing activities of its members but in the revitalization "of the staid elements" as in the time of the Fourth Aliyah. In the bourgeois, middle-class circles there is talk once again, especially in Jabotinsky's articles, "that the significance of physical labor wanes where there is no crisis in the world, when there is only a crisis of physical labor," and therefore the hakhshara and pioneer aliyah are superfluous.[38]

However, not only the Revisionists but also other Zionist circles friendly to pioneering came to the conclusion that the pioneering hegemony had reached its end. The accusation against the pioneers was that their demands deprive the ordinary person of the right to emigrate. "Why, after a year's hakhshara, does the pioneer have the right to emigrate while the artisan who has worked at his trade all his life is not privileged to receive a certificate."[39]

Yitzhak Gruenbaum and Moshe Kleinbaum (Sneh) also criticized the pioneer aliyah. In an article in "Heint" (Today), Gruenbaum writes that when none wanted to go to the Land of Israel, the pioneer was the trail-blazing element, but in times when many wish to emigrate, "He-Halutz has been pushed back and has had to make room for other working elements." And also: "We must busy ourselves with saving sorely troubled Jewish communities."[40] Gruenbaum also defends the right of the employers in the Land of Israel to import workers individually: i.e., special specialists whom he needs, and not through the national institutions. "Every manufacturer has the right to bring specialists with whom he worked in the lands of the Diaspora or whom he knows to be experts."[41]

Gruenbaum's arguments, especially the first one, are an echo of the tragic dilemma faced by the Zionist Organization in those years, especially after Hitler came to power. The pressure was great, the alternatives almost nil. It was a struggle of people who insticntively felt that they were condemned to go under and who tried in every which way to save themselves.

As a result of this tendency, the pioneers' share in the labor aliyah fell to 40-50% at a time when the pioneer movement was no longer asking for 90% as in 1929-1931 but only for 60-75%.[42]

The pioneer movement's wrangle over the participation of the hakh-shara members in the labor aliyah was based on arguments of principle foremost of which was that even in the prosperous times, and especially in these times, the Land of Israel needs not a capitalist emigration but an avant-garde, activist, pioneering aliyah.[43]

In the battle against the pioneer aliyah Tabenkin sees an expression of the middle-class ideology struggle which serves to support reaction. Fear of the hakhshara and pioneering has forged a unity in the entire middle-class camp, from the (right religious) Agudat Israel to the radical General Zionists and Revisionists. His conclusion was that the battle is not only against the hakhshara and the kibbutz but against the hegemony of the Labor Movement and the Histadrut in general.[44]

The pioneer movement characterizes the attackers of the hakhshara as "bankrupt, Sabbath and Festival Zionists"; but to it Zionism is not a matter of politics. Its members have sacrificed their lives to realize Zion-ist aims.[45]

The demands for the primacy of the pioneering aliyah in times of prosperity as well, is undergirded not only as an expression of selfish interests but as an objective-historic necessity: "The right of aliyah is not an objective right of every Zionist but is dictated by the interests of Zionism in the Land of Israel."[46] The Land needs not ordinary immi-grants but pioneers, so that the Land of Israel not become a second Diaspora. The hakhshara member is more important than the artisan, not because he has learned a skill during his hakhshara but becuase the hakh-shara "educated him to fulfill national-colonizing tasks and to be pre-pared for any, even the most difficult, work."[47]

Different from the other kinds of aliyah, especially the popular, which were sectarian and only concerned with their private or group fate, the kibbutz hakhshara aliyah, according to the pioneer argumentation, is in the general national interest because it alone is able to prepare the Land for the broad masses: "Favorable or unfavorable circumstances come and go, but the one who wants to build a sturdy structure based upon them will, in the end, betray Zionism . . . and this is not the way of the pioneer movement."[48]

The general tone of the pioneer offensive against the tendency to minimize the pioneer aliyah was that as long as pioneering fulfills the Zion-ist goals, and as long as one cannot depend upon the popular elements to be able to solve the Jewish problem, the demands of the hakhshara movement must be satisfied.[49]

The question is whether very often the particular interest of the hakhshara movement was not interpreted as an objective-historic necessity which carries a general national significance, just as the other avant-garde movements interpreted their ideologies as expressions of the historic-deterministic processes and themselves as their bearers.

The feelings of bitterness of the pioneer movement in all of its shadings against the Zionist establishment for not valuing its important avant-garde role in the national renaissance process, are best expressed in the following lines of Berl Katznelson's: "It was not an outstretched hand . . . that raised and caressed He-Halutz. It is very little missed." It is a step-child of Zionism. "One can cause it misery . . . tear it apart, destroy it. It doesn't matter. Is there a dearth of weeds? Whom and what did the Zionist Organization not pursue? . . . To what demands did it not turn an ear? Only to those of the pioneer movement 'that grows by itself.' The assumption was that it would not lack, that it would not cease. No one bemoaned himself when He-Halutz did not exist; no one wept that it was small. On the contrary, some are afraid lest it grow, become strong and influential . . . afraid for their privileges; others are striken with terror for their very being, which gives them no rest but continues to demand, to obligate. It is that pious man 'alone with his measure of carob fruit the entire week' and . . . it is upon him that the whole world of the Land of Israel depends."[50]

Still further: it revolutionized the Diaspora reality, brought new ideas to the Jewish ambience: "the Bund raised the Jewish worker from the filth," but did nothing for the productivization of the declassed Jewish masses. Nor did it stand against the centrifugal process of the Jewish community. This He-Halutz did. "It made the Jewish youth a bridge to the working class." Time at hakhshara became a symbol of new moral and communal values; through it the honor of every work was raised "and it also influenced others: ORT, and the producer-cooperation of the Bund."[51]

CHAPTER 8

THE LAST CHAPTER: 1936-1939

The negative phenomena of crisis and decline in the hakhshara move-ment indicate the extent to which the mass growth of hakhshara in 1932-1935 was in great measure the result of circumstances—because the Land of Israel was the only one accepting Jewish emigrants in great numbers—and not a direct result of the structural-ideological pro-pioneering and pro-Zionist development among the Jewish youth. In all of the organiza-tions, from He-Halutz to the Revisionists, this period lasts until the begin-ning of World War II and is characterized by the restrengthening of the avant-gardist character of the movement. The "ordinary pioneer" type, i.e. the older youth without any phase of education in a youth movement, vanishes almost completely. He is replaced by members of the youth movements. In these years they are the major components of the hakh-shara. Without them it would have completely disappeared. "Those going to hakhshara now are almost exclusively members of the youth move-ments."[1]

The roots of this development lie in the realm of general foreign affairs, i.e., independent of the internal developmental processes of the move-ment. We refer to the Italo-Abyssinian War and the economic crisis and unemployment which accompanied it, (the number of unemployed at the end of 1935 in the Land of Israel numbered 5000), as well as to the Arab disturbances that begin in April 1936 and lasted intermittently until 1939. These developments resulted in restrictions on emigration to the Land of Israel.[2]

The reaction in the Zionist movement to the crisis was immediate. Not only did the external opponents strengthen their anti-Land-of-Israel and anti-Zionist propaganda, but also "in the Zionist camp itself, voices of doubt began to be heard. . . Zionists suddenly saw that the time is difficult and concluded. . . that the youth need not be prepared for aliyah because there is none."[3]

As the crisis grows more severe, so does the depression spread through the broad strata of the people. Gone are the days "when father and mother brought their children to He-Halutz or hakhshara." Just the opposite. "We hear again this Jew or another saying that only fools are ready to suffer for years on hakhshara . . . ."[4]

This atmosphere also penetrated the ranks of the hakhshara movement. Optimism and the job offensive are replaced by defensiveness and disorientation. "Communal and cultural helplessness and ideological retreat"[5] prevail in its ranks.

After the doors of the Land of Israel were closed to new immigrants, the situation of the Polish Jews became catastrophic and the atmosphere stifling as a result of the extreme antisemitic government policy accompanied by a series of excesses and pogroms. Opportunistic and nihilistic leanings spread among part of the youth. There is talk of the devastation of the Jewish youth, of a cynical attitude toward ideologies. There is a spreading atmosphere of "grab and eat," a feeling of its bein the eve of destruction.[6] Understandably, in such an atmosphere it is very difficult to conduct a ramified educational and hakhshara activity.

The first victim of these developments was the branch (the first local stage of membership in He-Halutz before hakhshara), the weakest link in the chain of the hakhshara movement. In an article on the 20th anniversary of He-Halutz, the fact is emphasized that the branch has almost totally been destroyed. Thus the hakhshara movement lost its peripheral mass and reservoir from which most of the ordinary pioneer-candidates had been recruited for hakhshara. The pioneer hakhshara movement thereby lost the older, unorganized youth element. It social character changed.[7]

Those who left or finished the hakhshara played a not insignificant role in demoralizing the branch. Coming back home and waiting for aliyah a long time, part of them became doubtful, spread apathy and cynicism, scoffed at the younger ones who still believed in their pioneering ideals and yearned for hakhshara.[8]

The expressions of crisis on the hakhshara were more complicated and far-reaching.

The stopping of aliyah did not have the same immediate catastrophic effects upon the hakhshara as upon the branch, but it did also strongly influence its development in a negative sense. One of the chief features that were characteristic of the hakhshara at all times, and especially in the period of its mass growth, was the rotation of its members. After being there a certain length of time, a maximum of a year or two, they left for the Land of Israel. This did put a seal of temporariness upon it but, at the same time, it made the point that its goal was not to build collective, permanent, cells of life in the Diaspora. Its essence lay in preparing the members for their colonizing, avant-gardist tasks in the Land of Israel. Now the situation changed radically. The rotation ceased. Instead of a year, the members had to live on hakhshara four years or more.[9] In its aggressive, expansive euphoria, the movement was psychologically unprepared for the crisis nor had it prepared its members for such an eventuality. Therefore the new situation called forth, especially in the first period, in the 1936-1938 years, strong reactions of despair and helplessness. "The idealism is disappearing; the people are getting older; and the question of 'tachlis' (the practical end result) is becoming all the more sharp." In such a situation, many of the young people concluded that "it is not worthwhile to go to hakhshara. If it does not guarantee a future why waste the years?[10]

The more the chances of aliyah became slimmer, the greater became the camp of those who left the hakhshara. "Many members have lost their patience and returned to the small town."[11] The number of hakhshara members fell in a single year by 25%.[12] This trend continued later as well.[13] The situation stabilized to a certain degree at the end of 1938 and the beginning of 1939. The new situation forced a reduction in the numbers of hakhshara centers. The remaining members were moved to larger cities where the living conditions and work opportunities were better and where hands were in short supply.[14]

The new situation also had a certain positive influence on the hakh-shara's lifestyle. If in the period of the great expansion there had been a certain barracks quality to hakhshara life, the closing of the doors of the Land of Israel forced it to take on more stable forms. The members went from temporary, poorly paying work to skilled labor of a higher wage. Workshops and agricultural auxiliary systems were established. The living standard became higher and the living conditions better. The number of ill, a problem which had plagued the hakhshara in its aggressive years, dropped. The longer period on hakhshara also allowed for a deepening of the cultural activity, so that often the hakhshara life was on a higher level than in the small town. This however did not effect the psyche of the members. There was a feeling of fatigue in the hakh-shara over the length of time there, over the long wait from the redemption: for the certificate. Every bit of political news was interpreted in terms of its effect on aliyah and, of course, on the fate of the individual. "The hakhshara member is perhaps the most unfortunate of people with whom one must commiserate. . . . Many hakhshara members do not like it despite the fact that compared to the life of the proletarian youth, life in the hakhshara is like living in a palace and not in an Arab hut."[15]

The crisis really was the result of objective causes, but its mass start renewed once more the debate between the supporters of the avant-garde course, on the one hand, and the mass direction, on the other.[16]

The pioneer youth movements saw in the crisis, in the disappearance of the ordinary pioneers, a vindication of their concept that the essentially avant-gardist pioneering hakhshara cannot be built upon an emigrant, coincidental element lacking long-term ideational education, which has joined the movement in order to find a solution for its personal problems and not out of ideal motives. The pioneer youth movements were not against having such pioneers in the movement, but they did not believe that it could be turned into a mass movement. Therefore they held fast to the viewpoint that the backbone of the hakhshara movement must be the youth organizations. Ha-Shomer Ha-Tza'ir recollects that at the time of the popular mass growth people thought that the role of the youth movement was over. The crisis smashed those illusions and showed that it is the solid foundation of pioneering in the grave crisis years.[17]

The supporters of a mass pioneering movement in the times of crisis also did not discard their concept based upon the premise that the objective

Jewish reality demands a mass pioneering movement because "our course has proven itself," as Yitzhak Tabenkin asserts in 1938.[18] They do in fact admit that "in these trying times the kernel which steadied He-Halutz has been the youth movement," which educated to fulfillment, to maximalism, yielding on no ideational values.[19] At the same time, however, they rejected the viewpoint that only the youth movements will build the hakhshara work. No youth movement by itself can assure a reserve for hakhshara. Therefore once must not be satisfied with them but go out on an offensive to return the ordinary pioneer to the ranks of the hakhshara movement.[20]

Objective factors brought on the crisis. The movement had no control over them, but the severity and depth of the crisis is not the result of these factors alone. To blame for it, especially in the destruction of the branch, i.e., of the hakhshara's personnel-reserve, are, according to the proofs of the bloc, the youth movements that isolated themselves in their own ranks and did not send into the branch the somewhat more intellectual forces that were able to offer the branch a cultural and communal appearance: "It seems that many of those who fought the trend to mixed branches and hakhsharot are sorry today that these ranks have been lost."[21] The conclusion is that the avant-gardist youth movements err in thinking that the problem of a mass hakhshara has been taken care of. The conclusions about the character of He-Halutz have indeed lost their sharpness, but the problem of the young masses, the 20-25 year-olds who are idling around in the towns without a future has not been resolved. The hope is expressed "that when conditions in the Land of Israel will change and a large aliyah will become possible, many of them will return to He-Halutz and hakhshara. If our movement does not intend to give up on them, we must not eliminate even today the problem of the general nature of He-Halutz. The branch will yet become a meeting place for the youth that has not found its way into any organization . . . . Therefore, in these days of the liquidation of communal organizations, the branch has great meaning."[22]

Without any concessions in their principles and ideological concepts, both sides simultaneously sought ways of overcoming the crisis. Starting from the premise that it is not necessary to change the ideology nor its methods and ways of implementation for they have not lost their relevance and therefore need no revision, the conclusion was that the only way to overcome the crisis was to deepen the ideational education which was neglected in the mass growth period. The hakhshara, by dint of its idea, must conquer the difficult feelings of apathy. The weakness is that it lacks the great vision. The goal must be to qualitatively elevate each individual and transform him into an active bearer of the idea.[23]

In the organizational realm as well, efforts were made to mobilize the young people on hakhshara. Hands were lacking there. A somewhat paradoxical situation developed: precisely in the difficult economic times the hakhsharot stabilized and sought working hands, and the young people in the small town, whose situation was hopeless, were not in a rush to go. The youth movements took upon themselves the task of finding new reserves.[24]

To combat the difficulties better, in May 1937 in Jerusalem, a World Organization of Pioneer Organizations was formed. It set itself the following tasks: to defend and protect the unity of the pioneer movement in the crisis period, fighting cooperatively for its rights and for increasing its financial means in order to maintain the hakhshara; to avoid competition between the different hakhsharot in job-seeking; to coordinate the medical help; and jointly to represent the hakhshara in the Zionist Organization and other communal institutions.[25]

These efforts were crowned with certain successes. Already in mid-1938 there is a feelingthat the hakhshara has merged from the severe blow. In the first period, there is not yet any talk of expansion, only of protecting what exists. The situation on the hakhshara stabilizes itself.[26] There is warning however against easy optimism after the disappointments of the past.[27] Gradually the new trend becomes more prominent. The hakhshara even begins to enlarge a bit. A fishing hakhshara is set up in Gdynia, the Polish Baltic port. The cultural work becomes ramified and deepened. There are reports of hundreds of new hakhshara members replacing the older members who have made aliyah despite the White Paper of March 1939.[28] This trend did not achieve any full development due to the outbreak of the war.

The reasons for that transformation lie both in the waves of new pogroms that flooded over Poland in 1938-1939 and brought young people to the pioneer ranks once more, and also in the beginning of a broad scale illegal aliyah to the Land of Israel. It enabled the haksharot to be emptied of the older, embittered members, and to be filled with new young generation of members from the youth movements, saturated with enthusiasm and ready for sacrifice.

The illegal aliyah, which opened a new perspective for the hakhshara movement, had actually ebgun in the middle of 1934 when the ship "Vellos" had brought 350 pioneers to the Land of Israel. On its second trip, this ship spent three months at sea, after having been turned back from the shores of the Land of Israel, and finally returned to Poland. This misadventure resulted in a three-year hiatus in the illegal aliyah.

The difficult situation of thousands of hakhshara members who for years had survived hakhshara, exerted a strong pressure which led to the revitalization of the illegal immigration idea. In 1937 Klosow demanded its renewal of the Zionist leadership in the Land of Israel, but only at the beginning of 1938 does He-Halutz, of its own initiative, without the knowledge of the Land of Israel, begin to organize the illegal immigration again, from scratch, on a rather small scale. The Revisionists also organize their own aliyah. The Land of Israel harnesses itself to the work only at the end of 1938. In 1939, the illegal immigration wave swells to embrace hundreds of people, in spite of the British regime's beefed up battle against it, especially after the issuance of the anti-Jewish White Paper in the spring of 1939.[29]

This emigration created a small safety value which enabled the hakhshara movement in Poland to try anew to develop new initiatives in the area of strengthening and even expanding the hakhshara. But it did not go beyond the attempt because of the outbreak of the war. Only after the war does the illegal immigration, the "berihah" (the Flight) become a mass-phenomenon encompassing hundreds of thousands of Jews. But then the circumstances were different.

NOTES

Notes to Preface

1. See I. Oppenheim, "The Attitude of the He-Halutz Movement in Poland Toward Avodat Ha-Hove" (Productivization in the Diaspora), *Maasef, Journal of the History of the Jewish Labor Movement*, Part 1, no. 15 (1985), pp. 119-131; Idem, Part 2 (1986), pp. 89-95.

2. I. Oppenheim, "Chapters in the History of the He-Halutz Hakhshara in Poland Between the Two World Wars," in Joshua A. Fishman (ed.), *Studies in Polish Jewry 1919-1939*, Yivo Institute for Jewish Research (New York 1974), pp. 229-335.

Notes to Introduction

1. On the First Aliyah, Hibbat Tzion, its accomplishments and temptations, see: Moshe Braslavsky, *Tenu'at Ha-Po'alim Ha-Erez Yisraelit* (Heb.) (The Land of Israel Labor Movement), vol. I, (Ein Harod 1955), pp. 11-16; also Braslavsky, *Po'alim Ve-Irguneihem Ba-'Aliyah Ha-Rishona* (Heb.) (The Workers and Their Organizations in the First Aliyah), (Ein Harod 1953). Zvi Rosenstein (Even-Shoshan), *Toledot Tenu'at Ha-Po'alim Be-Erez Yisrael, Sefer Rishon* (Heb.) (The History of the Labor Movement in the Land of Israel, Book One) (Tel-Aviv 1955), pp. 11-33; M. Eliav, (ed.), *The First Aliyah* (2 vols.), (Jerusalem 1981).

2. The literature on the Second Aliyah is a very rich one. The following are but a few examples. See: Braslavksy, *Tenu'at Ha-Po'alim*, vol.

I, pp. 62-134; Rosenstein, op. cit., pp. 61-245. Berl Katznelson, *Ketavim* (Heb.) (Writings), vol. XI (Tel-Aviv 1959), pp. 126-211. Berakha Habass, (ed.), *Sefer Ha'Aliyah Ha-Sheniyah* (Heb.) (The Second Aliyah) (Tel-Aviv 1947). On the various pioneering groups in Russia, see: Yehuda Slutzki, "Ha-Ra'ayon Ha-Haluzi U'Tnu'ot Haluziot Shonot Lifnei Milhemet Ha-'Olam Ha-Rishonah" (Heb.) (The Pioneer Idea and the Various Pioneer Movements before World War I), in *Asufot,* a compendium on the history of the Labor Movement, vol. no. 12 (Tel-Aviv, July 1968). On the influence of the Second Aliyah on the Russian and Polish He-Halutz, see below in Chapter 1.

3.   On the ambivalent relationships between the pioneering hakhshara movements, the Zionist Organization, and the Zionist-Socialist parties, see below in Chapter 7.

4.   Ya'akov Eshed, "Ziyyunim" (Heb.) (Notes), in *He-Halutz Ha-Tza'ir,* the organ of the Bogrim of the He-Halutz Ha-Tza'ir Organization, no. 19, (Warsaw, January 1934), p. 5.

5.   On the sociological and psychological differences between He-Halutz and the autonomistic youth movements, see below in Chapter 5.

6.   On the Russian He-Halutz in the person of Joseph Trumpeldor, see: Braslavsky, *Tenu'at Ha-Po'alim,* vol. I, pp. 261-282; Even-Shoshan, op. cit., vol. I, pp. 358-379; Moshe Basok, ed., *Sefer He-Halutz, An Anthology* (Heb.) (The He-Halutz Book), (Jerusalem 1940), pp. 5-130; Leib Spizman, ed., *Halutzim in Poilin Antologia* (Yid.) (The Pioneers in Poland Anthology), (New York 1959), pp. 12-21; Israel Oppenheim, "He-Halutz Be-Russiah Be-Shanim 1918-1922," (Heb.) (He-Halutz in Russia in the Years of 1918-1922), *Asufot, Ketavim Le-Heker Tenu'at Ha-Po'alim Ha-Yehudi* (Heb.) (Asufot, Writings for the Study of the Jewish Labor Movement), May 1971, pp. 3-51. On the influence of the Russian He-Halutz on the formation of He-Halutz in Poland, see below in Chapter 1.

7.   Leib Spizman, op. cit., "First Years in Poland," pp. 22-32. These may have been groups that had already organized even prior to the World War and had stopped their activity. In time, after the Germans had settled in, they renewed their work.

8.   Leib Spizman, ibid., pp. 27, 31, 143, 235. The figures relate especially to the general He-Halutz. About other pioneer organizations, see Chapter 6.

Notes to Chapter 1

1.   On the various pioneer groups prior to World War I, see Slutzki, op. cit.; A., "Tze'irei Tzion Ve-He-Halutz" (Tze'irei Tzion and He-Halutz) in Yehuda Erez, ed., *Sefer Z. S.* (Heb.) (The Zionist-Socialist Book), (Tel-Aviv 1963), pp. 273-275.

2.   Y. Kalvir, *Be-'Ir Ha-Birah Ha-Polanit*, (Heb.) (In the Polish Capital), on the twentieth anniversary of He-Halutz (Kibbutz Ashdod Ya'kov, May 1938) (stencil), p. 22. Also see: Dr. Meir Peker, *Zarys Rozwoju "Hechaluc"–Pionier w Polsce* (Summary of the Development of He-Halutz in Poland) (Warszawa 1930), pp. 3-4. There too the fact is stressed that at the same time He-Halutz movements arose in America and Russia. See: Moshe Kliger, *Ikrei He-Halutz Ha-Tza'ir* (Heb.) (The Principles of He-Halutz Ha-Tza'ir), Report of the 2nd Nationwide Conference of He-Halutz Ha-Tza'ir, 1931, p. 23. Israel Oppenheim, op. cit., ibid. On the establishment of the American He-Halutz, see: "He-Halutz" (Yid.), (New York 1917). Z. Cutler, *He-Halutz, Zein Entwiklung, Ziel un Wegen un Tetigkeit* (Yid.) (He-Halutz, its Development, Goal, and Activity), (New York 1921). Spizman, op. cit., p. 7.

3.   See: "He-Halutz," (Yid.) dedicated to the pioneer movement, appearing twice a month, No. 2, (Warsaw), May 6, 1919. Pioneer groups were organized in a similar way in other places. See ibid. Also, Aaron Berdichevsky, "Chapters of He-Halutz History in Poland" in L. Spizman, op. cit., pp. 192-193. Also ibid., p. 22. Eliahu Dobkin, "On the History of the Third Aliyah," ibid., pp. 82-83; "Immigrants from Volkovysk," ibid., pp. 86-88.

4.   About the ideological development in its first phase, see below.

5.   *Dos Yiddishe Folk* (Yid.) (The Jewish People), Zionist weekly, (Warsaw no. 33), October 1917.

6.   Spizman, ibid., p. 22.

7.   On the relationships between the Russian He-Halutz, the Ze'irei Tzion, and the Zionist Organization, see: I. Oppenheim, op. cit., pp. 4-14; Eliahu Montzik, "Nizanei He-Halutz Be-Russiah" (Heb.) (The Buds of He-Halutz in Russia) in *Measeif Li-Tenu'at He-Halutz* (an anthology of the He-Halutz movement) (Warsaw 1930), pp. 99 ff.; *He-Halutz Be-Russiah, Toledot He-Halutz Ha-Bilti Legali Be-Russiah* (Heb.) (He-Halutz

in Russia, the History of the Illegal He-Halutz in Russia), (Tel-Aviv 1933), pp. 12 ff.

8.   *Dos Yidishe Folk*, no. 1, January 1918; Spizman, p. 34.

9.   Ibid. This fact is worth stressing because it shows us that He-Halutz, at the start, did not see itself as a youth movement like Ha-Shomer Ha-Tza'ir, nor did it develop a specific youth ideology. Neither did it negate the political parties as such. Many of the He-Halutz members were, at the same time, active members of the Tze'irei Tzion or the right wing Po'alei Tzion Party. A few years later He-Halutz also established its own youth movement, He-Halutz Ha-Tza'ir. For the reasons for this, see below, Chapter 5.

10.   *Unser Atid* (Our Future), no. 15, Vilna, October 2, 1918, Spizman, p. 24.

11.   Correspondence in *He-Halutz* (Yid.), no. 2, May 16, 1919. About other regional conferences, see ibid., no. 3, May 27, 1919.

12.   Ibid., no. 1, April 14, 1919. A call was also issued by the Provisional Central Committee (P.C.C.) with the agenda of the conference and the delegates' voting regulations. Ibid., no. 2, May 6, 1919.

13.   Ibid., no. 3, May 22, 1919.

14.   Ibid.

15.   Ibid.

16.   Ibid, no. 4, June 26, 1919.

17.   Ibid.

18.   Ibid.

19.   Ibid., on the differences of opinion as far as the structure of the Russian He-Halutz and its relationships with the Zionist organizations and the Zionist-Socialist parties, see the decision at the Petrograd He-Halutz Conference to remain independent and, as in Poland, only to accept the discipline of the Zionist Congress and not of the national organization. See: Dan Pines, *He-Halutz Be-Kur Ha-Mahapeikha* (Heb.) (He-Halutz in the Crucible of the Revolution), (Tel-Aviv 1936), p. 31; also see; note 7 above.

20.   *He-Halutz* (Yid.), no. 3, May 27, 1919, par. 4.

21.   Ibid.

22.   Ibid.

23.   Ibid.

24.   Ibid.

25.   See: *Hahlatot Ve-Taarikhim 1918-1935* (Heb.) (Decisions and Dates 1918-1935) (Warsaw 1935), p. 5. On the ideological developments which bolstered the independence of He-Halutz and brought it closer to Labor-Zionism, see below.

26.   On the other pioneering orgnaizations, see below, Chapter 6.

27.   *Decisions and Dates,* p. 6.

28.   *He-Halutz* (Yid.), nos. 8-9, December 12, 1919.

29.   Ibid.

30.   Spizman, p. 30.

31.   *Kuntres, Bitaon Mifleget Ahdut Ha-'Avodah Be-Erez Yisrael* (Heb.) (Kuntres, the Organ of the Ahdut Ha-'Avodah Party in the Land of Israel), no. 92 (Tel-Aviv), 22 Elul, 1921.

32.   *Befraiung* (Liberation), the Central-Organ of the Folk-Section of the Tze'irei Tzion Party in Poland, no. 19(76), (Warsaw, November 1922).

33.   Spizman, ibid., pp. 31-32; Berdichevsky, ibid., p. 191.

34.   Benjamin West, ed., *Naftulei Dor, Toledot Tze'irei Tzion Be-Russiah* (Heb. anthology) (A Generation's Struggles, the History of Tze'irei Tzion in Russia), vol. I & II, (Tel-Aviv 1948, 1956); Moshe Braslavsky, op. cit., vol. II, pp. 67-282; *Me-asef Li-Tnu'at He-Halutz* (Heb.) (Collection for the He-Halutz Movement Compendium), pp. 99-100; Oppenheim, ibid., pp. 4-16.

35.   See below.

36.   *He-Halutz* (Yid.), No. 3, May 27, 1919.

37.   Ibid.

38.   Ibid.

39.   Yehuda Reznitzenko (Erez), in *Weg* (Yid.) (The Way), "Tzu der Frage fun Hakhshara un Halutzishe Yugend-Bawegung" (On the Question of Hakhshara and the Pioneer Youth Movement), (Tel-Aviv no year), p. 10. At the first Tze'irei Tzion conference in Poland, September 1918, this generality even aroused opposition from part of the Tze'irei Tzion members who called for not joining He-Halutz. At the conference in 1919 the party demanded autonomy for its pioneer groups in He-Halutz, as well as direct influence upon He-Halutz through its party representatives in the He-Halutz Central Committee. See Berdichevssky, ibid., p. 191; Yitzhak Broides, "Ershte Trit fun He-Halutz in Vilna," (Yid.) (The First Steps of He-Halutz in Vilna), in Spizman, p. 39.

40.   Reznitzenko, ibid.

41.   "Der Ruf Noch Arbet" (Yid.) (The Call to Work), by J. H. (Joseph Heftman–I. O.) in *He-Halutz*, no. 3, May 27, 1919.

42.   See below, Chapter 7.

43.   "Oifruf tzu di Halutzim" (Yid.) (Call to the Pioneers) of the Warsaw He-Halutz in *Dos Yidishe Folk,* no. 33, October 1914.

44.   J. H., "The Call to Work," ibid.

45.   Spizman, p. 23.

46.   About the debate between the "idealists" i.e., the avant-gardists, and the "materialists," i.e., the supporters of mass He-Halutz at its start, see: E. Montzik, "Im Ha-Istadiah Ha-Shlishit" (Heb.) (At the Third Stage), in *He-Halutz un Zeine Oifgaben* (He-Halutz and its Tasks) (Warsaw 1919), also *Sefer Z. S.,* p. 101. About Trumpeldor's views on this matter see: Joseph Trumpeldor, "He-Halutz, Mahuto U-Te'udotav Ha-Kerovot" (Heb.) (He-Halutz, its Essence and Immediate Tasks), cited according to *Sefer He-Halutz* (Heb.) (The He-Halutz Book), pp. 18-28. The same in *Me-asef Li-Tnu'at He-Halutz,* pp. 259-263. I. Oppenheim, ibid., pp. 2-9, 10-14. In our opinion, there was no direct influence at that time of the Russian He-Halutz upon Poland. This is evident sometime later when the Russian pioneers came to Poland on their way to the Land of Israel. On their influence upon the ideological development of the Polish He-Halutz, see below.

47.   Spizman, p. 24.

48.   *He-Halutz* (Yid.), no. 4, June 29, 1919.

49.   Waxman, ibid.

50.   Ibid., no. 3, May 27, 1919.

51.   This ideology was revived later on by the Revisionist Betar under different circumstances. See below, Chapter 6.

52.   For a more precise analysis of the relationships, its ideology, practical reasons, and concrete expressions, see below, Chapter 7.

53.   *He-Halutz* (Yid.), no. 1, April 14, 1919.

54.   Pines, op. cit., p. 20. *He-Halutz* (the illegal), ibid., p. 18.

55.   *Kuntres,* no. 26, Shevat 1920.

56.   J. H., "Der Alveltlicher He-Halutz" (Yid.) (The World-Wide He-Halutz), in *He-Halutz,* no. 8-9.

57.   Ibid., no. 11, February 19, 1920. It should be stressed, however, that it did not identify with all of his conclusions and states that "some passages in this article" it feels "are open to discussion." It is possible that the majority of He-Halutz was still far from Socialism. Despite this, the

article is of interest to us because it reflects certain tendencies which will later prevail in He-Halutz. Therefore we shall cite it more.

58. All quotations are from there.

59. *Befraiung,* no. 11, March 14, 1921, according to Spizman, p. 30.

60. About the role of the Tze'irei Tzion in the development of the pioneer groups in Russia before the war, and the He-Halutz movement after the war, see: Benjamin West, op. cit., vol. I; Pines, op. cit., chs. 1-4; Yehuda Erez, ed., *Sefer Z. S.,* Index of names. Yehuda Slutzki, op. cit., *Asufot,* no. 2. The labor tradition of the Tze'irei Tzion movement bore an anti-Marxist character. Its Socialism was strongly influenced by "Narodnik" and later "S. R." (Social Revolution Party in Russia) ideas as well as being based upon the immanent Jewish national tradition of the Prophets. Furthermore, in the Polish Tze'irei Tzion, after the world war, there developed against it a more crystallized Socialist class-outlook. See: Zev Levinson, "Bereshit Ha-Tenu'ah" (Heb.) (At the Start of the Movement), in *Naftulei Dor,* vol. I, pp. 33-45. On the influence of the Marxist Right Po'alei Tzion Party upon the He-Halutz development: "The appearance of the right wing of the Po'alei Tzion. . .strongly influenced the Jewish Zionist youth, whose pioneering took on a Zionist-Socialist interpretation before even setting foot on the soil of the Land of Israel." Thus Y. Kalvir, op. cit., (n. 2 above), p. 22.

61. *Befraiung,* no. 11, March 14, 1921.

62. Hakhshara in various regions. *Befraiung,* no. 4, September 1923, according to Spizman, pp. 52-53.

63. The following is based upon Berdichevsky, ibid., p. 193; Yehuda Reznizenko, "He-Halutzim Yotzei Russiah Ve-Ukraina Be-Polin" (Heb.) (The Russian and Ukrainian Pioneers in Poland) in *Sefer He-Halutz,* pp. 93-95; Pines, ibid., p. 139; E. Dobkin, "Hathalat Irguno Ha-Olami shel He-Halutz" (Heb.) (The Beginning of the He-Halutz World Organization) in *Measef Li-Tnu'at He-Halutz,* pp. 176-180. "Li-Ve'idateinu He-Sheniyah, Berlin" (About Our 2nd Convention in Berlin) *He-Halutz Berlin* 11 Adar, 1923, p. 11; *Ve'idateinu Ha-Sheniyah* (Heb.) (Our 2nd Convention), (Talks, Discussions, Resolutions at the 2nd He-Halutz Conference), (Berlin, March 1923), p. 26.

64. About the participation of the Russian pioneers in creating the He-Halutz movement in Lithuania and Roumania as well as in other countries, see n. 63, above.

65.   See above, the beginning of this chapter.

66.   Moshe Basok, "Be-'Einei Ha-Yeled" (Heb.) (In the Child's Eyes) in *Sefer He-Halutz,* pp. 53-55.

67.   Eliahu Dobkin, *Mahut Ve-'Ikrei He-Halutz* (Heb.) (The Essence and Principles of He-Halutz), programmatic talks at the 2nd He-Halutz Nationwide Conference in Poland, July 27-30, 1921, quoted from the original manuscript which the late Mr. Dobkin was kind enough to let us copy from his personal archives. We take this opportunity to thank him for his cooperation.

68.   Ibid.

69.   "Hahlatot Ha-Ve'idah Ha-Arzit Ha-Sheniyah shel He-Halutz Be-Polin," par. b in *Hahlatot Ve-Taarikhim,* p. 6.

70.   Zalman Rubashov (Shazar), "Darko shel He-Halutz La-Histadrut Ve-Li-Tenu'at Ha-Po'alim" (Heb.) (He-Halutz's Path to the Histadrut and the Labor Movement), the opening address at the 2nd He-Halutz World Conference, in *Ve-'idateinu Ha-Sheniyah,* p. 6.

71.   About them, see Chapter 6.

72.   *Measef Li-Tenu'at He-Halutz,* p. 204. Also see the resolutions of the 4th Nationwide Conference of the Polish He-Halutz, *Hahlatot Ve-Taarikhim,* p. 6. On the Po'alei Tzion influence upon He-Halutz and the development of Socialist tendencies in its ranks, see A. Weiner, "Mit der Ferter Aliyah fun Poilin (He-Halutz in Polesia) (Yid.) (With the Fourth Aliyah from Poland: He-Halutz in Polesia), Kibbutz Gevat, according to Spizman, pp. 151-158.

73.   *Hahlatot-Ve-Taarikhim,* p. 52.

Notes to Chapter 2

1.   The unending efforts of the maskilim to change the economic and social structure of the Jewish people are an important chapter in its history of the last two hundred years. The literature about its plans, viewpoints, and recommendations is enormously rich. A few examples must suffice: Gothold Ephraim Lessing, *Die Erziehung des Menschengeschlecht* (Berlin 1785); the important book of Christian Wilhelm von Dohm, *Ueber die buergerliche Verbesserung der Juden* (Berlin 1781, 1783). For the plans of the Jewish maskilim, see: Simon Dubnow, *History of the Jews in Russia and Poland,* vols. I-II (Jewish Publication Society of America,

Philadelphia, 1916 and 1918; Ben-Zion Dinur, "Sheeilat Ha-Geulah U-Der-akhehah Be-Reishit Ha-Haskalah U-Pulmus Ha-Emanzipaziah" (Heb.) (The Question of Redemption and its Ways at the Start of the Enlightenment and the Emancipation-Dispute) in *Be-Mifneh Ha-Dorot* (Generational Turning Point) (Jerusalem 1955), pp. 229-354; Jacob Katz, *Masoret U-Mashber* (Heb.) (Tradition and Crisis) (Jerusalem 1960), Part 3, chs. 21, 23-25; Raphael Mahler, *Divrei Ymei Yisrael Be-Dorot Aharonim* (Heb.) (A History of Israel in the Last Generations) (Merhaviah 1956, 1970) vols. 4-5, pp. 42-48, 153-316; R. Mahler, *Ha-Hasidut Ve-Ha-Haskalah* (Heb.) (Hasidism and the Enlightenment) (Merhaviah 1961), especially pp. 72-77. As we know, the masses in general had no confidence in these plans and in not a few instances opposed them. An example is the "reception" which the Jews in the Pale of Settlement prepared for Dr. Max Lilienthal when, as representative of the Russian government, he tried to reform the Jewish school and educational system. The reason for the mistrust lay in the fact that Jews saw the maskilim as emissaries of the ruling power whose real intent was to assimilate them against their will. See: Dr. M. Lilienthal, *Maggid Yeshu'ah* (Heb.) (Herald of Salvation) (Vilna 5603/ 1842); Jonah ben-Amitai, *Maggid Emet* (Heb.) (Herald of Truth) (Leipzig 1843); B. Mandelstam, *Kovez Mikhtavim Mitokh 'Hazon La-Mo'ed'* (Heb.) (Collection of Letters from 'Vision of the Future') (Vienna 1877) published by the Hebrew University in Jerusalem, 1966.

2.   M. Buber, *Der Jude,* 1918, cited according to *Sefer He-Halutz,* pp. 28-29.

3.   Ibid.

4.   David Ben-Gurion, "Ver Vet Unz Dos Land Geben" (Yid.) (Who Will Give Us the Land) in the brochure: *He-Halutz, Zeine Princzipn un Oifgaben* (Yid.) (He-Halutz, Its Principles and Tasks), (New York 1917), pp. 3-7, especially p. 5. Also see there the articles of Yitzhak Ben-Zvi: "Di Naie Pionirung Bewegung" (Yid.) (The New Pioneer Movement), pp. 8-10, and Yaakov Zerubabel: "He-Halutz un Zeine Oifgaben" (Yid.) (He-Halutz and its Tasks), ibid., p. 19.

5.   About the hakhshara in Russia and its stages of development, see: J. Trumpeldor, op. cit., p. 13; *Measef Li-Tenu'at He-Halutz* (Heb.), pp. 261-262; *Sefer Z. S.* Index; I. Oppenheim, op. cit., pp. 16-28.

6.   I. A., "Tze'irei Tzion Ve-He-Halutz" (Heb.) (The Tze'irei Tzion and He-Halutz) in *Sefer Z. S.,* pp. 274-275; Y. Slutzki, op. cit., pp. 15-18.

7. Eliezer Kaplan, "Mi-Yamim 'Avaru' (Heb.) (Of Days Past) in *Naftulei Dor,* p. 48.

8. I. A., op. cit., p. 275.

9. Spizman, op. cit., p. 22.

10. Ibid., p. 22. Also see the call of the Provisional Central Committee of He-Halutz of December 27, 1919 to the Jewish youth to study agriculture, ibid.

11. *He-Halutz* (Yid.), no. 2, May 6, 1919.

12. On the founding of hakhsharot in other cities such as Grajewo, Bendin, Shedletz, Rippin, Kolo, etc., ibid., no. 8-9, December 11, 1919. Also Spizman, op. cit., pp. 40, 49, 50, 51, 78-79, 80-81, 89, 90-91.

13. *He-Halutz* (Yid.), no. 2, May 6, 1919.

14. Ibid.

15. Ibid.

16. Ibid.

17. I. H.: "Der Ruf Noch Arbet" (Yid.) (The Call to Work), ibid., no. 3, May 27, 1919.

18. Ibid.

19. Ibid., no. 4, June 29, 1919.

20. Ibid., no. 5, August 18, 1919.

21. Ibid.

22. Ibid.

23. About the urban aversion of the Free German Youth Movement and its expressions of protests against urban civilization, see: Dr. Charlotte Luetkens, *Die deutsche Jugendbewegung (Ein Soziologischer Versuch)* (Frankfurt A/M 1925); Walter Z. Laquer, *Young Germany: A History of the German Youth Movement* (London 1962). About the influence of the German youth movement on the Jewish youth and especially on Ha-Shomer Ha-Tza'ir, see: Elkanah Margalit, *Ha-Shomer Ha-Tza'ir Mei-'adat Ne'urim Le-Marxism Nahapkhani* (Heb.) (Ha-Shomer Ha-Tza'ir from Youth Group to Revolutionary Marxism), (Tel-Aviv 1971), pp. 17-52. Without a doubt, the currents in Ha-Shomer Ha-Tza'ir did more or less influence certain circles of the He-Halutz movement.

24. Berman, *He-Halutz* (Yid.), no. 3, May 27, 1919.

25. Ibid.

26. Joseph Heftman, "Der Program fun He-Halutz" (Yid.) (The Program of He-Halutz), ibid. Also see the expressions of others who took part in the discussions there.

27.   Ibid., no. 3.

28.   Attempts to create farms were made again in 1922-1924, such as in Grushdin, near Gora Kalvaria; "Trumpeldoriah" near Vilna; "Kfar Yosef" near Plonsk, etc. But after a short 2-4 year period of existence they disbanded. Thus He-Halutz, the largest pioneer movement which included thousands of members in its hakhshara ranks, had only two agricultural operations, the aforementioned in Grochow and the Ha-Shomer Ha-Tza'ir hakhshara in Chenstochowa. Other pioneer organizations also had a few farms. This is somewhat paradoxical: a movement educating for life on the soil and working the land is forced by objective circumstances to conduct its hakhshara almost 100% in the city. The reasons for this development are as follows: He-Halutz lacked the large amount of capital necessary to invest in farms which were unrentable because of the low prices of agricultural products in Poland; the competition of the Polish agricultural workers, who suffered from high unemployment and whose wage was very low; as well as the ideological development in the means and ends of the hakhshara, which later focused on preparing members for all sorts of work. All of these factors caused almost the entire hakhshara of the 30's, the period of He-Halutz's great growth, to be in the city.

29.   See correspondence from Shedletz, *He-Halutz* (Yid.), no. 2, May 6, 1919.

30.   Ibid., no. 4, June 29, 1919. On the efforts in Zamosc see, too, Zvi Gabah, "Di Ershte Halutzim" (Yid.) (The First Pioneers), in the memorial volume *Zamosc Bi-Geonah Ve-Shivrah* (Heb.) (Zamosc at its Height and Degradation), according to Spizman, pp. 82-86.

31.   *He-Halutz* (Yid.), no. 4.

32.   Ibid.

33.   See Zamosc, where it is reported that the estate owner did not engage any Christian farm workers because the pioneers' work was cheaper. Ibid., no. 8-9, December 12, 1919. This charge was repeated often in the thirites when the hakhshara was concentrated in the city. See below, Chapter 7.

34.   Ibid.

35.   A. Joseph, "Di Halutzimm in Kremenetz" (Yid.) (The Pioneers in Kremenetz) in *Pinkas Kremenetz* (Kremenetz Ledger) quoted according to Spizman, p. 89. About the positive attitude of Jewish landowners to the pioneers in Kolo, Tomashov-Lubelski, Lovitch, see *He-Halutz* (Yid.), no.

2, May 16, 1919; Grodno, ibid., no. 5, August 18, 1919; ibid., no. 8-9, December 11, 1919.

36. Eliahu Montzik in his report: "Die Yesodos fun Kolonizatzia un di arbeit fun He-Halutz in Eretz Yisroel" (Yid.) (The Foundations of Colonization and the Work of He-Halutz in the Land of Israel); also the agronomist Oppenheim in his report: "The organization of the practical work of He-Halutz in the Land of Israel does not require large farms. It needs small ones. Therefore the hakhshara should prepare a "small-scale peasantry." Ibid., no. 4, June 29, 1919.

37. It is reported from Zamosc that: "Our kevutza (small group) is a closed one, built on cooperative foundations. These foundations were laid down at the very start of the group's formation and the same principle has been carried out . . . in our jouney." Ibid. Also see *Hahlatot Ve-Taarikhim,* p. 16.

38. Which defines He-Halutz as a non-party Zionist avant-garde of national and social liberation whose goal is to create "a Jewish labor community which subsists upon its own work" without exploiter and exploited. Ibid., p. 15.

39. Ibid., p. 15, par. 1.

40. Ibid., p. 15, paragraphs 2-3.

41. Ibid., pp. 15-16, par. 4.

42. Ibid., p. 16, par. 5. Agriculture was also mentioned in the resolution but especially for the female members. Ibid., par. 6. The trade hakhshara was once again on the He-Halutz agenda in 1931, but already on a different level and under different circumstances. Then the hakhshara's center of gravity was the permanent hakhshara-kibbutz where the member lived on a collective basis until his aliyah, sometimes for half a year; and when the doors of the Land of Israel were closed, for 3-5 years. Then the plenary session of the He-Halutz Central Committee decided that only those members then living on a kibbutz would be considered for trade courses; only by special permission of the Central Committee; and on condition that the skill be necessary for the Land of Israel. Ibid., p. 33.

43. Decisions of He-Halutz headed: "Tasks," points 1-3 in *Dos Yidishe Folk,* no. 1, January 3, 1918.

44. *He-Halutz* (Yid.), no. 11 (2), February 19, 1920.

45. Ibid., no. 8-9, December 11, 1919.

46. Ibid., no. 4, June 29, 1919.

47.   Yehuda Erez (ed.), *Sefer Ha-Aliyah Ha-Shelishit* (Heb.) (The Third Aliyah Book) (Tel-Aviv 1969), pp. 26, 56, 76-77; Moshe Braslavsky, *Labor Movement* vol. I, pp. 185-188; Zvi Even-Shoshan, op. cit., Book 2 (Tel-Aviv 1966), pp. 48-49.

48.   See n. 42.

49.   See David Ben-Gurion report at the 2nd Histadrut Conference in January 1923.

50.   *Befraiung,* no. 4, September 1923.

51.   I. Shvum, "Tokhnit Ha-'Avodah shel Mahleket Ha-Hakhshara" (Heb.) (The Work Plan of the Hakhshara Department) in *He-Halutz,* the organ of the World He-Halutz Organization (Warsaw-Berlin 1923-1924). Further, *He-Halutz,* Hebrew volume no. 2-3, May 1923, pp. 12-13.

52.   Ibid., p. 14.

53.   It is the period of inflation in Poland.

54.   Ibid., p. 55.

55.   I. Shvum, "Ha-Hakhshara, Report of the 3rd Nationwide Conference of He-Halutz in Poland," see in *He-Halutz* (Heb.) vol. no. 4, September 1923, p. 28. The reporter was in error. ORT too had developed its own ideology, albeit not a Zionist one, but its activity was not merely philanthropic-practical. It too was suffused with ideational motifs. See for example, the periodical *ORT Yedi'ot* (ORT Information) (Berlin 1925-1931); *Achtsik Yohr ORT,* pages of history and documentation, (Yid.) (Eighty Years of ORT) (ORT Geneva 1960).

56.   Ibid., vol. no. 2-3, May 1923, p. 15.

57.   *Hahlatot Ve-Taarikhim,* pp. 16-18.

58.   Ibid., paragraphs 4, 5.

59.   Ibid., par. B.

60.   Ibid., p. 18. This demand foreshadows the future collectivist tendencies which became dominant in He-Halutz in the later years.

61.   E. Dobkin, *Din Ve-Heshbon Mi-Polin* (Heb.) (Report from Poland) in *Ve-'idateinu Ha-Sheniah* (Berlin 1923), pp. 12-18.

62.   Zev Levinson, "Din Ve-Heshbon Ha-Merkaz Ha-Olami Ha-Zemani" (Heb.) (Report of the Provisional World Central Committee), ibid., p. 23.

63.   Moshe Shapiro, ibid., p. 35.

64.   E. Dobkin and D. Cohen, ibid., pp. 36-37.

65.   David Ben-Gurion, "Hakhshara Halutzit" (Heb.) (Pioneering Preparation), an address at the He-Halutz World Council, Danzig, 1924. See *Sefer He-Halutz,* pp. 167-171.

66. *Ve-'idateinu Ha-Sheniah,* p. 55, paragraphs a-e; *He-Halutz* (Heb.), vol. 2-3, May 1923, pp. 24-25.

67. Ibid., para. 1.

68. Zvi Even-Shoshan, op. cit., pp. 64-66; M. Braslavsky, op. cit., pp. 274-276.

69. M. Braslavsky, ibid., p. 275. Also see there the descriptions of the feelings of despair.

70. Ibid., p. 276.

71. Eliezer Shmueli, *Perakim Be-Toldot Ha-Zionut U-Tenu'at Ha-Avodah* (Heb.) (Chapters in the History of Zionism and the Labor Movement), part 3, (Tel-Aviv 1959), p. 336.

72. *Hahlatot Ve-'Taarikhim,* p. 98.

73. *He-'Atid,* the bi-weekly of the He-Halutz World Organization (Warsaw 1925-1935), no. 54, November 14.

74. Ibid.

75. It is interesting to underscore the fact that Ha-Shomer Ha-Tza'ir in 1927-1928, still demanded trade hakhshara of its members, not as individuals but in the ranks of the hakhshara kibbutz. The purpose was to prepare the kibbutzim for the reality of the Land of Israel which does not allow the newly arrived immigrants to settle upon the land immediately. These young kibbutzim were forced at the outset to live in the colony or city and support themselves from salaried work until they could make the shift to settlement, i.e., to settle on and build up their own land area. See: the decisions of the Kibbutz Artzi Council "About the Hakhshara in the Diaspora" in *Ha-Shomer Ha-Tza'ir 'Iton Ha-Bogrim,* (Heb. bi-weekly), (Ha-Shomer Ha-Tza'ir Older Youth Newspaper) (Warsaw 1927-1939), no. 12, May 30, 1928. But after a short time this movement also adopted the position of the entire He-Halutz.

76. Meir Bogdanovsky, "Ha-Hitpathut shel Ha-Histadrut He-Halutz Ha-'Olami" (Heb.) (The Development of the World He-Halutz Organization), Report of the 3rd He-Halutz World Conference, March 1926, according to *Measef Li-tnu'at He-Halutz,* pp. 185-192.

Notes to Chapter 3

1. Yitzhak Gruenbaum, *Neumin Be-Sejm Ha-Polani* (Heb.) (Speeches in the Polish Sejm) (Jerusalem no date), p. 260.

2. *Din Ve-Heshbon Ha-Hanhalah Ha-Zionit La-Kongress Ha-Zioni Ha-14* (Zionist Administration Report to the 14th Zionist Congress) (London 1925), p. 253.

3. *Korrespondentzblatt der Einwanderungstelle des Hilfsvereins des deutschen Judentums* (Berlin 1927), from *Din Ve-Heshbon Ha-Hanhalah Ha-Zionit La-Kongress Ha-Zioni Ha-15* (Heb.) (Zionist Administration Report to the 15th Zionist Congress) (London 1927), pp. 212, 243-249.

4. Ibid., pp. 243-245. In 1926, the immigrant total was 6,809, of whom 311 had capital. Invited by relatives—1,167. Worker-Certificates 5,055. Landworkers—715. Skilled laborers, 1,033; unskilled, 1,003; businessmen, 135; technicians and free professions, 133; unemployed, 2,564. See ibid.

5. Shmueli, op. cit. (Ch. 2, n. 67), p. 341.

6. *Din Ve-Heshbon Ha-Hanhalah Ha-Zionit La-Kongress Ha-Zioni Ha-16* (Heb.) (Zionist Administration Report to the 16th Zionist Congress) (London 1929), p. 201.

7. Apollinari Hartglass, "Milhamot Yehudei Polin al Zekhuyoteihem Ha-Ezrahiyot Ve-Ha-Leumiyot," (Heb.) (The Battles of the Jews of Poland for Their Civil and National Rights) in Israel Heilperin (ed.), *Beit Yisrael Be-Polin* (Heb.) (The House of Israel in Poland), vol. I (Jerusalem 1948), p. 142.

8. *Zionist Administration Report to the 15th Zionist Congress,* pp. 261-262.

9. Chaim Arlosoroff, "Die Oifgabe fun He-Halutz in Itztiken Moment" (Yid.) (The Task of He-Halutz at This Moment), a report at the 3rd He-Halutz World Conference, Danzig 1926.

10. *Zionist Administration Report to the 15th Zionist Congress,* p. 262, in *Davar,* the daily Labor Movement newspaper (Tel-Aviv, March 10, 1936).

11. For the reasons that new pioneering organizations arose and the He-Halutz battle for the unity of the entire pioneer movement, see below, Chapters 5-6.

12. In 1932, 39%, see: *Pinkas Ha-Histadrut Ha-Klalit shel Po'alei Eretz Yisrael* (Heb.) (The Ledger of the General Histadrut of the Workers of the Land of Israel), no. 8 (Tel-Aviv) January 1938, pp. 22-24.

13. *He-'Atid,* no. 35, April 30, 1926.

14. Ibid., no. 35, no. 103, September 30, 1930; *Sefer He-Halutz,* p. 185.

15. *He-Halutz* (Heb.) vol. III-IV, June 1924, pp. 31-34.

16. Meir Bogdanovsky, "Ha-Aliyah Ve-He-Halutz" (Heb.) (The Aliyah and He-Halutz), ibid., p. 2ff.

17. *Befraiung,* September 11, 1925, from Spizman, pp. 173-174.

18. *He-'Atid,* no. 103, September 20, 1930.

19. Ibid., no. 35, October 16, 1927.

20. Ibid.

21. Ibid. In 1927 the English government greatly limited the aliyah of the pioneers.

22. *Ashdot Ya'akov,* on the 20th anniversary of He-Halutz, 1938, p. 31.

23. *He-Halutz* (Yid.), no. 6, September 8, 1919.

24. Yehoshua Manor, "Ha-Hakhshara Be-Or Ha-'Aliyah" (Heb.) (The Hakhshara in the Light of Aliyah). *He-'Atid,* no. 63, January 31, 1929.

25. Ibid. See also Joseph Baratz, "Darko shel He-Halutz" (Heb.) (The Way of He-Halutz), *He-'Atid,* 24-25, July 26, 1925.

26. The opponents of hakhshara argued that He-Halutz in general is necessary when aliyah is restricted i.e., as a temporary organ, "not at a time of free aliyah." *Measeif Li-Tenu'at He-Halutz,* p. 301. Y. Manor, ibid.

27. Meir Bogdanovsky, "Le-Hakhsharat He-Halutz Ba-Golah" (Heb.) (About the He-Halutz Hakhshara in the Diaspora) (Davar 1925) according to *Sefer He-Halutz,* p. 180.

28. Ibid., p. 181. Also see P. Samet, "Saviv La-Vikauh shel Ha-Hakhshara" (Heb.) (About the Hakhshara Debate), *He-'Atid,* no. 64, February 15, 1924.

29. *He-'Atid,* no. 13, April 30, 1925.

30. Ibid.

31. Joseph Trumpeldor, "He-Halutz, Mahuto U-Te'udotav Ha-Kerovot Be-Yoteir," (He-Halutz, Its Essence and Most Immediate Tasks). This is a brochure which appeared in Russian, in Petrograd, in October 1918, before the All-Russian He-Halutz Conference which was held in January 1919. Cited from *Measeif Li-Tenu'at He-Halutz,* p. 261.

32. *He-'Atid,* no. 12, April 3, 1925.

33. *Sefer He-Halutz,* p. 182.

34. See Ben-Gurion's address against these tendencies at the World Council of He-Halutz in Danzig, 1924, from Spizman, pp. 166-171.

35. Joseph Bankover, "'Ha-Koveish'" Ba-'Aliyah Ha-Revi'it" (Heb.) (Kibbutz Ha-Koveish in the Fourth Aliyah), *Sefer He-Halutz*, pp. 183-185.

36. Ibid., p. 185. Moshe Shapiro, "Le-Beirur Ha-Matzav" (Heb.) (To Clarify the Situation), *He-'Atid*, no. 16, May 22, 1925. Also see a response by one of the initiators of the aliyah kibbutz, ibid., no. 18, June 25, 1925.

37. *Sefer He-Halutz*, p. 186.

38. See further about setting up the permanent hakhshara-kibbutz.

39. *He-'Atid*, no. 13, April 30, 1925.

40. Spizman, pp. 143, 144, 151, 154, 196.

41. Moshe Shapiro, op. cit., ibid., no. 16, May 22, 1925.

42. Joseph Bankover, "Li-Sheeilat Ha-Kibbutz" (Heb.) (On the Kibbutz Question), *He-'Atid*, no. 18, June 25, 1925.

43. *He-'Atid*, no. 36, May 21, 1926; *Hahlatot Ve-Taarikhim* (Heb.) (Decisions and Dates), p. 106.

44. *Hahlatot Ve-Taarikhim*, pp. 42-43.

45. *Hahlatot Ha-Ve'idah Ha-Olamit Ha-Shlishit* (Heb.) (Decisions of the 3rd He-Halutz World Conference), Danzig, March 1926, p. 227. Even at the 4th World Conference of He-Halutz in Berlin, 1930, when the permanent hakhshara became the chief instrumentality of the pioneering hakhshara, the Central Committees in the various countries are asked to organize aliyah kibbutzim once more, in light of their success in the Land of Israel, see *He-'Atid*, no. 104-105, October, 1930.

46. E. Dobkin, "Likrat Tekufah Hadashah" (Heb.) (Toward a New Era), *Measeif Li-Tnu'at He-Halutz*, p. 283; *He-'Atid*, no. 64, February 15, 1929.

47. *Din Ve-Heshbon Ha-Hanhalah Ha-Zionit La-Kongress Ha-Zioni Ha-15* (Heb.) (Report of the Zionist Administration to the 15th Zionist Congress), (London 1927), pp. 405-409. Jonah Goldberg, "Gordoniah" in the brochure *Di Yugend Bawegungen in Tzionism* (Yid.) (The Youth Movements in Zionism), written by the leaders of each Zionist youth movement (Warsaw 1934), p. 66; and see the resolutions of the He-Halutz World Council in 1927, in *Measeif Li-Tnu'at He-Halutz* (Warsaw 1930), pp. 233-234. The other pioneer organizations that arose in the years of the Fourth Aliyah also suffered greatly from the crisis. *Netivah* (Path), published bi-weekly by the Tze'irei He-Halutz Ha-Mizrahi and Ha-Po'el Ha-Mizrahi, Warsaw, no. 8.

48. See A. Berdichevsky, *Perakim Le-Toldot He-Halutz Be-Polin*

(Heb.) (Chapters in the History of He-Halutz in Poland), p. 268; A. Barsky (Aaron Berdichevsky–I. O.), "Briev Tzu Haverim" (Yid.) (Letters to Friends), monthly supplement to *He-'Atid,* July-September 1926.

49.   B. Minkovsky, "Beirurim" (Heb.) (Clarifications), *He-'Atid,* no. 48, February 21, 1927.

50.   *Ashdot Ya'akov* on the 20th Anniversary of He-Halutz, p. 31; *Measeif Li-Tnu'at He-Halutz,* p. 209.

51.   Aharon Weiner, "Im Ha-Aliyah Ha-Reviit Mi-Polin" (Heb.) (With the Fourth Aliyah from Poland), Kibbutz Gevat, quoted from *Sefer He-Halutz,* p. 202; "Din Ve-Heshbon Mei-Ha-Plenum shel Merkaz He-Halutz" (Heb.) (Report from the Plenary Session of the He-Halutz Central Committee), *He-'Atid,* no. 38, June 26, 1926. A. Ber-sky, op. cit., monthly supplement to *'Atid* July 1926, and "Klapei Penim" (Heb.) (Looking Inward), ibid., no. 42, August 31, 1926. A. T-Sh (Tarshish–I. O.) "Tafkideinu" (Heb.) (Our Functions), *He-'Atid,* October 18, 1926. B. Minkovsky, "Beirurim" (Heb.) (Clarifications), *He-'Atid,* no. 48, February 21, 1927.

52.   *He-'Atid,* no. 29, June 1926.

53.   On the beginnings of He-Halutz Ha-Tza'ir, see Spizman, pp. 229-248.

54.   A. Weiner, op. cit., p. 202.

55.   A. Ber-sky (Berdichevsky–I. O.), "Briev tzu Haverim" (Yid.), monthly supplement to *He-'Atid,* July 1926.

56.   Ibid.

57.   *Hahlatot Ve-Taarikhim,* pp. 20-22. Decisions of the 4th Nationwide Conference in 1925 and of the Plenary Session in 1926.

58.   "Le-Siyyum 'Onat Ha-Kayyiz" (Heb.) (At Summer Season's End), *He-'Atid,* no. 44, October 18, 1926.

59.   A. Berdichevsky, "Li-Gemar Ha-Mo'eiza" (Heb.) (After the Conclusion of the Council), *He-'Atid,* no. 52, August 31, 1927.

60.   Moshe Braslavsky, *Hakhshara in Poilin* (Yid.) (The Hakhshara in Poland), (Warsaw 1934), pp. 26, 27.

61.   *Din ve-Heshbon Ha-Hanhalah Ha-Zionit La-Kongress Ha-16* (Heb.) (Report of the Zionist Administration to the 16th Congress) (London 1929), pp. 194-195. M. Braslavsky estimates the number of members on permanent hakhshara at 900; in Galicia, about 300 on permanent hakhshara and over 200 on temporary hakhshara. Ibid.

62. Of about 1500 sawmills in Poland in 1931, more than half were in Jewish hands. See: Raphael Mahler, *Yahadut Polin dein Shtei Milhamot 'Olam: Historiah Kalkalit-Sozialit Le-Or Ha-Statistika* (Heb.) (Poland Between Two World Wars: An Economic-Social History in Light of the Statistics) (Tel-Aviv 1968), pp. 84, 95-96.

63. Moshe Braslavsky, "Le-Hearat Karkhei He-Halutz" (Heb.) (Toward Lighting the Path of He-Halutz), *He-'Atid,* no. 126, October 15, 1934.

64. Moshe Shapiro, "Likrat Mo-ezet He-Halutz Be-Polin" (Heb.) (Toward the He-Halutz Conference in Poland), *He-'Atid,* No. 16, May 22, 1925.

65. On Klosow's first steps, see: Sh. Even-Zohar, "Die Grindung fun Klosow" (Yid.) (The Founding of Klosow) in Spizman, pp. 202-204.

66. The literature on Klosow is quite abundant. See: M. Braslavsky, *Di Hakhshara in Poilin* (Yid.) (The Hakhshara in Poland), pp. 12-18; Spizman, pp. 144, 158, 202-204, 366-373; *He-'Atid,* no. 2, January 30, 1925; ibid., no. 156, September 15, 1934; *Dos Vort, Togzeitung fun der Lige fun Arbetenden Eretz Yisroel* (Yid.) (The Word, Daily of the League for Labor Palestine) Warsaw, no. 23, January 26, 1934. *Sefer Kibbutz Klosow,* (Heb.) (The Kibbutz Klosow Book), A. Fialkow (ed.), Beit Lohamei Ha-Getaot and Ha-Kibbutz Ha-Meuhad, 1978.

67. In time, a third hakhshara kibbutz, Tel Hai, was established in the Grodno-Bialystok area. See: Yehoshua Pundak, "Der Meshek Shaharit" (Yid.) (The Shaharit Unit) in Spizman, pp. 204-206; A. Berdichevsky, "Geschichte fun He-Halutz in Poilin" (Yid.) (History of He-Halutz in Poland), ibid., pp. 197-198; *He-'Atid,* no. 44, October 18, 1926. *Shahariah, The Story of a Hakhshara Kibbutz,* S. Segal and A. Fialkow (eds.), Beit Lohamei Ha-Getaot and Ha-Kibbutz Ha-Meuhad, 1983.

68. *Hahlatot Ve-Taarikhim,* p. 19.

69. Ibid., p. 20.

70. *He-'Atid,* no. 44, October 18, 1926.

71. *Hahlatot Ve-Taarikhim,* p. 98.

72. Ibid., p. 93. *Unsere Yedios* (Yid.) (Our News) (of the He-Halutz Central Committee in Poland, 1931-1939. Published monthly, but became a weekly from the 25th number, July 5th; later, on April 4, 1935 it became a bi-weekly; from December 11, 1936 it again became an irregular periodical). Warsaw, no. 71, February 5, 1932.

73.   *Hahlatot Ve-Taarikhim*, pp. 22-24.

74.   Gordoniah periodical. Published by the Z. S. of Gordoniah, Lwow, vol. VI (11), January 1928, pp. 7-8.

75.   *Hahlatot Ve-Taarikhim*, pp. 24-25.

76.   For a report of the convention and its discussions, see: M. B-Y (M. Braslavsky–I. O.), "Pegishat Kibbutzei He-Halutz Be-Polin" (Heb.) (Meeting of the He-Halutz Kibbutzim in Poland), *He-'Atid*, no. 99-100, 1931, in *Sefer He-Halutz*, pp. 321-323. Also see Braslavsky's *Hakhshara in Poilin* (Yid.) (Hakhshara in Poland), pp. 19-20.

77.   *Hahlatot Ve-Taarikhim*, pp. 26-30.

78.   Ibid., pp. 30-33.

79.   See the decisions of the He-Halutz World Council about the freedom to organize in every colonizing form, *Measeif Li-Tenu'at He-Halutz*, p. 234.

80.   *He-'Atid*, no. 66, March 15, 1929; ibid., no. 102, September 10, 1930; ibid., no. 129, March 30, 1932; *Ha-Shomer Ha-Tza'ir,* Warsaw, no. 12-15, August 25, 1930; *Hahlatot Ve-Taarikhim*, pp. 34-39, 43-46, 54; Avraham Tarshish, "Yie'udei He-Halutz" (Heb.) (The Goals of He-Halutz), *He-'Atid*, on the 20 anniversary of He-Halutz, Warsaw, March 31, 1938.

81.   This youth movement joined He-Halutz on the basis of broad internal autonomy. The agreement between He-Halutz and the World Shomer Ha-Tza'ir was signed in 1926 during the 3rd World Conference of He-Halutz in Danzig; but only after negotiating for three years did the Ha-Shomer Ha-Tza'ir in Poland join He-Halutz. Then representatives of Ha-Shomer Ha-Tza'ir entered the Central Committee of He-Halutz and liquidated the financial and economic independence of its hakhshara kibbutzim which, from then on, were under the administrative supervision of He-Halutz. Ever after the lengthy negotiations, bitter disputes erupted between the majority in He-Halutz and the youth movements of Ha-Shomer Ha-Tza'ir and Gordoniah, which joined He-Halutz in 1930. See below, Chapter 5. For the details of the agreement see: *Ha-Shomer Ha-Tza'ir* (Heb.) vol. III, (Warsaw-Lwow, July 1927).

82.   Ibid., no. 12-15, August 15, 1930; no. 7, April 1, 1931; no. 10, November 1, 1931.

83.   *Hahlatot Ve-Taarikhim*, p. 32. On the course of the discussion at the plenary session, see: *He-'Atid*, no. 114-115, March 31, 1931; ibid., no. 118, April 15, 1931.

84.   About the "wandering", see the next chapter.

85.   Circular no. 8 of the top leadership of Ha-Shomer Ha-Tza'ir in Poland (Warsaw, October 21, 1932), p. 11. Ha-Shomer Ha-Tza'ir for years steadfastly insisted that its hakhshara was not a permanent one. And in 1935, at the 4th World Conference of Ha-Shomer Ha-Tza'ir, the difference between the "permanent hakhshara" of the "He-Halutz majority" and the "prolonged (longer) hakhshara" of Ha-Shomer Ha-Tza'ir is emphasized. See: *Din Ve-Heshbon shel Ha-Ve'idah Ha-'Olamit Ha-Reviit shel Ha-Shomer Ha-Tza'ir* (Heb.) (Report of the 4th Ha-Shomer Ha-Tza'ir World Conference) (Warsaw 1936), pp. 86-113. In our opinion, the difference is only one of semantics, not of essence.

86.   *Le-Sha'ah Zo* (Heb.) (For the Time Being), plenary session of the He-Halutz Central Committee, Warsaw, October 1932, p. 30.

87.   "Sheeilot Ha-Hakhshara" (Heb.) (The Hakhshara Problems), a discussion about hakhshara at the last He-Halutz plenary session, *He-'Atid*, no. 114-115, March 31, 1931.

88.   Avraham Berdichevsky, ibid., no. 116, April 15, 1931.

89.   Moshe Braslavsky, "To Light the Way . . . " (Heb.), *He-'Atid*, no. 126, October 15, 1931.

90.   Ibid.

91.   Certain circles of the Russian He-Halutz saw the kibbutz hakhshara as a positive model for bringing the Jewish masses to labor and productivity, even for those who have no intention of immigrating to the Land of Israel. Generally, the idea was not implemented. But the Russian He-Halutz did take an active part in organizing Jews in the Crimea at the start of the twenties. See, for example, Pines, op. cit., pp. 93-94, 134-135.

92.   In Poland, too, they entertained similar notions. In 1927, Aryeh Tartakower published a number of articles in which he proposed changing the He-Halutz operations to cooperatives. His premise was that He-Halutz is a part of the productivization process of European Jewry. Despite the difference between the hakhshara kibbutz and Jewish cooperation, he felt there is a common denominator. It is the will to break the parasitic life prevalent till now and "change the Jewish masses into a healthy, creative factor in general Jewish life." If He-Halutz became an active factor in the Jewish cooperation, it would have an opportunity to become its leading factor and lead it onto the path of consumer and producer cooperatives.

He-Halutz must revolutionize the "rotten" Jewish life. The author argues against the pioneer movement's isolation from the Jewish masses.

"To a large part of the movement, the people's woes are alien." He calls
for giving up the hakhshara which is exclusively for the Land of Israel. The
Jewish proletariat is under anti-Zionist influence. If He-Halutz would accept his plan, he believes, it would be possible to free it of that influence.
He proposes that the hakhshara yield a bit in its main goal in order to become a major factor in the restructuring of Diaspora Jewry socially and
economically. He proposes that the hakhshara give up its collectivist principles and build up the Jewish productivity-cooperation. He-Halutz should
fulfill this task along with its major one, the pioneering preparation for
the Land of Israel. See: "He-Halutz Ve-Ha-Kooperaziah" (Heb.) (He-
Halutz and Cooperation), *He-'Atid,* no. 47, January 22, 1927. Tartakower,
"'Al Harhavat Ha-Gevulin" (Heb.) (On Expanding the Boundaries), ibid.,
No. 59, November 30, 1928.

He-Halutz responded negatively to these proposals, largely in opposition to the practice of the Russian He-Halutz. "He-Halutz had always indirectly influenced productivization in the Diaspora, but we will never assume the task of preparing workers who will remain in the Diaspora . . . .
As always, the exclusively Land of Israel self-fulfillment is the chief content of He-Halutz." See: E. Dobkin, "Ha-Mazav Ba-Tenu'ah Ha-'Olamit
shel He-Halutz" (Heb.) (The Condition of the World He-Halutz Movement), from a report to the He-Halutz Council, October 1927, in *Measeif
Li'Tenu'at He-Halutz,* p. 124.

It was nearly ten years after this proposal had been rejected that
Yaakov Leschinsky, the distinguished economist, again proposed a similar
plan after he had visited a few hakhshara kibbutzim. The visit impressed
him greatly: "The most beautiful and valuable thing in He-Halutz is that
before it improves the world it wants to improve itself. . . . Before it
preaches Socialism for others, it institutes justice and equality, Socialism
and righteousness and decent human relations for itself." Yaakov Leschinsky, "A Bazuch in a Halutzim Kolonyeh" (Yid.) (A Visit in a Pioneer
Colony) in *Dos Neie Vort,* Organ of the League for Labor Palestine, no.
139, May 28, 1937.

Leschinsky saw in the hakhshara kibbutz one of the main solutions for
the productivization process of Jews in general and of the Jewish youth in
particular, whose situation was catastrophic as a result of the world crisis
and the Fascist, antisemitic policy of the Polish government.

In a series of articles which he published in the *Yiddishe Ekonomik* (Jewish Economy) in 1937-1938, he suggests the establishment of non-Zionist hakhshara kibbutzim. In his opinion, the Bund and other non-Zionist parties should also participate in this project together with He-Halutz. "At the center of the non-Zionist kibbutzim should be the youth and not the country. The preparation (of the youth—I. O.) should be for the goal of assuming the task of changing Jewish life in every country." In spite of the similarity to the pioneer hakhshara kibbutzim, the general hakhshara kibbutzim must make their chief task to teach the hakhshara member a skill: "For one year the young man will get used to work and for two years he will learn a skill." Yaakov Leschinsky, "Vegn a Construktiven Plan far Poilishe Yiden" (Yid.) (About a Constructive Plan for Polish Jews) in *Yiddishe Ekonomik,* Warsaw 1937, pp. 129-148, 209-222; 1938, pp. 1-2, 92-115, 297-322. Neither the non-Zionist parties nor He-Halutz reacted to this initiative. I. Oppenheim, "The Attitude of the He-Halutz in Poland Toward the Avodat Ha-Hoveh (local political activity) in the Diaspora," *Measef* (Journal of the History of the Jewish Labor Movement), no. 15, 1985, Part I, pp. 119-131.

93.   E. Gurevich, "Ha-Vikuah 'al Ha-Hakhshara Be-Polin" (Heb.) (The Debatever Hakhshara in Poland) at the He-Halutz plenary session, *He-'Atid,* no. 114-115, March 31, 1931.

Notes to Chapter 4

1.   Only in 1924-1925, when masses of young people joined the movement, was there a reaction from the leftist, anti-Zionist parties, but this was only for a short time. After the crisis of the Fourth Aliyah, the discussion about He-Halutz took on a generally anti-Zionist character. The internal development of He-Halutz had no public echo.

2.   In 1929 the Land of Israel absorbed only 10% of the Jewish emigration from Poland. In 1932 this figure had grown to 39.9%, and in 1935 to 80.6%. In 1937 it dropped to 37.6% because of the British immigration restrictions. On the average, from 1929-1937, the Land of Israel received 43.7% of the Jewish emigration from Poland; Argentina, 18.6%; other countries (including the United States) only 37.5%. See: Dov Weinryb, "Yehudei Polin Mi-Huz Le-Polin" (Heb.) (The Polish Jews Outside Poland) in Israel Halperin (ed.), *Beit Yisrael Be-Polin* (Heb.) (The House of

Israel in Poland), vol. II (Jerusalem 1954), pp. 141-192. Between 1929-1938, 271,508 people emigrated to the Land of Israel: in 1933, 30,328; in 1934, 42,395; in 1935, 61,854; in 1936 the number already fell to 29,729; and in 1937, only 10,556; the same in 1938. See Spizman, p. 127.

On the pauperization of the Polish Jews in the thirties, see R. Mahler, op. cit., pp. 189-195. On the struggle of the Jewish minority for its national political and civil rights, see: Apollinari Hartglass in *Beit Yisrael Be-Polin,* vol. I (Jerusalem 1948), pp. 128-151, especially 146-151.

Also see: I. Marcus, *Social and Political History of the Jews in Poland* (Berlin, New York, Amsterdam 1983) and E. Melzer, *Political Strife in a Blind Alley: The Jews in Poland 1935-1939* (Tel-Aviv 1982).

3. *Hahlatot Ve-Taarikhim,* p. 100. "Finf Yohr Po'alei Tzion Tetigkeit" (Yid.) (Five Years of Po'alei Tzion Activity), 1936, quoted by Spizman, pp. 323-327. *Sefer He-Halutz,* p. 417. In Galicia, in 1931, the number of pioneers of all the groups was 1,008; in 1935, 7,315. The growth halted in 1936-1937. The number on hakhshara in Poland drops to 2,000, and in Galicia, to 500. See Zvi Even-Shoshan, op. cit., vol. II, pp. 25-26. The drop is a result of the aliyah restrictions.

The aforementioned numbers indicate much about the character of the pioneer movement. They show that to a great extent the growth was not a factor of inner, organic development but of developments in the Land of Israel. Since the Land of Israel had become the main target of emigration, masses of young people joined hakhshara not for ideological reasons but as the only way to emigrate. After aliyah ceased, many of these members left the movement. Hakhshara, no longer a mass phenomenon, to a great extent resumed its avant-gardist organization character as in the twenties and beginning of the thirties.

4. Simon Segal, *The New Poland and the Jews* (New York 1938), p. 36.

5. About the political and economic developments in the Land of Israel during these years, see: M. Braslavsky, op. cit., vol. II, pp. 137-165; A. Margalit, op. cit., pp. 161-178; David Ben-Gurion, "Mir un di Araber" (Yid.) (We and the Arabs) (Warsaw 1934), *Yedi'ot Merkaz Mapai* (Heb.) (News from the Mapai Central Committee) (Tel-Aviv 1930-1931), *Ha-Po'el Ha-Tza'ir* (Weekly of the Mapai Party) (Heb.) (Tel-Aviv 1929-1931). The situation changed for the better in 1932. The prosperity lasted until the outbreak of the disturbances in 1936.

6.   R. S., "Hitpathut Ha-Hakhshara Be-Polin" (Heb.) (The Development of the Hakhshara in Poland), *He-'Atid*, no. 23, June 1935.

7.   M. Braslavsky, "Bi-Drakhim" (Heb.) (On the Road), *He-'Atid*, no. 122, July 20, 1931, pp. 122-123; no. 123, August 31, 1931.

8.   At this opportunity it is worth noting that Ha-Shomer Ha-Tza'ir claimed for itself the credit of being the first: "We were the first to begin the great achievements of the hakhshara movement in Poland." See Feivel Gavze, "Le-Mo'ezet Brit Ha-Kibbutzim Be-Polin" (Heb.) (To the Council of the Associated Kibbutzim in Poland), (the association of Ha-Shomer Ha-Tza'ir kibbutzim established in 1931 for the purpose of coordinating the activity of the Ha-Shomer Ha-Tza'ir's hakhshara kibbutzim), *Ha-Shomer Ha-Tza'ir*, no. 2, February 1931. This argument was put forward at the time of the most bitter debate between Ha-Shomer Ha-Tza'ir and the bloc, see below, Chapter 5. It is difficult to render an impartial decision in this matter. Certain it is that there was only a short span of time between when the hakhshara kibbutzim of the "General Bloc" and those of the Ha-Shomer Ha-Tza'ir set out to wander, because they were all caught by the crisis at the same time and therefore had to take to the roads.

9.   Moshe Braslavsky, ibid., and in Spizman, pp. 352-353.

10.   M. Braslavsky, ibid., according to Spizman, pp. 360-362. *Ha-Shomer Ha-Tza'ir* years 1932-1934; *He-'Atid* years 1932-1934. About the hakhshara organizations not part of He-Halutz, see below, Chapter 6.

11.   An outstanding example is the hakhshara kibbutz in Lodz which succeeded not only in penetrating factories hitherto closed to Jews but also set up its own large shops which successfully penetrated the domestic and foreign markets. About this development of the Lodz hakhshara kibbutz, see the volume dedicated to it: Shlomo Even-Shoshan (ed.), *Sippuro shel Kibbutz Hakhshara: Ha-Kibbutz 'Al Shem Borovchov in Lodz and Be-Nohiah* (Heb.) (The Tale of an Hakhshara Kibbutz: The Borochov Kibbutz in Lodz and Nohiah), (Tel-Aviv 1970). In the other industrial cities as well, the hakhshara members managed, on a somewhat smaller scale, to get into different fields which had previously been closed to Jewish labor. See—Zvi Rosenstein, "Zekhutenu La-'Avodah" (Heb.) (Our Right to Work), *He-'Atid*, no. 132, June 1932; Gershon Ostrovsky, "Mir un der Bund" (Yid.) (We and the Bund), *Yedi'ot*, no. 19, June 1933.

12.   See Mahler, op. cit.

13.   About the relationships between the hakhshara and the non-Zionist parties, see below, Chapter 7. About the struggle in Lodz, see references in the index of the book about this kibbutz. Also see above, n. 10.

14.   S. Horowitz, "Di Ersheinung fun Freiheit" (Yid.) (The Appearance of Freiheit), *Yugent Freiheit* (Youth Freiheit), the central organ of the Socialist Farband of the Jewish Labor Youth Freiheit in Poland, Warsaw, November 1927; *Yovel Bletter fun Freiheit* (Yid.) (Anniversary Pages of Freiheit), no. 1, October 1935; and especially, *Unser Freiheit* (Yid.) (Our Freedom), main organ of Freiheit (Freedom), Warsaw 1930 and further. For example, H. Zelatinsky, "Di Fragen fun Unser Tetigkeit in Golus" (Yid.) (The Questions of Our Activities in the Diaspora), ibid., no. 3, February 1937; Sh. Israeli, "Fragen" (Yid.) (Questions), ibid., no. 2, January 1937; Leib Spiezman, "Etappen" (Yid.) (Stages), ibid., no. 3, March 1936; I. Sheinbaum, "Nisyonis un Dergreichungen" (Yid.) (Attempts and Achievements), ibid., no. 4, March 1937; *Mitn Ponim Tzu Zikh* (Yid.) (Facing Oneself), reports, discussions, and resolutions of the National Council of Freiheit, November 11-14, 1934 (Warsaw 1934), p. 14.

15.   *Measeif Li-Tenu'at He-Halutz,* pp. 315-316; M. Braslavsky, "Lehaarat Darkei He-Halutz" (Heb.) (Lighting the Way of He-Halutz), *He-'Atid,* no. 124, October 1, 1931; *Be-Sha'ah Zo,* p. 30; Benjamin, "Eiranut Politit" (Heb.) (Political Awareness), ibid., no. 19, June 1, 1935; *Unsere Yedies* (Yid.) (Our News), no. 78-79, December 1937. About the extremely negative attitude of Ha-Shomer Ha-Tza'ir to the Jewish rights campaign, see Meir Ya'ari, "Darkenu Be-Golah" (Heb.) (Our Course in the Diaspora) in *Sefer Ha-Shomrim,* an anthology on the 20th anniversary of Ha-Shomer Ha-Tza'ir, (Warsaw 1934), pp. 526-532; Nathan Bistritsky, "Mitzvot U-Ma'asim" (Heb.) (Commandants and Deeds), ibid., pp. 141-142; Zvi Luria, "Di Golus Politik in Eretz Yisroel Arbet un Mir" (Yid.) (Diaspora Politics in the Land of Israel and We), *Nei-Yugent* (New Youth) a one-time publication of Ha-Shomer Ha-Tza'ir, Warsaw, December 15, 1936. There were however a few voices in Ha-Shomer Ha-Tza'ir as well that demanded more Diaspora activity. This demand was tied to the general radicalization of the Jewish youth. See, for example, *Ha-Shomer Ha-Tza'ir* no. 16, November 1, 1931.

16.   According to the census of January 20, 1935, the hakhshara

members came from the following homes: businessmen and merchants, 29.9%; artisans, 20.2%; petty merchants, 9.2%; free professions, 2.9%; entirely without a profession, 26.9%; without parents, 3.8%; the rest unknown. See: Dr. Meir Peker, *Zagadnienie przysposobienia emigrantow do Palestyny* (Problems of Skill Preparation for Immigrants to the Land of Israel), a report presented to the session of the Polish Government's Emigration Commission at the Institute for the Study of National Issues, (Warsaw 1936), pp. 18-21; *He-'Atid,* no. 103, September 30, 1930. "The small town, not the large city, is the basis of He-Halutz," writes an emissary from the Land of Israel in Poland. "Were it not for the shtetl, I would long ago have despaired. The large city is worthless. It is cynical and contemptuous of every activity." *Unser Yedios* (Yid.) (Our News), no. 2, Warsaw, February 15, 1935. Somewhat different was Ha-Shomer Ha-Tza'ir's composition, sometimes almost school youth. In the thirties, the common-folk elements grow, but the participation of the high schoolers is still significant. See Baruch Linkovsky, "Ba'ayot Ha-Tenu'ah" (Heb.) (Problems of the Movement), *Ha-Shomer Ha-Tza'ir,* no. 1, Warsaw, March 15, 1935; S. Zaromb, "Di Brider un Shvester" (Yid.) (The Brothers and Sisters), *Unser Yedies,* no. 9, June 21, 1935.

17.   M. Braslavsky, "Ba-Drakhim" (Heb.) (Under Way), *He-'Atid,* no. 11, February 1935.

18.   Israel Sheinbaum, "Mif'al Ha-Hakhshara Shelanu" (Heb.) (Our Hakhshara Work), ibid.

19.   See below, the chapter on the hakhshara outside of He-Halutz.

Notes to Chapter 5

1.   We have treated the internal growth of He-Halutz in a separate chapter because of its special place as the most significant organization in the general hakhshara movement. Of 375 hakhshara kibbutzim in Poland (outside Galicia) with 13,756 members, according to the census of September 1, 1935, He-Halutz had 176 hakhsharot with 8,612 members, i.e., 62.4%; the General Zionist He-Halutz had 56 hakhsharot and 1,562 members, 11.35%; the religious He-Halutz Ha-Mizrachi, with 55 hakhsharot and 1,649 members, 11.98%; the Revisionists with 38 hakhsharot and 771 members, 5.5%. The rest belonged to Agudas Israel, the Jewish-Staters (the Grossmanists, who had split off from the Revisionists when the latter left

the Zionist Organization), and WIZO. See Dr. Peker, op. cit. (Polish), p. 9. The internal development of He-Halutz also strongly influenced the development of other movements. In Galicia the situation was similar, except for eastern Galicia, where the strength of the General Zionist He-Halutz reached 27.81% and that of the general He-Halutz, 43.59%. Ibid., pp. 9-10.

2.   About the reasons for these youth groups' coming into being and how this took place, see Spizman, pp. 229-248.

3.   A general Zionist movement with certain religious tendencies, whose center was in Galicia but which also had branches in Poland. See B. Yehieli, *Akiba, Zionist Youth Movement* (Moreshet and Sifriyat Poalim 1988).

4.   Busliah: the hakhshara organization of the "Hitahdut" (Unity) Party.

5.   Meir Bogdanofsky, "He-Halutz Ve-Ha-No'ar" (Heb.) (He-Halutz and the Youth), *Measef Li-Tenu'at He-Halutz,* p. 300.

6.   A. Margalit, op. cit., pp. 161-296.

7.   On this chapter see Baruch Rabinoff, "Ma'amadeinu Be-He-Ha-lutz" (Heb.) (Our Standing in He-Halutz), *Ha-Shomer Ha-Tza'ir,* no. 18, November 1, 1931; M. Bogdanofsky, "He-Halutz Ve-Ha-No'ar" (Heb.) (He-Halutz and the Youth), *Measeif Li-Tenu'at He-Halutz,* pp. 300-301; "The Decisions of the 3rd He-Halutz World Conference," ibid., pp. 230-231; L. Levite, "Ha-Shomer Ha-Tza'ir Ve-He-Halutz" (Heb.) (Ha-Shomer Ha-Tza'ir and He-Halutz), *He-'Atid,* no. 126, September 15, 1931.

8.   "Hahlatot Ha-Mo'eizah Ha-'Olamit Ha-Shlishit shel He-Halutz" (Heb.) (Decisions of the 3rd He-Halutz World Council), ibid.

9.   *Hahlatot Ve-Taarikhim,* p. 66. Also see *He-'Atid,* no. 61, December 15, 1928 which analyzes Ha-Shomer Ha-Tza'ir's approach to He-Halutz as the first step toward full unification.

10.   *Sefer Ha-Shomrim* (Warsaw 1934), p. 129.

11.   *He-'Atid,* no. 104-105, October 1, 1930.

12.   Ya'akov Hazan, "Ha-No'ar Ve-He-Halutz" (Heb.) (The Youth and He-Halutz), *He-'Atid,* no. 109, January 1, 1931; No. 111, February 1, 1931. Also see Avrahm Lipsker, "Le-Mazeveinu Bi-Tenu'at He-Halutz Be-Polin" (Heb.) (On Our Condition in the He-Halutz Movement in Poland), *Ha-Shomer Ha-Tza'ir,* no. 7, April 1931. On the similar stand by Gordoniah, see Yona Goldberg, "21 Nekudot" (Heb.) (21 Points), *He-'Atid,* no. 20, June 15, 1935. In these years the discussion of this theme

occupies an important place in the pioneer press. See *Unser Freiheit*, 1931-1935; *He-Halutz Ha-Tza'ir*, Central Organ of He-Halutz Ha-Tza'ir in Poland, (Warsaw 1930-1935; *He-'Atid*, 1930-1935; *Yedies*, 1931-1936; *Gordoniah* (letter) (Yid.) Writings from the Top Leadership of Gordoniah (Warsaw 1931-1933); *Ha-Shomer Ha-Tza'ir*, 1930-1936.

13.   *Hahlatot Ve-Taarikhim*, pp. 64-67.

14.   "Gilui Da'as fun He-Halutz Ha-Tza'ir" (Yid.) (An Explanation by He-Halutz Ha-Tza'ir), *He-'Atid*, no. 104-105, October 1, 1930.

15.   *He-'Atid*, no. 118-119, June 1; no. 120-121, June 30, 1931.

16.   *Hahlatot Ve-Taarikhim*, p. 67.

17.   A. Lipsker, ibid., no. 7, April 1, 1931.

18.   *Hahlatot Ve-Taarikhim*, pp. 32, 35-36.

19.   About Russia, see Benjamin West (ed.), *Naftulei Dor* (Yid). (Struggle of a Generation), (the History of the Tze'irei Tzion in Russia), vol. I (Tel-Aviv 1941); Dan Pines, *He-Halutz Be-Kor Ha-Mahapeikhah*, ibid.; "He-Halutz Be-Russiah: Le-Toldot He-Halutz Ha-Bilti Legali Be-Russiah" (Jerusalem 1940), *Measeif Li'Tenu'at He-Halutz; Sefer He-Halutz*. About the tendency to unity in the Polish He-Halutz, see above, Chapter 1.

20.   *He-'Atid*, no. 80, October 15, 1929; ibid., no. 104-105, October 1, 1930; no. 108, December 15, 1930; no. 109-11, January 1, 1931; no. 114-115, March 31, 1931, etc.

21.   See below.

22.   See below.

23.   See the anthology *Ahdut Ha-'Avodah* (Tel-Aviv 1930), pp. 130 etc.

24.   L. Levite, "Ha-Ve'idah Ha-Sheminit shel Ha-Shomer Ha-Tza'ir" (Heb.) (The 8th Ha-Shomer Ha-Tza'ir Convention), *He-'Atid*, no. 117, April 30; no. 118, June 1, 1931. Levite is less extreme in his attitude to Ha-Shomer Ha-Tza'ir than other members of the bloc.

25.   Israel Otiker, "He-Halutz," in the brochure *Di Yugent Bawegungen in Tzionism (geshriben durch di Firer fun der Zionistisher Yugent Baweggungen)* (Yid.) (The Youth Movements in Zionism written by leaders of the Zionist youth movements) Warsaw 1934), pp. 112-113.

26.   Zvi Luriea, "'Emdateinu Be-He-Halutz" (Heb.) (Our Status in He-Halutz), *Ha-Shomer Ha-Tza'ir*, no. 15-17, August 25, 1930.

27.   The attempt did not succeed. There were more party pioneer organizations in Poland.

28.   Ya'akov Hazan, "He-Halutz Ve-Ha-No'ar" (Heb.) (He-Halutz and the Youth), *He-'Atid*, no. 104-105, October 1, 1930.

29.   "Tazkir Ha-Shomer Ha-Tza'ir Ve-Hordoniah Le-Va'ad Ha-Po'el shel Ha-Histadrut" (Heb.) (Memorandum from Ha-Shomer Ha-Tza'ir and Gordoniah to the Executive Committee of the Histadrut), *Ha-Shomer Ha-Tza'ir,* no. 14-15, November 15, 1933; A. Lipsker, "Le-Mazaveinu Bi-Tenu'at He-Halutz Be-Polaniah" (Heb.) (On Our Situation in the He-Halutz Movemnt in Poland), *Ha-Shomer Ha-Tza'ir,* no. 2, April 1, 1931; "Zeh Mul Zeh" (Heb.) (One against the Other), editorial article, ibid., no. 2, January 15, 1933; Yehuda Schwartzbard, "Darkeinu Be-Hakhshara U-Ve-He-Halutz" (Heb.) (Our Course in the Hakhshara and in He-Halutz), ibid., no. 14-15, November 15, 1933; Schwartzbard, "Einheit in der Bawegung" (Yid.) (Unity in the Movement), *Dos Vort,* no. 9, March 1934; Nahum Ben Menahem, "Be-Kinosei Halutzim" (Heb.) (At Pioneer Conventions), *Ha-Shomer Ha-Tza'ir,* no. 5-6, April 1, 1934; Baruch Rabinoff, "Erev Ve'idat He-Halutz" (Heb.) (On the Eve of the He-Halutz Convention), ibid., no. 7, April 1934.

30.   *Din Ve-Heshbon Mei-Ha-Ve'idah Ha-Revi'it Ha-'Olamit shel Ha-Shomer Ha-Tza'ir* (Heb.) (Report of the 4th World Ha-Shomer Ha-Tza'ir Convention), in Pofrad (Czechoslovakia), 10-16 October, 1935 (Warsaw), p. 100.

31.   Ibid.

32.   E. Monchik, "Nizanei He-Halutz Be-Russiah" (Heb.) (The First Beginnings of He-Halutz in Russia), *Measef Li-Tenu'at He-Halutz,* pp. 99-100; Monchik, "Der He-Halutz un Zeine Oifgaben" (Yid.) (He-Halutz and its Tasks), *Sefer He-Halutz* (Warsaw 1920), pp. 4-16. Also see Pines, *Index.*

33.   *Le-Sha'ah Zo* (Heb.) (For This Hour), minutes of the He-Halutz Central Committee (Warsaw, October 1932), pp. 19-60.

34.   See *He-'Atid,* no. 92-93, April 15, 1930; ibid., no. 18, May 15, 1935.

35.   Nahum Benari, "'Al Ha-Hinukh Ha-Kibbuzi" (Heb.) (On the Kibbutz Education), *He-'Atid,* no. 152, April 1933.

36.   Meir Ya'ari, "Darkeinu Ba-Golah" (Heb.) (Our Course in the Diaspora), *Sefer Ha-Shomrim* (The Hashomer Ha-Tza'ir Book), pp. 529-532.

37.   Ibid.

38.   Moshe Basok, "Lema'an Goral Meshutaf" (Heb.) (For a Common Fate), *He-'Atid,* no. 138, November 30, 1932.

39.   A. Lipsker, *Ha-Shomer Ha-Tza'ir,* No. 7, April 1, 1930.

40. Meant here is the mass growth of He-Halutz.

41. Feivel Gavze, "Problemot Brit Ha-Kibbutzim" (Heb.) (The Problems of the Brit Ha-Kibbutzim), *Ha-Shomer Ha-Tza'ir*, No. 14-15, November 15, 1933. Idem, "Al Ha-Mivneh Ha-Penimi shel He-Halutz" (Heb.) (On the Internal Structure of He-Halutz), ibid., no. 11-12, October 1, 1933. Zvi Lurie emphasizes the role of Ha-Shomer Ha-Tza'ir in the regeneration of He-Halutz. Thanks to its influence, the avant-garde point of view had a respected place in the movement. See Zvi Lurie, "Le-Ma'amadeinu Be-He-Halutz" (Heb.) (About Our Standing in He-Halutz), ibid., no. 16, November 1, 1931; Rabinoff, "Li-Sheeilat Tenu'at Ha-No'ar Be-He-Halutz" (Heb.) (On the Question of the Youth Movement in He-Halutz), ibid., no. 4, February 15, 1931.

42. Kibbutzim of the Hitahdut Party.

43. A small religious group which identified in the Land of Israel with the general Histadrut rather than with Ha-Po'el Ha-Mizrahi.

44. *Dos Vort,* no. 141, December 1933.

45. See n. 39 above.

46. The point of view of the bloc and the youth movements in 1938. See: Zeev Bloch (someone very active in Ha-Shomer Ha-Tza'ir), "'Im Ha-Panim La-No'ar" (Heb.) (Facing the Youth) and A. Tarshish, "Yi'udei He-Halutz" (Heb.) (Goals of He-Halutz), both in *He-'Atid,* on the 20th anniversary of He-Halutz, (Warsaw, March 1938).

47. *Hahlatot Ve-Taarikhim,* pp. 35-36.

48. Yitzhak Tabenkin, *He-'Atid,* no. 146, November 1, 1933.

49. M. Basok, "10 Yor Klosov (Yid.) (Ten Years of Klosow), an introduction to the Klosow celebration), according to Spizman, p. 367.

50. *He-'Atid,* no. 65, March 1, 1929; ibid., no. 68, December 15, 1929.

51. The representatives of the youth movements admitted that the bloc is more dynamic than the others, but they attributed it to various objective factors. See: David Rosenbaum, "Mi-Sheeilot Ha-Sha'ah" (Heb.) (Contemporary Questions), *Ha-Shomer Ha-Tza'ir,* no. 5-6, March 15, 1932.

52. All the various aforementioned arguments were offered at that plenary session of the He-Halutz Central Committee. See: *Le-Sha'ah Zo* (Heb.) (For This Hour), pp. 30-60.

53. Y. Shapiro, ibid., p. 48.

54. For the minority arguments, see ibid., pp. 30-60. Yehuda Gotthelf, "'Al Ha-Organiyut Ha-Kibbutzit" (Heb.) (On the Organic Nature of

the Kibbutzim), *Ha-Shomer Ha-Tza'ir,* no. 2, February 1, 1933; Feivel Gavze, "Hakhshara Me-'Urevet Ve-Otonomit" (Heb.) (The Mixed and Autonomous Hakhshara), ibid., no. 11-12, October 1, 1933; Y. Schwartzbard, "Darkeinu Be-He-Halutz Ve-Ha-Hakhshara" (Heb.) (Our Course in He-Halutz and the Hakhshara), ibid., no. 14-15, November 15, 1933.

Notes to Chapter 6

1. In spite of the stormy development of the different pioneering organizations, He-Halutz remained the most meaningful of them all in Poland (outside the two Galicias) according to the Palestine Office census of February 28, 1934 which indicates the following composition:

General He-Halutz	184 hakhsharot with 6,367 members	62.33%
He-Halutz Ha-Mizrahi	70 hakhsharot with 1,522 members	15.10%
Betar	35 hakhsharot with 469 members	4.70%
He-Halutz He-Medinati (the Jewish Staters)	16 hakhsharot with 257 members	2.58%
Zionist Organization	7 hakhsharot with 120 members	1.20%
WIZO	1 hakhsharot with 68 (girls)	.18%
Agudas Yisroel	no figure hakhsharot with 156 members	1.56%
General Zionist He-Halutz	72 hakhsharot with 1,232 members	12.35%
Sum Total	385 hakhsharot with 10,191 members	100.00%

See: *Din Ve-Heshbon fun der Hoipt-Leitung fun Torah Va-'Avodah for di Yoren Tishrei 5693–Tishrei 5696* (Yid.) (The Report of the Torah Va-'Avodah Top Leadership for the Years October 1932–September 1935) (Warsaw 1936), p. 48.

In 1935, the percentage of participation of the general He-Halutz grew a bit according to the June 1935 tally: General He-Halutz, 67.60%; He-Halutz Ha-Mizrahi, 12.09%; He-Halutz Ha-Klal Tzioni, 12.65%; Betar, 4.45%; He-Halutz Ha-Medinati, 2.90%; WIZO, 0.31%. See ibid.

In all of Poland (including both Galicias) the picture is a bit different. The general He-Halutz participation drops; that of He-Halutz Ha-Klal Tzioni, Betar, and Agudas Yisroel increases. The numbers are based on a census of September 1, 1935:

General He-Halutz	250 hakhsharot with 11,196 members	59.2%
General Zionist He-Halutz	99 hakhsharot with 2,655 members	14.1%

He-Halutz Ha-Mizrahi	72 hakhsharot with	2,152 members	11.4%
Betar	62 hakhsharot with	1,396 members	7.3%
Agudas Yisroel	44 hakhsharot with	903 members	4.4%
He-Halutz Ha-Medinati	24 hakhsharot with	586 members	3.2%
WIZO	5 hakhsharot with	70 (girls)	.4%
Sum Total	556 hakhsharot with	18,958 members	100.0%

See Dr. Peker, op. cit., p. 10. For figures on the situation in Galicia in 1933, see: *Hanoar-Hacijoni, Organ Han. Hac. w Polsce* (The Zionist Youth, the organ of the Zionist Youth in Poland), no. 2-2, Luty-Marzec (February-March) 1934, p. 54.

2.   Until 1932 it was called He-Halutz Ha-Merkazi. See: Aryeh Shpalter, "Di Tetigkeit fun He-Halutz Ha-Klal Tzioni," according to Spizman, pp. 299-300.

3.   About the beginning phase of He-Halutz Ha-Merkazi see: Baruch Kasterinsky, "Zikhronot Mei-Ha-Yamim Ha-Heim" (Heb.) (Memories of Those Days), in Yohanan Cohen (ed.), *Sefer Ha-No'ar Ve-Ha-'Oved Ha-Zioni* (Tel-Aviv 1961), pp. 120-121.

4.   About this organization see further on in this chapter.

5.   About the ideological development of He-Halutz, see above, Chapter 1.

6.   Aaron Berdichevsky, one of the leaders of the general He-Halutz condemns this step most harshly and characterizes it as a diversionary attempt of bourgeois Zionism "to break the unity of the pioneer movement," Spizman, p. 192. In our opinion this judgment is not justified for, as we have seen above, the Zionist leaders were not very happy with this new organization. Their distrust of it was fed by a negative historical experience. This was expressed in the welcoming address of General Zionist leader Dr. Noah Davidson at the Founding Congress of He-Halutz Ha-Merkazi. "We General Zionists have no luck with youth. In the past we believed in the Tze'irei Tzion youth which had organized under the leadership of Eliezer Kaplan. But they left us and went left to Socialism. May the youth that have now organized in He-Halutz remain with us and continue the work which we have begun." See Kasterinsky, ibid., p. 121. Berdichevsky's version is therefore unjustified.

7.   See *Measeif Li-Tenu'at He-Halutz,* p. 204. In general, the Congress was influenced by the stormy development of private initiative in the Land of Israel, notable for its severe criticism of pioneering and the kibbutz and labor colonization. It was called the pampered pet of Zionism

and there was a demand to undo it as an anachronism and remnant of the past no longer needed for the future. The only one who defended the collectivist labor colonization from a broad historical perspective was Chaim Weizmann. See: Getzel Kressel, "Di Tzionistishe Kongressen" (Yid.) (The Zionist Congresses) in *Faren He-Halutz* (Tel-Aviv 1946), pp. 49-50.

8. *Measeif Li-Tenu'at He-Halutz,* p. 204.

9. See the memorandum of the He-Halutz World Organization to the 16th Zionist Congress in 1929, in which are cited the following main principles which were adopted at the 3rd He-Halutz World Conference in Danzig in 1924: "a) the duty of doing physical labor; b) Hebrew labor culture; c) ties with the labor histadrut in the Land of Israel; d) active participation in activities for a labor Land of Israel." The memorandum also emphasizes the fact that the largest majority of Zionist youth is united in its ranks and demands that the decisions of the 13th Congress be renewed. Ibid., pp. 203-204.

10. The following lines about the genesis of this youth movement are based upon the following sources: Reuben Be-Shem (Dr. Feldshu), *Yugend Tzionism* (Yid.) (Youth Zionism) (Warsaw 1934); Moshe Kol (Colodney), "Leveinah 'al gabei Leveinah" (Heb.) (Brick upon Brick), in *Sefer Ha-No'ar Ve-Ha-'Oved Ha-Zioni,* pp. 19-24; Moshe Gertner, "Yihudo shel Ha-No'ar Ha-Zioni Ve-Tafkidav" (Heb.) (The Uniqueness of Ha-No'ar Ha-Zioni and its Functions), ibid., pp. 55-87; M. Rabinowitz, "Be-Derekh Ha-Meshutefet" (Heb.) (Along the Road Together), *Ha-No'ar Ve-Ha-'Oved Ha-Zioni,* no. 3-4, February-March 1934; Shmuel Domb, "Vegen Heimishe Zachen," (Yid.) (About Homey Things), Bloi-Veiss Algemeiner Tzionistisher Yugent Blatt (Blue-White General Zionist Youth Paper [monthly journal]) of Ha-No'ar Ha-Tzioni and He-Halutz Ha-Klal Tzioni, Warsaw no. 2 (10), April 15, 1935.

11. Moshe Kol, ibid., p. 20. Also see R. Ben-Shem, ibid.

12. J. K., ibid., pp. 15-16.

13. *Sefer Ha-No'ar Ve-Ha-'Oved Ha-Zioni,* pp. 91-95; *Ha-No'ar Ve-Ha-'Oved Ha-Zioni,* no. 4-5, December 1933. The Akiva movement after a short while, split off in 1934 and joined the general He-Halutz.

14. See for example: Yehuda Erez (ed.), *Sefer Z. S.;* Benjamin West (ed.), *Naftulei Dor,* pp. 19-25.

15. *Sefer Ha-No'ar Ve-Ha-'Oved Ha-Zioni,* pp. 78-90.

16. Ibid., pp. 20-22, 97-99, 124; Reuben Ben-Shem, op. cit., pp. 13-14.

17. R. Ben-Shem, ibid., pp. 13-14.

18. Ibid.

19. See later in this chapter about the exclusivist kibbutz orientation of the General Zionist youth movement.

20. Moshe Schneider, *Der Veg fun Ha-No'ar Ha-Tzioni* (Yid.) (The Path of Ha-No'ar Ha-Tzioni), (Warsaw, no year), pp. 7-10.

21. Moshe Kol, "Ha-Derekh shel Ha-Sintezah Ha-Leumit" (Heb.) (The Course of National Synthesis), in *Sefer Ha-No'ar Ve-Ha-'Ovid Ha-Zioni,* pp. 17-18.

22. *Sefer Ha-No'ar Ve-Ha-'Oved Ha-Zioni,* p. 134.

23. Ibid., par. 7.

24. Ibid., p. 135.

25. See: "Ha-Ahdut Ha-Leumit" (Heb.) (The National Unity), in *Ha-No'ar Ha-Tzioni,* no. 1, January 1934.

26. About the discussion on the relationship to the Histadrut, see M. Gertner, *Sefer Ha-No'ar Ve-Ha-'Oved Ha-Zioni,* pp. 56, 312-320, 325-357.

27. Yehezkel Kaufmann, "Milhemet Ma'amadot Be-Yisrael" (Heb.) (Class War in the Land of Israel), in *Sefer Ha-No'ar Ve-Ha-'Oved Ha-Zioni,* pp. 41-45; Ben-Gera, *Oifen Veg fun He-Halutz Ha-Klal Tzioni* (Yid.) (On the Course of He-Halutz Ha-Klal Tzioni) (Warsaw 1933), pp. 12-15.

28. *Sefer Ha-No'ar Ve-Ha-'Oved Ha-Zioni,* pp. 100, 101, 102.

29. Moshe Schneider, op. cit., pp. 16-17.

30. Ibid. Also see: *Yedi'ot Ha-Hanhagah Ha-Rashit shel Ha-No'ar Ha-Zioni Be-Polaniah* (Heb.) (News from the Head Leadership of Ha-No'ar Ha-Zioni in Poland), no. 1, (Warsaw, October 1933). (Bulletin appearing irregularly.)

31. Yerahmiel Eshel, "'Al Hagshamah 'Azmit" (Heb.) (On Self-Realization), in *Ha-No'ar Ha-Zioni,* no. 4-5, November 1933.

32. Ibid., Ben-Gera, "Vegen Unser Kibbutzim" (Yid.) (About Our Kibbutzim), in *Bloi-Weiss,* no. 30, (Warsaw, November 1934). M. Singer, "Hashkafateinu Ha-Kibbuzit" (Heb.) (Our Outlook on the Kibbutz), cited according to an article in the monthly journal of Akiva, *Divrei Akiva,* in *He-'Atid,* no. 158, October 15, 1934.

33. A. L. Bloch, "Farn Velt Rat" (Yid.) (Before the World Council), in *Bloi-Weiss,* no. 7(10), April 15, 1935.

34. See: *Hanoar-Hacijoni* (Polish monthly and later a bi-weekly journal), no. 1, January 1934.

35.   See above, Chapter 4. Space will not allow a broader treatment of this specific development of the hakhshara kibbutzim of Ha-No'ar Ha-Zioni in the ranks of He-Halutz Ha-Klal Zioni. For that, see: *Yedi'ot Ha-No'ar Ha-Zioni*, no. 7, October 27, 1933; no. 4, May 9, 1935. *Ha-No'ar Ha-Zioni*, no. 1-2, Tevet-Shevar 5693; Jan. 1933, no. 7-8, Tammuzy 569, July 1933; *Hanoar-Hacijoni* (Polish), no. 1, January 1934; no. 10, May 1935; no. 20, November 1935; no. 22, December 1935; no. 6-7 (33-34), January 1938; no. 13 (55), May 1939. *Sefer Ha-No'ar Ve-Ha-'Oved Ha-Zioni*, pp. 395-397, 405-408; *Sefer He-Halutz*, pp. 463-464; *Dos Vort*, no. 80, April 4, 1934; *Bloi-Weiss*, no. 1, November 31, 1934; no. 3, December 14, 1934; no. 5(8), March 15, 1935; no. 6(9), March 30, 1935; no. 9(12), August 2, 1935; no. 5, December 20, 1937.

36.   For the development of the general He-Halutz from an amorphous ideological and general Zionist movement to its outspokenly Zionist-Socialist character, see above, Chapter 1. About the ideological background to the emergence of He-Halutz Ha-Merkazi, see: Eliezer Pomerantz, "Noch dem Fareinikung" (Yid.) (After the Union), *Bloi-Weiss*, no. 1(4), January 1935.

37.   *Ekronot He-Halutz Ha-Klal Zioni* (Heb.) (The Principles of He-Halutz Ha-Klal Zioni) (Warsaw 1934), pp. 2-3.

38.   Referred to are the hakhsharot of the General Zionist He-Halutz, not Ha-No'ar Ha-Zioni. The latter conducted a limited hakhshara activity even in the crisis years, especially at the end of the period. This movement's first group went to hakhshara in 1928. On Ha-No'ar Ha-Zioni see *Sefer Ha-No'ar Ve-Ha-'Oved Ha-Zioni*, p. 91.

39.   For details about the difficulties of the first period in Lodz, the unwillingness of the Jewish manufacturers to employ pioneers, and the Polish workers' opposition to them, see: A. Shpalter, "Pe'ulat He-Halutz Ha-Klal Zioni" (Heb.) (The Activity of He-Halutz Ha-Klal Zioni) in *Sefer He-Halutz*, p. 338.

40.   Mordecai Rabinowitz, "Ha-Mazav Ba-Hakhshara" (Heb.) (The Situation in the Hakhshara), a speech at the Council of General Zionist Hakhsharot-Mo'ezet Kibbutzei He-Halutz Ha-Klal Zioni (Warsaw 1931), pp. 31-36.

41.   J. K., "Anahnu Ve-He-Halutz Ha-Klal Tzioni" (Heb.) (We and the He-Halutz Ha-Klal Zioni), *Yediot Ha-No'ar Ha-Zioni*, no. 11, October 1934.

42.   See *Sefer Ha-No'ar Ve-Ha-'Oved Ha-Zioni,* pp. 407-408. From this we see that there is a certain analogy between the position taken by Ha-No'ar Ha-Zioni in He-Halutz Ha-Klal Zioni and that of Ha-Shomer Ha-Tza'ir and Gordoniah in the general He-Halutz. The internal percentage of the 1,395 members in He-Halutz Ha-Klal Zioni is also similar. In August 1935 there were 920 at 38 hakhsharot of He-Halutz Ha-Klal Zioni and 470 members at 18 hakhsharot belonged to Ha-No'ar Ha-Zioni. See: *Mo'ezet Kibbutzei Ha-Klal Zioni,* p. 36. For the percentile participation of the youth movements in the general He-Halutz, see: *Yediot Ha-No'ar Ha-Zioni,* no. 2, January 12, 1934; ibid., no. 5, May 9, 1935; ibid., no. 7, May 1936.

43.   Joseph Simkowitz, in *Sefer Ha-No'ar Ve-Ha-'Oved Ha-Zioni,* p. 405. For a general overview of developments from 1936-1939, see the concluding chapter below.

44.   See *Netivah,* the bi-weekly of the religious-national youth and labor in the Land of Israel and the Diaspora, (Jerusalem), no. 8-9, March 28, 1934.

45.   *Dos Yidishe Folk,* no. 19, May 9, 1918.

46.   Ibid., no. 20, May 16, 1918.

47.   *Netivah,* no. 8-9, March 28, 1934.

48.   See above, Chapter 1.

49.   All quotations are from Nehemiah Avinah, "Yahasim" (about He-Halutz Ha-Mizrahi) (Heb.) (Relationships), *He-'Atid,* no. 12, 1925.

50.   *Netivah,* February 21, 1927.

51.   *Dos Yidishe Folk,* no. 30, July 25, 1918.

52.   Compare to the General Zionist He-Halutz and the general He-Halutz, the Torah Va-'Avodah movement was a roof organization of various more or less radical segments that joined it at different times: He-Halutz Ha-Mizrahi, Tze'irei Mizrahi and, at the end of the twenties, the scout organization Ha-Shomer Ha-Dati. The religious girls' organization Beruriah also was part of the Torah Va-'Avodah movement. See *Netivah* ibid., "Ha-Shomer Ha-Dati" (Heb.), organ of the top leadership of Ha-Shomer Ha-Dati in western Galicia, irregular, (Cracow), June 1931. *Ezra,* Report of the Central Committee "Ezra," an organization for pioneers and immigrants to the Land of Israel, for the year 1936/37 (Lwow, May 1937), p. 34.

twenties, the scout organization in Ha-Shomer Ha-Dati. The religious girls' organization, Beruriah, also was part of the Torah Va'Avodah movement. See *Netivah,* ibid., "Ha-Shomer Ha-Dati" (Heb.) (The Religious Scout), organ of the top leadership of Ha-Shomer Ha-Dati in western Galicia, irregular, (Cracow, June 1931). *Ezra,* Report of the Central Committee "Ezra," an organization for pioneers and immigrants to the Land of Israel, for the year 1936/37 (Lwow, May 1937), p. 34.

53.   See Spizman, p. 192. A further symptom of the crisis is the fact that the organ of the movement, *Netivah,* carries almost nothing about the religious hakhshara in the June 1926–September 1927 years.

54.   Shlomo Zalman Shragai, "Hakhsharateinu" (Heb.) (Our Hakhshara), *Netivah,* no. 15, September 1926.

55.   See above, Chapter 2.

56.   S. Z. Shragai, ibid.

57.   *Netivah,* no. 8(29), February 1928. Similar resolutions were adopted at the 4th plenary session of the Tze'irei Mizrachi Executive Council in 1929, ibid., no. 9(54), January 1929; at the 5th Nationwide Conference of Tze'irei Mizrachi in Poland in 1930, ibid., no. 11-12 (81-82), March 1930.

58.   Ibid., no. 22-23, November 1932.

59.   Ibid., no. 24(45), September 1928.

60.   S. Z. Shragai, "Ha-Po'el Ha-Mizrahi" (Heb.), *Netivah,* January 1930.

61.   Ibid.

62.   Ibid.

63.   On He-Halutz Ha-Tza'ir, see Chapter 2.

64.   See *Oholeinu,* the organ of Ha-Shomer Ha-Dati, published by the Executive Leadership (Warsaw-Cracow-Lwow), no. 4, July 1939.

65.   L. A., "Mi-Toldot Tenu'ateinu" (Heb.) (From the History of Our Movement) in *Ha-Shomer Ha-Dati, its Course and Aim,* issued once, Cracow, 1930, p. 3.

66.   *Ha-Shomer Ha-Dati,* organ of the Executive Leadership in Cracow, issued once, June 1931.

67.   See the decisions of the 2nd Session of the Tze'irei Mizrahi Main Council in Poland. The formation of Ha-Shomer Ha-Dati groups is hailed and their support is urged. *Netivah,* no. 22(43), September 1938. Also

see the decisions of the 4th Session of that Council, ibid., no. 9(58), 1929; no. 11-13(98-100), March 1932.

68. Actually, the 2nd Convention in 1932 was the first to have a nationwide character, i.e., delegates from Galicia participated for the first time. But in the historical tradition of Ha-Shomer Ha-Dati this conference is considered the first.

69. One can clearly see the conscious analogy to Maimonides' Thirteen Principles which are of a purely religious nature whereas those of Ha-Shomer Ha-Dati are religio-educational.

70. *Ha-Shomer Ha-Dati,Darko U-Matarato* (Heb.) (Its Course and Task), (Cracow 1930), pp. 2-3.

71. *Ha-Shomer Ha-Dati,* June 1933.

72. Ibid. For a comparison of the demands of Ha-Shomer Ha-Tza'ir in the general He-Halutz, see above, Chapter 6. For the similar developments between He-Halutz Ha-Klal Zioni and Ha-No'ar Ha-Zioni, see the beginning of this chapter.

73. *Ha-Shomer Ha-Dati, Darko U-Matarato* (Heb.) (The Religious Scout, His Course and His Goal), p. 5.

74. *Oholeinu* (Heb.) (Our Tent), November 1935, p. 16.

75. Ibid., p. 15, on the establishment of aliyah kibbutzim and the difficulties of deepening the Socialistic-kibbutz idea in Ha-Shomer Ha-Dati. Also see *Netivah,* no. 3-4, October 1934; no. 13, December 1936; *Oholeinu,* November 1935, p. 12.

76. *Ha-Shomer Ha-Dati,* no. 1, 1936.

77. *Niv He-Haver* (Heb.) (The Member's Expression), published by Hever Kibbutzei Ha-'Aliyah (The Association of Aliyah Kibbutzim) of Ha-Shomer Ha-Dati (Warsaw 1938), pp. 13, 63, 100. *Netivah,* no. 3-4 (111-112), January 1937.

78. Joseph Wiener, "Mi Anu?" (Heb.) (Who Are We?), *Ohleinu,* April 1934.

79. Ibid. Also see: Moshe Krone, "Morei Ha-Derekh" (Heb.) (The Guides), *Oholeinu,* December 1934.

80. Ibid. A similar ambivalent tension situation developed between He-Halutz and the Zionist-Socialist parties with which He-Halutz shared common theoretical-ideological foundations but differed on their implementation. He-Halutz, being radical, accuses the parties of opportunism, short-sightedness, and hollow activity. The chapter on the relationships

between He-Halutz and the Zionist-Socialist parties is multi-faceted and requires a separate, broader treatment, but for lack of space these few words which offer only a mere hint of this complicated theme must suffice.

81. *Din Ve-Heshbon Mi-Pe'ulot Ha-Hanhagah Ha-Rashit Li-Tenu'at Torah Va-'Avodah Be-Polaniah, October 1932-October 1935* (Heb.) (Report of the Activities of the Executive Leadership of the Torah Va'avodah Movement, September 1933-September 1936) prepared for the 7th Conference (Warsaw 1936), p. 15; *Heint* (daily) (Yid.) (Today), no. 255, November 5, 1935. It is interesting to note that Ha-Shomer Ha-Dati was negative about mass growth, seeing it as contrary to the avant-garde ideology. "We have not exerted ourselves to artistically inflate the hakhshara. We have not forced our mass membership to go out to hakhshara and have not put our minds to the question of a great aliyah." See: *Report of Ha-Shomer Ha-Dati at the 3rd Conference* (Warsaw 1937), pp. 23-24. The elitist Ha-Shomer Ha-Dati point of view is to a certain degree similar to that of Ha-Shomer Ha-Tza'ir to mass hakhshara. See above, Chapter 5. It also draws its nourishment from the same ideational and psychological sources, from a youth movement whose education is selective and exclusively toward the kibbutz. In this connection, a few words about the structure of this movement. The Torah Va-'Avodah organization is, as aforementioned, a roof organization for the following movements: Tze'irei Mizrahi, He-Halutz Ha-Mizrahi, Ha-Shomer Ha-Dati, and the girls' organization, Beruriah. He-Halutz Ha-Mizrahi was the hakhshara and aliyah division for the entire association. The relationship between Ha-Shomer Ha-Dati and He-Halutz Ha-Mizrahi also in certain measure remind one of the tensions between the autonomistic youth movements and the "Bloc" in the general He-Halutz, with one difference: the general He-Halutz educated solely for the kibbutz whereas the Torah Va'Avodah movement educated also toward other forms of labor living, in the city, in the colony, in the moshav, and the like. Thus Ha-Shomer Ha-Dati complains that He-Halutz Ha-Mizrahi does it an injustice in matters of hakhshara and aliyah, and this creates frictions between the two. In 1936 a joint agreement was signed in which it was hoped that relationships would improve. See ibid., p. 24.

82. *Report*, ibid.; *Heint*, ibid.

83. Zvi Kurtz, "Darkeinu Be-Hakhshara Ve-'Aliyah" (Heb.) (Our Course in Hakhshara and Aliyah), *Oholeinu*, no. 11, February 1934.

84.   *Report*, p. 17.

85.   Ibid., pp. 17-18; *Netivah*, no. 16, January 1937.

86.   Beruriah—named after the wife of the distinguished Tanna (Mishnaic Sage) Rabbi Meir—who the Aggadah reports was a personality in her own right. See: H. N. Bialik and Y. H. Rawnitzki, *Sefer Ha-Aggadah* (Heb.) (The Legends Book) (Tel-Aviv 1953), pp. 190-191, 330, 349, 435.

87.   *Netivah*, no. 3-4 (111-112), January 1933.

88.   *Report*, p. 18.

89.   On the tensions between the radical youth which considered itself avant-garde and the adult, older Orthodoxy which opposed pioneering, see the Benjamin Mintz article, "Lomir Machen a Heshbon; Vos Hoben Mir Geton far Eretz Yisroel" (Yid.) (Let Us Make an Accounting; What Have We Done for the Land of Israel), *Togblatt* (Daily Newspaper), no. 243, September 20, 1933.

90.   *Togblatt*, no. 289, September 15, 1933; *Der Moment* (Yid.) (The Moment), daily newspaper, no. 63, March 14, 1934.

91.   Noah Prilutsky, "Vegen a Ligen Kegen Yiddishen Antisemitism" (Yid.) (Abut a Lie Against Jewish Antisemitism), *Der Moment*, No. 72, March 25, 1934.

92.   *Togblatt*, No. 288, September 14, 1933; no. 290; no. 290, September 17, 1933; *Der Moment*, no. 63, March 14, 1934.

93.   Despite the fact that after the split in Revisionism two hakhshara organizations were formed, that of Betar and that of the Grossmanist-Jewish Staters, we shall treat them together because their ideological approach to the hakhshara problem was similar and almost identical.

94.   *Tel-Hai* (monthly) published by the High Command of Brit Trumpeldor (Yid.-Heb.) (Warsaw), no. 1, December 1924; no. 9, October 1930. *Ha-Medinah* (weekly), Riga, later Warsaw, and (bi-weekly), no. 17, November 26, 1935.

95.   Zelig Lerner, "Rechtliche Gevalt Tetigkeit" (Yid.) (Righteous Forceful Activity), an article of praise for Mussolini and Pilsudski, both leaders who saved their countries and peoples from the Communist tohu-bohu, while the democracies were not skilled enough to solve the living problems of their peoples. See *Tel-Hai*, no. 1(3), February 1930.

96.   See an interview with Aharon Propes, a Betar leader, in *Ha-Medinah*, no. 18-19, June 23, 1933.

97. *Syrion* (Polish), a monthly, no. 1, February 1936. The following quotation can serve as an indication of how far the Betar ideology reflected the extremely nationalistic spirit of the thirties: "Our God–Zionism, Renaissance, Realization of the idea. . . . Our redemption conception– to be a nation, a real nation . . . a nation sound in body and spirit." M. Merhaviah, from "Fun Shmuessen" (Yid.) (From Conversation), *Tel-Hai*, no. 1, December 1929.

98. Ibid., no. 2, December 1929. It may also be of interest that Betar's first hakhshara groups, just as those of He-Halutz, were formed in Volhynia and spread from there throughout all of Poland. See *Ha-Medinah*, no. 3 (25), February 16, 1934.

99. Benjamin Lubotsky (Dr. Benjamin Eliav), "Halutzism" (Yid.) (Pioneering), *Tel-Hai*, no. 3(5), April 1930.

100. Ibid. Also see: M. merhaviah, "Mei-Az 'Ad Ha-Yom" (Heb.) (From Then Till Now), *Tel-Hai*, no. 2(4), March 1930.

101. *Ha-Medinah*, no. 6, March 19, 1933.

102. See Jabotinsky's criticism of the hakhshara at the 2nd World Conference of Betar in Cracow, *Der Moment*, no. 66, January 7, 1935; the critique of the hakhshara at the session of the 6th Revisionist Conference in Poland, ibid., no. 50, February 27, 1934; *Tel-Hai*, no. 1(2), January 1931.

103. Zvi Berest, Die Fach Hakhshara" (Yid.) (The Trade Hakhshara) in *Ha-Medinah*, no. 4, May 3, 1931.

104. Eliezer Shostak, "Bilbul Ha-Mahuyot Ve-Ha-Musagim" (Heb.) (Confusion of Categories and Content), *Ha-Medinah*, no. 6, March 19, 1933; idem, "Be-Shulei Vikkuah Rezini" (Heb.) (On the Brink of a Serious Discussion), ibid., no. 3, February 16, 1934. The following lines draw upon these articles.

105. All quotations are from "Confusion of Categories . . .", *Ha-Medinah*, ibid.

106. I.e., increasing the number of certificates. These were distributed percentage-wise according to the number of members on hakhshara.

107. Eliezer Shostak, "On the Brink . . .", ibid.

108. Ibid.

109. Moshe Goldberg, "Men Farbesert di Hakhshara in Poilin" (Yid.) (The Hakhshara in Poland Is Being Improved), *Ha-Medinah*, no. 13, May 2, 1933.

110. *Tel-Hai,* no. 5-6, June-July 1930. It is in the same Klosow where the first permanent hakhshara kibbutz of He-Halutz was established. The geographical identity is not accidental. The relationships between both hakhshara groups were very bad. The He-Halutz members saw the Betar pioneers as competitors, a tool used by the employers. In general, the relationships between the two movements were tense as a result of opposing ideational and political positions. The press in those years is full of reciprocal attacks.

111. Ibid., no. 4, May 1930; no. 5-6, June-July 1930.

112. *Ha-Medinah,* no. 2, February 19, 1933.

113. See "A Shmuess miten Netziv" (Yid.) (A Conversation with the Commandant) by Aharon Propes in *Ha-Medinah,* no. 18-19, June 23, 1933. About the numbers a year later, compare n. 1 above. These numbers show the chance character of this hakhshara. It is worth adding that according to Betar's own reports its membership was 70,000, mostly in Poland, i.e., that a negligible number of its members was on hakhshara. See Jabotinsky's address at the Betar World Conference, *Der Moment,* no. 6, January 7, 1935.

114. *Din Ve-Heshbon Mi-Pe'ulot Ha-Nezivut bein Ha-Ve'idah Ha-Shelishit, Be-October 1935, Ve-Ha-Revi'it, Be-Mai 1936* (Heb.) (Report of the Command Activities between the 3rd Conference, October 1935, and the 4th, May 1936), (Warsaw, June 1936), pp. 29-30.

115. Ibid., p. 29.

116. This is tied in with private agreements between employers and Betar, not through the Jewish Agency, i.e., a break in the national solidarity.

117. Ibid., pp. 30-33. Also see *Ha-Medinah,* no. 1(37), January 9, 1937.

118. Aryeh Goldin, "Hakhshara Problemem" (Yid.) (Problems of Hakhshara), *Tel-Hai,* no. 5-6, June-July 1930.

119. Eliezar Shostak, "On the Brink . . .", *Ha-Medinah,* no. 3(25), February 16, 1934. Also see: *'Avodateinu, Din Ve-Heshbon Mi-Mifkedet Betar Be-Galiziah Ha-Ma'aravit Ve-Ha-Mizrahit* (Heb.) (Our Activity, A Report from the Betar Command in Western and Eastern Galicia) (Lemberg 1936), p. 17. In light of these negative experiences, Moshe Joelson demands the elimination of hakhshara as a Betar category and the institution of new concepts such as "agronomy," "the theory of labor." *Ha-Medinah,* no. 2, February 19, 1933; also Alexander Epstein, "Far di

Rat-Zitzung fun di Raion-Kommandaturen in Poilin" (Yid.) (For the Council Session of the Regional Commands in Poland), ibid., no. 6, March 19, 1933.

120. Joseph Krust, "Referat vegen Hakhshara" (Yid.) (Report on Hakhshara) in *Mo'azot Mifkadot Galiliyot shel Betar Be-Polaniah* (Heb.) (Betar Regional Command Councils in Poland), (Warsaw 1933), pp. 10-11.

121. Ibid. Also see the discussion and the reports about the serious demoralizing influence of hakhshara upon its members. The point is made that the trade hakhshara is no more than a fragment of the entire Betar activity. Ibid., pp. 14-19.

122. The Betar member had to obligate himself to work for two years in labor battalions in the Land of Israel at the behest of the movement. About these, see for example, Moshe Helman, "Di Arbets-Plugot" (Yid.) (The Labor Battalions) in *Ha-Medinah,* no. 9, March 5, 1933; no. 14, May 14, 1933; no. 18-19, June 23, 1933; no. 1 (23), January 17, 1934; no. 15 (33), November 24, 1935.

123. Decisions of Regional Command Councils. . . , p. 30.

124. Eliezer Shostak, "On the Brink. . .", *Ha-Medinah,* no. 3 (25), February 16, 1934.

125. Dr. Gershon Yunitshman, "Ha-Derekh Li-Plugot Ha-'Avodah" (Heb.) (The Way to Labor Battalions), *Ha-Medinah,* no. 6 (24), April 30, 1935.

126. Y., Ben-Ami, "Mi-Pinkaso shel Me-Vakeir" (Heb.) (From a Visitor's Notebook), *Tel-Hai,* no. 7, August 1930. Also see *'Avodateinu,* "Din Ve-Heshbon Mi-Mizrah Galiziah 1932-1934" (Heb.) (Our Work, Report from Eastern Galicia 1932-1934) (Lemberg 1934), pp. 17-18.

127. See notes 119-120.

128. *Decisions of the 2nd World Betar Convention* (Cracow, January 6-9, 1935), pp. 11-12.

129. *Ha-Maf'il,* organ of He-Halutz Ha-Medinati in Poland (Yid.-Heb.) (Warsaw, April 1935), p. 1.

130. Israel Ka'ach, "Di Hakhshara Frage" (Yid.) (The Hakhshara Question), ibid., p. 13.

131. Ibid., pp. 2-3.

132. Zvi Waxman, "Kibbutz Problemem" (Yid.) (Kibbutz Problems). The article was presented as the personal opinion of the author and not as the official position of the movement. Ibid., p. 15.

133.   Ibid., p. 7. According to other sources there were only 15 locations with 353 members. See the Ezra report of 1936-1937 (Lemberg 1937), pp. 31-32.

Notes to Chapter 7

1.   Berl Katznelson, "He-Halutz," written on the 10th anniversary of He-Halutz, 1928, in *Der Oiftu fun Yungen Dor* (Yid.) (The Accomplishment of the Young Generation) (Warsaw 1936), p. 5.

2.   Eliezer Kaplan, "Mi-Yamim 'Avaru" (Heb.) (Of Days Past), in *Naftulei Dor,* p. 47.

3.   B. Katznelson, op. cit.

4.   Israel Oppenheim, op. cit., pp. 28-31.

5.   See above, Chapter 1.

6.   Special circular of the Zionist Central Committee Bureau "about organizing He-Halutz groups," *Dos Yiddishe Folk,* no. 10, March 7, 1918.

7.   About the question, see above, Chapter 1.

8.   J. H. (Joseph Heftman—I. O.), "Farkerperter Villen" (Yid.) (Embodied Will) *He-Halutz,* no. 1, April 14, 1919.

9.   Ibid.

10.   Ibid.

11.   *He-Halutz,* no. 2, May 6, 1919.

12.   *Ha-Po'el Ha-Tza'ir* 1919. Cited according to *Sefer He-Halutz,* pp. 76-77.

13.   Ibid.

14.   *Ha-Po'el Ha-Tza'ir* 1919. *Kuntres,* no. 12, 1919, according to *Sefer He-Halutz,* pp. 76-78.

15.   "He-Halutz," quoted from *Sefer He-Halutz,* pp. 77-78.

16.   *Ha-Aretz Ve-Ha-'Avodah,* organ of Ha-Po'el Ha-Tza'ir in the Land of Israel, January 1919, pp. 87-88. Quoted according to *He-Halutz,* no. 3, May 25, 1919, pp. 45-46.

17.   Details of this pioneering radical critique and the struggle for an unlimited emigration, see *Hahlatot Ve-Taarikhim,* pp. 9-13; *He-Halutz,* no. 3, p. 37; J. H. (Joseph Heftman), "Der Ruf Noch Arbet" (Yid.) (The Call for Work), ibid., pp. 38-39; no. 4, June 29, 1919, pp. 65-66; lead article, no. 5, August 18, 1919, p. 69. J. H., "Halutzim un Tzionim (Yid.) (Pioneers and Zionists), ibid., pp. 70-71; "Noch der Ferter Conferentz" (Yid.)

(After the 4th Conference), ibid., no. 6, September 8, 1919, p. 85; J. H., "Paris un Eretz Yisroel" (Yid.) (Paris and the Land of Israel), ibid., pp. 86-87. "Di Tzionistishe Conferentz" (Yid.) (The Zionist Conference), ibid., pp. 82-90. J. H., "Der Alveltlicher He-Halutz" (Yid.) (The World Pioneer), ibid., no. 8-9, December 11, 1919, pp. 114-115. Tanhum Berman, "Ha-Mahpeikha Ve-Hagshamatah" (Heb.) (The Revolution and its Implementation), ibid., p. 115; p. 132; no. 11, February 19, 1920, pp. 151, 159. Spizman, pp. 63-64, 124. According to the accusation of the pioneer movement, the Zionist leadership by its politics is impeding the labor aliyah. The 2nd World Convention of He-Halutz demands "that the organizing of the labor emigration be put into the hands of the labor movement," ibid., p. 133. The demand was raised after the British regime, in 1920, had restricted the labor immigration into the Land of Israel by establishing a certificate-quota and put the certificate distribution in the hands of the Zionist leadership. Also see: *Ha-Measeif Li-Tenu'at He-Halutz,* pp. 175-176, 222-223.

18.   Y. H., "The Call for Work," *He-Halutz,* no. 3, May 27, 1919, p. 39.

19.   "Zu der Ferter Conferentz" (lead article) (Yid.) (To the 4th Conference), ibid., no. 5, August 18, 1919, p. 69.

20.   Ibid. Also see the speeches of the He-Halutz delegates at this Conference in the same vein and the Zionist leadership's counter-attack upon He-Halutz accusing it of being an irresponsible association whose activity borders on adventurism. Yitzhak Gruenbaum was among the attackers of He-Halutz and an opponent of an elemental mass emigration so long as the conditions were not ripe. See ibid., no. 6, September 8, 1919, pp. 88-90.

21.   See *Sefer He-Halutz,* p. 417, n. 1.

22.   Ibid.

23.   For the discussion on this, see *He-Halutz* (Heb.), vol. IV, 1924; *He-'Atid,* no. 1, January 21, 1928. Nahum Benari, "Le-Darkhei He-Halutz" (Heb.) (On the Ways of He-Halutz), *Measeif Li-Tenu'at He-Halutz,* pp. 270-271. The battle against pioneering and pioneer aliyah became more extreme in the thirties, when the aliyah possibility in many cases literally meant saving lives.

24.   See, for example, *He-'Atid,* no. 39, July 6, 1926; no. 41, July 20, 1926; no. 45, November 19, 1926; no. 50, May 15, 1927; no. 52, August

15, 1927; no. 55, March 3, 1928; no. 58, February 15, 1929; no. 70, May 15, 1929; no. 81, November 1, 1929. *Measeif Li-Tenu'at He-Halutz,* p. 280. Spizman, pp. 149, 178-181.

25. See, for example, *Measeif Li-Tenu'at He-Halutz,* pp. 183-184, 190-192, 205-210; *He-'Atid,* no. 53, August 1927.

26. See above, Chapter 3.

27. "Ha-Sokhnut Ha-Yehudit U-Va'ayat He-Halutz" (Heb.) (The Jewish Agency and the Problem of He-Halutz), *He-'Atid,* no. 101, August 15, 1930.

28. Aryeh Tartakower, "He'arot Likrat Ha-Kongress" (Heb.) (Observations before the Congress), ibid., no. 118-119, June 1, 1931.

29. Ibid., no. 135, July 30, 1932.

30. *Unsere Yedies,* issued by the He-Halutz Center in Poland (a weekly and later a periodical journal), Warsaw, no. 12(47), August 15, 1935. See there also the approximate figures of the He-Halutz deficit.

31. Ibid., no. 13(48), September 15, 1935. *Dos Naie Vort* (a daily paper of the League for Labor Palestine), no. 130, October 1935.

32. *He-'Atid,* no. 104-105, November 15, 1930.

33. Dov Weinryb, "Yehudei Polin Mi-Hutz Le-Polin" (Heb.) (The Polish Jews Outside of Poland), in *Beit Yisrael Be-Polin* (Heb.) (The House of Israel in Poland), vol. II (Jursalem 1954), p. 192.

34. It began after the events of Av 1929.

35. Zvi Rosenstein, "Li-Ve'idateinu" (Heb.) (To Our Convention), *He-'Atid,* no. 103, September 30, 1930.

36. Yitzhak Tabenkin, "Di Sakkones vos Droen" (Yid.) (The Threatening Dangers), *Unsere Yedies,* no. 20, November 1932.

37. Ibid.

38. See the discussion with this argumentation, Zvi Rosenstein, "Negged Ha-Zerem" (Heb.) (Against the Stream), according to *Sefer He-Halutz,* p. 409.

39. *Heint,* January 5, 1935. See also Kleinbaum's critical article, ibid., January 7, 1935, quoted according to Unsere Yedies, no. 1(36), January 10, 1935. Also see *Heint,* no. 199, August 27, 1935.

40. *Yedies,* ibid.

41. *He-'Atid,* no. 136-137, October 30, 1932. *Hozeir shel Ha-Shomer Ha-Tza'ir,* (Heb.) (Ha-Shomer Ha-Tza'ir Circular), no. 8, Warsaw, October 21, 1932. *Dos Vort,* no. 59, September 10, 1933; no. 93, April 20, 1934;

no. 184, July 30, 1937. *Ha-Shomer Ha-Tza'ir,* Warsaw, no. 2, April 1, 1935; no. 11, September 30, 1936; no. 12, November 14, 1936. *Heint,* no. 199, August 27, 1935; no. 204, September 2, 1935; no. 207, September 5, 1935. *Finf Yor Po'alei-Tzion Tetigkeit* (Yid.) (Five Years of Po'Alei-Tzion Activity) (Warsaw 1936), p. 73. *Sefer He-Halutz,* pp. 418-420.

42.   *Le-Sha'ah Zo,* pp. 70-71.

43.   Tabenkin, op. cit., ibid.

44.   "Mo'ezet Kibbutz Klosow" (Heb.) (The Council Session of the Klosow Kibbutz), *He-'Atid,* no. 129, March 30, 1932.

45.   *Unsere Yedies,* no. 12(47), August 15, 1935.

46.   Zvi Rosenstein, "Against the Stream," quoted according to *Sefer He-Halutz,* pp. 409, 418-420. David Perlah, "Mif'aleinu Be-Hakhshara" (Heb.) (Our Hakhshara Work) in *Din Ve-Heshbon shel Ha-Ve'idah Ha-Olamit Ha-Revi'it shel Ha-Shomer Ha-Tza'ir* (Report of the 4th International Conference of Ha-Shomer Ha-Tza'ir), (Warsaw 1935).

47.   *Hozeir Ha-Shomer Ha-Tza'ir* (Heb.) (Ha-Shomer Ha-Tzair Circular), no. 8, October 21, 1932.

48.   See above, no. 39.

49.   Berl Katznelson, "He-Halutz," in *The Accomplishment...* (Warsaw 1936), p. 5.

50.   Idem, "Kegen di Mekratregim" (Yid.) (Against the Accusers), in *Unsere Yedies,* no. 1(36), January 18, 1935.

51.   Idem, ibid.

Notes to Chapter 8

1.   *Unsere Yedies,* no. 2, April 18, 1938.

2.   About the political and economic developments in the Land of Israel during this period, see: Zvi Even-Shoshan, *History of the Labor Movement* (Heb.) vol. III, (Tel-Aviv 1966), pp. 39-87; *Entziklopedia 'Ivrit* (Heb.) (The Hebrew Encyclopedia) vol. VI (Jerusalem 1957), pp. 545-556.

3.   *Nowa Mlodziez* (New Youth), organ of Ha-Shomer Ha-Tza'ir, Warsaw-Lemberg, no. 2, March 1936.

4.   *Ha-Shomer Ha-Tza'ir,* Warsaw, no. 3, February 1, 1938.

5.   Abraham Tarshish, "Oifen Front" (Yid.) (At the Front), *Unsere Yedies,* no. 78-79, December 15, 1937; *Sefer He-Halutz,* p. 516; *Hanoar Hacijoni,* no. 4(32), Warsaw, December 10, 1937, pp. 100-101.

6.   *Unsere Yedies,* no. 88, April 1938.

7.   A. Tarshish, "Yi'udei He-Halutz" (Heb.) (The Goals of He-Halutz), Anniversary number of *He-'A tid,* Warsaw, March 31, 1938. The situation was also no different in the other hakhshara movements. Among the General Zionists the branch almost disappeared completely. See *Bloi-Weiss,* no. 1, April 1938; *Sefer Ha-No'ar Ve-Ha-'Oved Ha-Tzioni,* pp. 43-46. The situation was no different with the religious hakhshara. See *Netivah,* September 16, 1937. On the crisis in the Revisionist hakhshara, see *Ha-Medinah,* no. 1(48), January 31, 1937. The youth groups that educated their cadres from childhood on also suffered from the crisis, but in smaller measure, because the composition of their membership was more homogeneous and better prepared ideationally. See "Der Velt-Seminar fun Ha-Shomer Ha-Tza'ir" (Yid.) (The Ha-Shomer Ha-Tza'ir World Seminar), *Unsere Yedies,* no. 81, March 15, 1938.

8.   *Netivah,* no. 1, September 16, 1937; *Unsere Yedies,* no. 87, March 1939. A discussion erupted over the members who had left hakhshara: should they be excluded from the movement or should efforts be made to draw them into the educational activity in order to neutralize their negative influence upon the younger generation and save them from the Left or from the generally prevalent demoralizing influence. See *Unser Freiheit,* no. 2-4, December 1936, February 1937.

9.   *Unsere Yedies,* no. 83, May 1938.

10.   *Netivah,* no. 1, October 15, 1936.

11.   See "Sippuro shel Kibbutz Hakhshara. . . Be-Lodz U-Venoteha" (Heb.) (The Story of the Kibbutz Hakhshara. . . in Lodz and its Branches), *Beit Lohamei Ha-Getaot,* 1970, pp. 141, 162, 254, 288.

12.   Hirsh Shner, "Halutzim in der Kibbutzisher Hakhshara, Loit a Tzeilung fun Oktober 1936" (Yid.) (Pioneers in the Kibbutz Hakhshara according to an October 1936 Count) in *Yidishe Ekonomik* (Warsaw 1937), pp. 204-206.

13.   In April 1937, the General Zionist hakhshara had only 750 members, i.e., about 30% of the 1935 number. See *Sefer Ha-No'ar Ve-Ha-'Oved Ha-Zioni,* p. 501; a comparison of the figures above in Chapter 6, no. 1. One can assume that the situation in the other hakhshara movements were no better.

14.   *Sefer Ha-No'ar Ve-Ha-'Oved Ha-Zioni,* pp. 413-416; *Story of the Kibbutz Hakhshara. . . in Lodz,* pp. 254-288.

15.   Yitzhak Tabenkin, "Be-Derekh Ha-Haghshamah" (Heb.) (On the Road to Fulfillment), *Mi-Bi-Fnim* (From Within), vol. V, 1938, according to *Sefer He-Halutz*, pp. 521-522. Also see *Unsere Yedies*, no. 80, February 1938; no. 86, December 1938; *Iggeret fun He-Halutz-Raion-Kommitet in Volin* (Yid.) (Letter from the He-Halutz Regional Committee in Volhynia), Lutsk, May 1937.

16.   See above, Chapter 5.

17.   Zev Bloch, "Facing the Youth," *Unsere Yedies*, anniversary number, Warsaw, April 1938. Aharon Fiks, "Le-Havraat Ha-Tenu'ah He-Halutzit" (Heb.) (Toward the Recovery of the Pioneering Movement), *Ha-Shomer Ha-Tza'ir*, no. 5, March 15, 1936; Isaiah Weiner, "Mi-Sheilot Ha-Hakhshara Be-Polin" (Heb.) (Questions of Hakhshara in Poland), ibid., no. 5, December 31, 1937; Adam Rand, "Yovel U-Meziut" (Heb.) (Anniversary and Reality), ibid., no. 2, March 1938; Zev Bloch, "Likrat Mo'ezet He-Halutz" (Heb.) (Toward the He-Halutz Council), ibid., no. 8, September 1938 and no. 9, October 1938.

18.   *Sefer He-Halutz*, p. 521.

19.   Feivel Bendori, "Moieren Durchbrechen un Lebens Festungen Oifshtelen" (Yid.) (Breaking Through Buildings and Building Life's Fortresses), *Unsere Yedies*, no. 86, December 1938.

20.   J. Perlis, "Oifn Rand fun Vinter-Arbet in Freiheit-He-Halutz Ha-Tza'ir" (Yid.) (On the Brink of Winter Work in the Freiheit-He-Halutz Ha-Tza'ir Movement), *Unsere Yedies*, no. 86, December 1938.

21.   A. Tarshish, *Sefer He-Halutz*, p. 516.

22.   *Sefer He-Halutz*, p. 517.

23.   Yitzhak Tabenkin, ibid., p. 522. Sh. Mintz, "Di Ideiishe Hershaft" (Yid.) (The Ideational Domination), *Unsere Yedies*, no. 66, September 11, 1936. *Hanoar Hacijoni*, no. 3(25), May 15, 1936.

24.   *Unsere Yedies*, no. 75-76, September 23, 1937; no. 79-80, December 1937, no. 83, May 1938.

25.   *Netivah*, no. 36, May 28, 1937.

26.   *Unsere Yedies*, no. 84, July 1938; no. 86, December 1938.

27.   Perlis, ibid.

28.   *Unsere Yedies*, no. 87, March 1939; no. 88, April 1939.

29.   For details about the illegal aliyah, see: Zvi Even-Shoshan, *History . . .* , vol. III (Tel-Aviv 1966), pp. 88-98.

INDEX

Abyssinian War, 6, 135
"Achvah", 48
Ahvah, 95
Akiva, 73, 92, 95, 176-177
Aliyah
    First, 2, 24-25, 28, 142
    Second, 2, 5, 24, 28, 34, 40, 51, 142-143
    Third, 6, 34, 39-40, 43, 51, 126
    Fourth, 5-6, 14, 32, 37-39, 41-43, 45-47, 49, 52, 55, 61, 72, 74, 92-94, 100, 102-105, 128-129, 131-132, 158, 164
    Fifth, 6, 39, 42, 52, 56, 63, 93, 100, 129, 131
Argentina, 40, 164
Arlosoroff, Chaim, 41
Atkin, 16
"Avodah," 48

Balfour Declaration, 8, 9
Bankover, Joseph, 48
Baranovich, 65
Barzel, 111
Basel, 128
Bendin, 9, 11, 13, 26, 126
Ben Gurion, David, 25, 37, 154, 157
Ben Zvi, Yitzhak, 25
Berdichevsky, Aaron, 175
Berlin, 36, 75-76, 78, 158
Berman, Tanhum, 28

"Beruriah", 109, 179-180, 182-183
Betar, 94, 113-121, 147, 173-174, 183-185
Bialystok, 11, 48, 66, 160
Bilu, 25, 113
Bistri, 95
Bnai Zion, 124
Bogdanovsky, S., 46
"Borochov," 66
Braslavsky, M., 59, 159
Brisk-Grodno, 19, 66, 93
Brisk, Lithuanian, 33, 93
Buber, Martin, 24
Bund, 31, 50, 60, 67, 69, 134, 164

Canada, 40
Carlsbad, 128
Chenstochowa, 152
Crakow, 17, 106, 180, 184

Danzig, 38, 104, 154, 157, 161, 175
Davidson, Noah, 175
Dobkin, E., 20-21, 49
Dombrowice, 57
"Dror," 19

Ein Harod, 114

"Freiheit," 68, 72, 77

Galicia, 6-7, 18, 20, 38, 65-66, 95,